Poor Relations

Sulli,

With many thanks for your help

Christopher Hawes

Poor Relations

The Making of a Eurasian Community
in British India 1773–1833

C.J. Hawes

CURZON

First published in 1996
by Curzon Press
St John's Studios, Church Road, Richmond
Surrey, TW9 2QA

© 1996 C.J. Hawes

*Typeset by LaserScript, Mitcham, Surrey
Printed in Great Britain by
Biddles Ltd, Guildford and Kings Lynn*

All rights reserved. No part of this book may be reprinted or reproduced or utilised in any form or by any electronic, mechanical, or other means, now known or hereafter invented, including photocopying and recording, or in any information storage or retrieval system, without permission in writing from the publishers.

British Library Cataloguing in Publication Data
A catalogue record for this book is available from the British Library

Library of Congress in Publication Data
A catalogue record for this book has been requested

ISBN 0–7007–0425–6

Contents

Preface vi
Acknowledgements xi
Abbreviations xiii
Glossary xiv
Illustrations xv

1 British Men, Indian Women, Eurasian Children 1

2 Charity and Children in Care 21

3 Eurasian Employment: A Limited Opportunity 36

4 Eurasians in the Official Eye 55

5 Towards a Reluctant Community 73

6 Eurasians Up Country and in the Indian States 93

7 The Eurasian Struggle for Self-Advancement 112

8 Political Protest: The East Indians' Petition of 1830 133

Aftermath 150
Biographical Appendix 158
Notes 171
Bibliography 199
Index 213

Preface

Today an Anglo-Indian community still remains in India, its families often linked to the Anglo-Indians who left in the mid-twentieth century, at the time of India's Independence, for new lives in Britain, Canada and Australia. They are the acknowledged descendants of the mixed race Eurasian children of the British *Raj*, officially described as 'Anglo-Indian' since 1911. Their origins date back to the first arrival of European traders in India at the start of the sixteenth century, but their importance to the study of British involvement in India first becomes clear in the sixty years from 1773 to 1833, when an explosion in the numbers of British Eurasians forced their presence, their needs, and their demands on to the social and political agenda of British India. By 1830 there were already many more Eurasians in India than British civilians. One hundred years later within a total of 300,000 of European descent, (civilians and soldiers included) living and working in India, Eurasians – Anglo-Indians – had become a clear majority of the population of Western descent, dress, religion, custom and life-style.[1] They counted themselves as members of British society and were widely employed, albeit generally in subordinate roles, in occupations of value to the operation of the imperial regime.

The general exploration and literature of British involvement in India is extensive and continues still. The lives and works of viceroys, bishops, governors, missionaries and officials have commanded attention. So too has the relationship between British colonial authority and Indians themselves. But Eurasians, who in their lives were often the Cinderellas of British society, are nowadays but a footnote to the historical account of British India. No definitive account exists for the crucial years of the late eighteenth and nineteenth century in which the numbers of Eurasians with British fathers rose from the hundreds to the thousands and at whose

Preface

conclusion they already formed, in British eyes at least, a distinct community. Why this neglect? Perhaps an answer may be sought in the marginality of Eurasians to the great affairs of colonial government. The working lives of many amongst them were spent in the offices of government in the early nineteenth century and in supervisory railway roles in the twentieth.[2] The poverty of many Eurasians was at all times a very public feature of the community.[3] Undoubtedly this embarrassed the *Raj* then and fits awkwardly into the British imperial story now.

There is the problem too for historians of the early Eurasian community that, in contrast to senior British officials and soldiers, there are no caches of letters home to their families in Britain nor tin trunks of manuscripts brought back on retirement from India to personalise events and policies through the experience of individuals. Nevertheless a wealth of contemporary sources exists to illuminate the circumstances of Eurasian lives, and the role ascribed to them by British authority. Leading Eurasians of the early nineteenth century, through petitions and letters in the English language press of India, were vociferous in their disappointed expectations of the role prescribed for them in the European society to which they belonged. This book is as much about the social as the political history of a community which formed reluctantly in response to outside considerations rather than through its own wish. An exploration of the reasons underlying the facts of its development, the conflict between the status and opportunity to which educated Eurasians aspired and the British allowed are important aims. So too is an examination of the lives of the historically most obscure and inarticulate – the poorest amongst Eurasians – the children of British soldiers. In describing the formation by the British of an unfavourable Eurasian stereotype – amiable, but allegedly unambitious and unfitted for major responsibility – a contrast is made between the achievement of Eurasians in Indian states where greater opportunity often existed for them than allowed in British India, pointing to the truth that educational advantage and occupational opportunity determine the social state of any community rather than any other consideration.

It has been left largely to Anglo-Indians themselves to record the development of their own community and its concerns.[4] More than half a century has passed since H. A. Stark, himself a distinguished educationalist descended from a Eurasian family long resident in Calcutta, published an account of the emergence of a Eurasian community in British India. He was the first to describe its early development, the lives of Eurasians prominent in attempting to improve the educational and job prospects of their fellows in the 1820s, and the unsuccessful agitation of that time to gain recognition for Eurasians as fully British.[5] His critical judgment of British treatment of their Eurasian relatives has been widely accepted.

More recent community writers: Frank Anthony, the long term leader of the Anglo-Indian community still resident in India, and Austin D'Souza, have accepted and reiterated Stark's argument that in the late eighteenth and early nineteenth centuries British policy set out deliberately to limit and stifle Eurasian ambitions, education, and job prospects.[6] Most recently the work of Evelyn Abel, which is of particular assistance in study of twentieth century Anglo-Indian concerns as India approached self government and eventual independence, echoes Stark's strictures on British policy towards Eurasians.[7]

The Anglo Indian historians of the 1930s and 1940s on whom we must still depend for most of what is publicly known of the development of a Eurasian community in British India had their own political agenda. It was to hold on to areas of public service employment traditionally reserved to the Eurasian community. The proposals of the Montague-Chelmsford commission in 1919 to advance Indianisation of government employment rang alarm bells in the Anglo-Indian community. Moves in the 1930s towards representative government for India threatened even greater competition for Anglo-Indian men, for whom public service was the largest employer.[8] Although the Eurasian activists of the early nineteenth century had failed to achieve their goal of parity with British nationals in India, from the late eighteenth century onwards Eurasians had always received a significant measure of economic protection. It was in this context that prominent Anglo-Indian historians sought to stress the British debt to their loyal community, to re-emphasise their Britishness, and attack past British policy towards them. Their agenda was political as much as historical.

Anglo-Indian criticisms of British policy deserve an impartial examination, as do British actions and the motives which inspired them. To attribute them to racial discrimination alone – present though it undoubtedly was – would be unduly simplistic, for the emergence of a sizeable Eurasian population in British India forced colonial authority to consider the issues which it raised. How were Eurasians to be catered for in education and employment? Were there enough jobs for their rising numbers? Were they natives of India or British, or somewhere in between? Could a large resident population of European descent, as events in other colonial regimes suggested, pose a threat to stability and order? How far was general policy, even when discriminatory in theory, modified in practice by officials in India?

The years between 1773 and 1833 were critical to the British role in India. They were the years in which it expanded rapidly from a primary purpose of trade to paramountcy amongst the continent's ruling powers. Sixty years of rapid transition changed the political map of India irreversibly, engaged the British Government in supervision of the vast territorial holdings of its agent, the East India Company, and raised new and complex problems in the government of a distant continent. A feature of these years was the replacement of the free-wheeling British trader/administrators of earlier years by a new breed of salaried officials imbued with the concept of a civilising British mission, a necessary rationalisation of their exercise of political power. This was thought best to be achieved by the exaltation of British 'character', the public display of Christian virtue, and social distancing of a ruling caste from those whom they ruled.

These events, and changing concepts of acceptable British social behaviour in India, swept up Eurasians almost accidentally into their consequences. It was not that a Eurasian population was a novelty. The colonial rivals of the British, Dutch, French, and the Portuguese particularly, had generated their own mixed race populations. From the very earliest days of a British presence in India there had always been a Eurasian population of British stock, though few in numbers. Its dramatic increase, already causing concern to British authority by the 1780s, directly and primarily related to the influx of British soldiers required to support the expansion of British interests in India.[9] The Eurasian 'problem', as it became, was thus essentially of military origin. As the numbers of British born Eurasians rose from hundreds to thousands – 20,000 is tentatively estimated by the 1830s – questions of 'class' as well as 'race' arose. Whilst there were many Eurasians who were the sons and daughters of military officers and covenanted civil servants, by far the most were the children of 'poor whites' – the military rank and file. A distinction in the treatment of Eurasians was clearly drawn between the education and employment appropriate to the Eurasian children of British 'gentlemen' – civil servants and officers – and the children of ordinary solders drawn from the poorest social classes of their mother country.

By the 1830s the social place of Eurasians in British India had been broadly determined. Though not accepted as British subjects they were recognised to be within the broad circles of British society in India, even though excluded from its higher reaches. For motives of philanthropy, obligation and expedience provision – always inadequate to the need – was made for their education and employment. A Eurasian social hierarchy existed reflecting the orders of British society, albeit at a lesser level. The better born, sons of British civil servants and military officers, held an overwhelming proportion of the best jobs in the junior ranks of Government service, a position already under threat from an emerging cadre of Western educated Indians. The army looked after the Eurasian children of its soldiers, taking the boys back as non-combatants and the girls as wives. But the 'safety net' thus provided for Eurasians was far from adequate for their numbers. That, and a marked reluctance on the part of Eurasians themselves to widen their occupational prospects into trade and commerce, swelled the numbers of those at the foot of society who lived pauperised in the major Presidency towns.

This then is not a book about the great and successful of British India, but about a community – largely but not wholly poor – which sprang from the artificial social conditions of colonial life. It depicts the emergence of a community which aspired to be accepted as wholly British but was denied its choice – a community which only reluctantly and with ill grace accepted its distinctive and secondary place within British colonial society.

Christopher Hawes
London 1996

Acknowledgements

I began my search for the origins and characteristics of a distinctive, albeit reluctant, Eurasian community in British India at the School of Oriental and African Studies, London in the late 1980s. I am consequently most grateful to Kirti Chaudhuri for encouraging my interest in its early days and especially to David Arnold, his colleague at SOAS, for his guidance and criticism of the doctoral thesis from which this present study has since developed.

Whilst conducting research in India I benefited from the ready assistance of the staff of the National Library, Calcutta, and would like to thank, amongst the many who helped me, Sunil Chaterjee, librarian of the Carey Library, Serampore for bringing to my attention important works by John Ricketts and James Kyd, both prominent in the Eurasian community of the 1820s. I also thank Cedric Spanos, Secretary of the East India Charitable Trust for access to the records of the foundation of the European Female Orphan Asylum; David Howard, Headmaster of St. Thomas's School, for information on the early days of the Calcutta Free School; and Monsignor D'Souza for the opportunity to examine the registers of Roman Catholic baptisms, marriages and burials in eighteenth and early nineteenth century Calcutta. I am much indebted to Neil O'Brien, Brian Sweeney, and to S.R. Ayer for their generous and practical help.

I am particularly grateful to the staff of the India Office Library and Records, the British Library, the National Army Museum, the Public Record Office, the Indian Institute at Oxford, and the Library of the School of Oriental and African Studies, for their courtesy and efficiency. I also received valuable help at the libraries of Rhodes House and Regent's Park College, Oxford, in exploring the involvement of Eurasians in the early days of British missionary activity in India. It is a pleasure to thank the Baptist Missionary

Society for their permission to consult and quote from their archival records housed in the Angus Library at Regent's Park College, Oxford. I am similarly obliged to the British Library, the Council for World Mission, the India Office Library and Records, the Methodist Missionary Society, the National Army Museum, the Public Record Office, Regent's Park College, and the United Society for the Propagation of the Gospel, for the use of and permission to quote from their archives.

To the many who have helped me with perceptive advice, information and practical help in the various stages of my work I offer very real thanks. Crystal Brown, Salli Dyson, and William Kirkpatrick have most generously provided family information. Rosemary Morton has prepared my typescript. Rosie Llewellyn-Jones, 'Mac' MacGregor, Robert Pinker, Theon Wilkinson, and the late Zoë Yalland, in particular, have given me consistent encouragement and constructive advice for which I am much in their debt. Though last, not the least, to Noreen and our family my gratitude for their continuing interest and support.

Abbreviations

LIBRARIES, COLLEGES, INSTITUTIONS

BL	British Library, London
IOL	India Office Library and Records, London
NLC	National Library, Calcutta
PRO	Public Record Office, London
RPC	Regent's Park College, Oxford
RH	Rhodes House Library, Oxford
SOAS	School of Oriental and African Studies, London

ORGANISATIONS

BACSA	British Association for Cemeteries in South Asia
BBI	Bengal Benevolent Institution
BEFOS	Bengal European Female Orphan Society
BMS	Baptist Missionary Society
BMOS	Bengal Military Orphan Society
CFS	Calcutta Free School
Company	The Honourable East India Company (HEIC)
CWM	Council for World Mission
LMS	London Missionary Society
MFOAM	Military Female Orphan Asylum, Madras
MMOAM	Military Male Orphan Asylum, Madras
PAI	Parental Academic Institution, Calcutta
SPCK	Society for the Promotion of Christian Knowledge
SPEP	Society for the Promotion of Education of the Poor
USPG	United Society for the Propagation of the Gospel in Foreign Parts
WMS	Wesleyan Missionary Society

Glossary

aumil	village headman.
batta	additional payment made to the Company's military officers when stationed at a distance from the main Presidency town or when on campaign.
chowkeydar	lawcourt attendant.
chuprassi	servant.
conjee	boiled rice water, used as a drink.
ghee	clarified butter.
kedgeree	rice and fish dish.
keraneeships	clerkships.
khazi	Muslim religious officer.
kutcheree	courthouse.
matross	Artillery gunner.
mofussil	Bengal outside Calcutta.
muhktar	village headman.
pagoda	gold or silver coin current in South India until the early nineteenth century. Worth approximately 3½ rupees.
pettah	marketplace.
peon	soldier, orderly.
purdah	state of seclusion in which Hindu women of caste and Muslim women commonly lived.
rait	peasant.
register/registrar	chief clerk in Government offices.
sadr amin	junior civil court judge.
sadr diwani adalat	court for civil suits and revenue disputes.
zemindar	landlord and tax collector.
zenana	apartments within which women lived in purdah.

Illustrations

The British Library, the National Army Museum, and the National Maritime Museum have kindly given permission to reproduce the works in their collections which appear within the body of the text.

I am also very grateful to Mrs. C. J. Jarrett for a further illustration, and to Mr. Theon Wilkinson for the portrait of Charles Weston which features on the jacket cover.

1

British Men, Indian Women, Eurasian Children

Once increasing numbers of young unmarried British males began to arrive in India from the start of the seventeenth century a mixed race population of British and Indian descent, small at first but later to grow rapidly, was inevitable. Many of these men were destined to spend all of their adult lives in exile from their mother country, for until the mid nineteenth century India was many months risky sail away from Britain. Few women were attracted by the prospect, yet, unless men were to remain lifetime celibates – an improbable scenario for most – wives were needed. In consequence colonial authority could not escape the responsibility either of providing suitable partners for their servants or else of devising the rules under which they might marry locally. When they did marry, authority decided the terms under which they would accept responsibility for the children of such marriages.

Earlier European colonists in India experienced the dilemma, met later by the British, of how to provide for unaccompanied males. *All* Western countries found it hard to get suitable women to make the journey out to Asia. Jacques Specz, a Dutch Governor-General on his way to Batavia in 1629, remarked of the women aboard his ship that: 'We lack nothing save so many honest girls and housewives in place of the filthy strumpets and street walkers who have been found in the ships'.[1] The Portuguese and Dutch soon recognised that a policy of local marriage, particularly for their soldiers, was inevitable. Alfonso de Albuquerque, the Portuguese Viceroy at Goa in 1510, is generally credited with initiating the policy.[2] The Dutch followed the precedent, and by the end of the seventeenth century were offering three months pay to those of their men who married locally.[3]

However, a policy of local marriage by Western men to Asian women ran into considerable cultural and religious problems as

European nations attempted to impose their domestic codes of marital behaviour in a non Christian environment. The insistence that only Christian marriages were to be recognised, and the absence of a concept of civil non-religious marriage, met the obstacle that local women had to be converted before they could marry. Though some women did convert, it is clear that the majority preferred not to. In consequence conventional morality was widely ignored by European men of all nations, occupations, and social degree. Most recent scholarship rebuts convincingly earlier assertions that many Portuguese men married Indian women and that irregular unions were rare.[4] Where Indian women *did* marry Portuguese men few were from the higher castes.[5] M.N. Pearson describes the behaviour of Portuguese men in Goa as 'concupiscence on a grand scale'.[6] Nor it seems did Dutch men behave any differently.

Colonial regimes, the British included, had no option but to tolerate a widespread disregard amongst their servants of the code of Christian marriage, for it could only have been avoided by an inflow of Western women into Asia comparable in numbers to that of immigrant males. Reasons of cost, and the general unavailability of suitable female candidates, ruled out that solution. The consequence was visited on the progeny of the unofficial unions of European men and Indian women. Their Eurasian children were illegitimate in Western eyes. As such, the question of whether their welfare was a matter of private or public responsibility played an important part in British attitudes to and treatment of its rising Eurasian population.

*

At first, in the early seventeenth century, the British East India Company had expected that its servants would lead a celibate life. They worked, dined and slept within the factory in a collegiate manner. Prayers were attended twice daily and offences of drunkenness, swearing or failure to return after the gates were closed at dusk brought a fine.[7] Before long behaviour was increasingly at variance with expectation, as some servants set up house outside the factory walls, and others kept Indian women within.[8] By the end of the seventeenth century the British were facing the same problem that the Portuguese and Dutch had met before them. Covenanted servants, the upper social level, were still expected to marry suitable local women – many of whom were of Portuguese Eurasian descent – or else to pay for wives to come out from

Britain. Irregular unions with Indian women were frowned upon. The partnership of Job Charnock – later to be the founder of Calcutta – with an Indian woman brought a censure from his superior in 1682 that it was 'to ye great scandal of our nation'.[9]

The greater problem, however, was how to cater for the needs of the larger numbers of inferior servants, mainly the military. A fundamental problem was the social background and unruly behaviour of such men. The Council at Fort St. George, Madras complained in 1741 that of the military recruits it had just received: 'It is not uncommon to have them out of Newgate, as several have confessed: however, those we can keep pretty much in order, but of late we have had some from Bedlam'.[10] Such men, whose lives were frequently to be spent wholly in India, needed wives but clearly could not afford to pay for their journey. The Company made sporadic early attempts to bring out women for them, but cost of transport and maintenance on arrival in India made it an expensive policy. Since it also was particularly difficult to get 'respectable' women to come out, the Company, with some reluctance it seems, endorsed a policy of local marriage for its soldiers. 'Induce by all meanes you can invent', the Company wrote in 1688 to its Council at Fort St. George, 'our souldiers (sic) to marry with Native women, because it will be impossible to get ordinary young women, as we have before directed, to pay their own passages although Gentlewomen sufficient do offer themselves'.[11]

The encouragement of local marriage accompanied by a special payment to each soldier who had his child baptised as a Protestant – a practice which continued until 1741 – has been interpreted as evidence of a 'new and deliberate official policy whereby intermarriages were encouraged and a mixed community brought into existence'.[12] But it seems more likely that the Company's new policy was not motivated by any great desire to create a mixed race community as such. Such a population was already there. What the Company in London and its agents in Madras wished to do was to *control* their servants' behaviour. The concern in London was that if the soldiers at Fort St. George lived with or married the many Portuguese women there the children would be brought up as Roman Catholics rather than Protestants.[13] The Company's officials on the ground were less worried about the religious issue, but more concerned that their soldiers should be married, 'to prevent wickedness'.[14] Married soldiers with family ties were clearly thought likely to be better behaved than bachelors.

The policy of the late seventeenth century foreshadows some of the issues which came to the fore as the Eurasian population in British India began to expand rapidly a century later – firstly, the need to socialise soldiers through marriage; secondly, attempts to limit the growth of a Eurasian population which might prove disloyal to British interests; thirdly, the establishment of Christian marriage as the baseline for any dependant's claim on the Company's financial support. A line was to be drawn between those Eurasian children born of lawfully married parents – 'honest parents' – and those who were illegitimate. The latter had come into life 'unofficially', as it were. As the mores of British colonial behaviour became stricter from the end of the eighteenth century, the claim of the illegitimate to public support could be countered by the argument that to grant it would be to condone disregard for what was socially approved behaviour.

*

By the later eighteenth century the private lives of most British men seemed almost wholly at variance with public policy. More lived with Indian women than were married, whether to Europeans, Eurasians or Indians. It seems that in Bengal between 1757 and 1800 only one in four British covenanted civil servants, one in eight civilian residents, and one in ten army officers married there. Amongst military other ranks the proportion was even smaller; between one in fifteen and one in forty-five. Even as late as 1828 only one in every ten soldiers was married.[15] Only a small minority of British residents married whilst in India, and the poorer they were the less likely they were to marry.

Contemporary wills and baptismal records illustrate the consequences of the British failure to marry. One in three of wills (83 of 217) in Bengal between 1780–85 contain bequests either to Indian companions or their natural children.[16] Those who left wills were naturally amongst the better-off in British society. Baptismal records in Bengal at the time show the remarkably high incidence of Eurasian children born to unofficial partnerships. Over half (54%) of the children baptised at St. John's, Calcutta between 1767 and 1782 were Eurasian and illegitimate. They were the children of high and low in British society: a son to Thomas Rumbold, then Second in Council at Fort William and later Governor at Fort St. George; a son to John Shore, then a junior merchant and later Governor-General; two daughters to Tilly Kettle, the painter; and children to men in a wide variety of professions and callings, from attorneys and surgeons to ships' mates, doctors and soldiers.[17]

These children were publicly recognised by their fathers and, by baptism, their membership of British society was established. Up country though, and particularly amongst the military rank and file, it is likely that a smaller proportion of Eurasian children were baptised than in the Presidency towns, and it may well be that the true percentage of illegitimate Eurasian births was higher than the one in two recorded at St. John's. Their numbers too were in inverse ratio to the better off in the British community. Most fathers of Eurasian children were 'poor whites'.

Though the prevalence of unofficial British partnerships with Indian women in early colonial India is well documented, little study has been made of the reasons for the phenomenon or of the nature of the relationships themselves. The frequency of marriage of British men to the Eurasian daughters of men of similar social status has been largely overlooked. Much more too is known about the behaviour of the British 'elite' than of 'poor whites'. Among military officers, for instance, stationed outside Presidency towns and often up country on campaign, access to marriageable British women was inevitably less easy than for their compatriots in Presidency towns. For the sergeants and private soldiers such opportunity was almost non existent. Indeed, an important aspect of the military social situation was its generation of an almost self-contained supply of wives from within its own ranks. The Eurasian daughters of officers married other officers. Daughters of the rank and file returned to the Company's army as wives to British soldiers or to the soldiers' Eurasian sons, who were allowed to serve with the army in non-combatant roles.

There were several reasons for the general disinclination to marry of so many of the British elite in India of the late eighteenth and early nineteenth centuries. The scarcity of marriageable British women was a constant, but there were other considerations as well. The cost of supporting a British wife and the 'class' suitability of those who were available were disincentives to many. By the end of the eighteenth century these questions of cost and class perhaps bulked larger than the supply of British women in India with pretensions to gentility, for their numbers had, temporarily at least, exceeded demand. The reforming zeal of Governor-General Lord Cornwallis had ensured that the opportunities for Company servants to make a fortune through trade had gone for ever. Most now had to live on their Company salaries and few found themselves 'in circumstances that invite matrimonial engagements; hence a number of unfortunate females are seen wandering for years in a single and unconnected state'.[18]

In the early years of their service in India most covenanted civil servants and military officers were often in debt and in no financial position to marry. British officers needed to attain at least the rank of Major and their civil service colleagues substantial positions before they could even contemplate the costs of supporting a British wife at the standard of life which polite society – and the wives themselves – deemed appropriate. James Rennell, then a Lieutenant writing home to England in 1770, put it succinctly:

> To tell you the truth a Man with small Prospects ought not to marry in this country as all the Ladies esteem themselves on an equal footing and consequently often endeavour to outshine one another in Appearance, the consequences often fall heavy on the Husband who pays for their ornaments tho' he does not wear them.[19]

It was ironic that Rennell himself married in India only two years later, but most young men felt that the Rs 25 to Rs 40 a month (approximately £50 a year) necessary to provide for the wants of an Indian companion and her attendants was 'a very comfortable figure', compared with the £600 a year needed to support a British wife with any degree of public style.[20]

If the cost of supporting a British wife was one disincentive to marriage, so too was the feeling amongst some British civil servants and army officers that the claims to gentility of many British women were tenuous at best. Surgeon John Stewart, writing to his brother from Cawnpore in 1785, remarked:

> Many of the women here are mere adventuresses from the Milliners shops on Ludgate Hill and some even from Covent Garden and Old Drury [well known areas of prostitution in late eighteenth century London]. They possess neither sentiment nor education, and are so intoxicated by their sudden elevation, that a sensible man can only regard them with indignation and outrage.[21]

Such women, out in India to make a marriage, brought neither dowry nor inherited lands with them as a marriage portion. Once married the union could not easily be ended – there were only 189 divorces granted by Act of Parliament in Britain between 1771 and 1830, and just eleven in India; none before 1801.[22] Small surprise then that many of the sons of minor gentry, army officers, clergy and the business classes who made up the British elite in India preferred not to marry there. Service abroad offered them the chance of a return home with savings and a pension enough for an advantageous marriage in Britain to women of their own social class.

Meantime it was no bar to a later marriage to have lived with and had children by an Indian companion. Despite his Eurasian son and daughter, the wealthy and rather elderly civil servant John Bristow married Emma Wrangham, the toast of Calcutta society, in 1782 who gave him four legitimate children.[23] Tolerance went further yet, for it was not unknown for a newly married British wife to take on the care of her husband's Eurasian children.[24]

★

Exploration of the lives of British men with their Indian companions is hampered by a dearth of colloquial written evidence. But an examination of the wills of British men at the end of the eighteenth century can tell us a great deal. It suggests that what may have seemed in Britain of the time and to later generations aberrant behaviour, was very normal to the men themselves. It shows too that many partnerships of Indian women with British upper class men were long term – marriages in all but legal name. Many wills suggest ties of affection, loyalty on both sides, and happy companionships. British men often asked their close friends to be executors and to care for their Indian partners, referring to them as 'well beloved', 'female friend', and 'worthy friend'. They were often left substantial bequests and annuities to maintain them after their partner's death. When Major Thomas Naylor in 1782 bequeathed to his companion Muckmul Patna Rs 4000, a bungalow and a garden at Berhampore, a hackery, bullocks, her jewels, clothes, and all their male and female slaves, he treated her as he might a wife.[25]

It is clear too that British men respected the traditional way of life and religious beliefs of their Indian womenfolk. The zenana of Khair un Nissa, the companion of James Kirkpatrick, within the Residency compound at Hyderabad and where she lived in purdah, was 'adorned with paintings and made cool by fountains'.[26] She, and others of her social standing, lived much as they would have done had they married Indian men of wealth. There was no pressure put upon them to convert to Christianity, and no evidence that any upper class Indian women did so. Some of these partnerships were formalised according to Muslim custom, for most women of social standing who lived with British officials were Muslims, 'the Hindus being far more scrupulous'.[27]

The men who made these long-term alliances saw them as

morally binding, even if they were not officially recognised. Colonel William Gardner, whose marriage to Mah Munzel Ool Nissa lasted forty happy years, clearly believed that, 'a Moslem lady's marriage with a Christian by a Khazi is as legal in this country as if the ceremony had been performed by the Bishop of Calcutta'.[28] Nevertheless, British men almost invariably had their children baptised as Christians and educated as Europeans. Indian companions could expect to have their children taken away at an early age and sent to Britain for their education. Major Samuel Kilpatrick, for instance, left the interest on Rs 12,000 to his companion, Nannah, so long as she remained unmarried, but requested that their two children be sent back to England for their education, asking his executors to ensure that they were brought up 'in the genteelest manner'. Nannah was to receive a gift of Rs 1000 when the time came for the children to be taken away, to be done 'with the greatest delicacy'.[29]

There seems to have been a tacit understanding between both man and woman, even at the higher social levels, that partnerships were for India only. Save in a very few cases, when British men returned home, the Indian companion stayed in India. If this was attributable to the inevitable social and cultural problems for an Indian woman in Britain it probably reflected too her unwillingness to leave for a life in old age far from the country of her birth and family. Though officers and civil servants may have had a choice, for the majority of the British and their Indian partners there was none. British soldiers were not allowed to take their Indian partners and Eurasian children back to Britain and quite often retired to an invalid colony such as Chunar.

In general most British upper class men found their choice of Indian partner restricted by the exceedingly limited opportunities of social contact between them and the higher ranks of Indian society, whether Hindu or Muslim. There were some exceptions in which the social standing of the woman matched or exceeded that of the man, and where the match originated in romance. Colonel Gardner's case was one of these. British wills, with dedications such as 'to Commaul; a girl formerly in my service', 'to Betsy, she having proved herself a faithful servant for many years', suggest that far more often the partnership started on a master-servant basis. Other wills make it clear that a payment to relatives of the girl was a common practice. Men were frank about the matter. Major-General Claude Martin of Lucknow, whose bequest founded the La Martinière Schools, noted in his will that he had acquired his much loved companion, Boulone, for a monetary payment. He explained that, though he had paid for Boulone and for other girls, 'they were not as we term slaves tho' paid a consideration for, but the sum I paid was a present to the relations that I might have a right on her'.[30] Similarly, Robert Grant, brother of Charles Grant, a future Chairman of the East India Company, bought his devoted Zeenut in 1778 from her uncle who sold her to pay off his gambling debts.[31] On occasions a girl was hired as a companion rather than bought outright.[32]

Their illegitimacy and mixed race descent counted against the Eurasian children of Indian mothers. But so too did adverse British perceptions of their mothers' morality. When Frederick Shore commented that, 'the women who live with Englishmen are, with few exceptions, common prostitutes by profession, bred to the trade', his judgement was harsh, perhaps a great exaggeration, but nevertheless widely accepted.[33]

*

One particular social group – the military – was, although Eurasian children were born to British fathers in all walks of life, responsible primarily for the rapid growth of a Eurasian population to a considerable size by the early nineteenth century. From a few hundred soldiers in the mid-eighteenth century the British military population in India had increased to 18,000 in the Royal and Company armies of 1790. The isolation of military life in early British India – often far from the Presidency towns, in cantonments set amidst a multitude of servants, camp-followers and traders who travelled with the regiment wherever it went – fostered the development of an extended 'service family' within which the Colonel and his officers assumed social responsibility for regulating all aspects of the private life as well as the public duty of the regiment. A patriarchal authority established codes of behaviour amongst its officers and men, determined whether and whom they might marry, and even settled disputes between its soldiers and their women.[34] The 'service family' embraced the women and children of its soldiers within its protection, support and discipline.

Soldiers, particularly junior officers and men, were generally the poor relations of the larger British community in India. Company officers, until they reached the rank of Major or obtained a civil appointment, were less well paid than either their counterparts in the civil service or even in the Royal Army. Promotion in the Royal Army was much faster than in the Company's. In the Company's service an officer could expect to serve at least 25 years to reach the rank of Major, compared to between 12–17 years in the Royal Army. There were few General officer appointments to which a Company officer might aspire. In 1784 no rank was open above Colonel, and in the Bengal Army only four such appointments between 931 officers. The situation had improved a little by the end of the century, but as late as 1826 there were still only eighteen Generals on the Company's establishment.[35]

Pay for junior officers was low – in 1831 a Lieutenant in the Company's Bengal European Regiment received, with half-batta, £282 a year and less if he was in either the Bombay or Madras armies. Most in consequence had great problems in living in the style expected of them as 'gentlemen'. Perhaps the case of Lieutenant Cullen of the Bengal Artillery, who admitted in 1827 that he had returned to England owing Rs 90,000 was exceptional, but hardly any young officers managed to avoid debt.[36] As the sons of parents with influence enough to obtain cadetships for their sons, but not enough money to buy a more desirable Royal commission, there were few Company officers with large parental funds or inherited wealth on which to draw in their early years of service.[37] In consequence the prospects for a young Company officer in the competitive British marriage market in India were poor indeed. The newly arrived Lieutenant Massey, visiting a ball in Calcutta in 1826, wrote home to his sister complaining that: 'Here at a plain blue coat [the dress of a covenanted civil servant] every tradesman wears in England, sheeps eyes without end are cast'. The red coat of an officer held little attraction to the opposite sex, 'save with light blue facings, or two large epaulets', denoting either a civil appointment or Colonel's rank.[38]

Most Company officers, unlikely to reach field rank and to accumulate enough money to retire home in comfort, were destined to become permanent exiles. Even in India they could not afford to marry until in their middle age. So they took Indian women as their companions, and as the numbers of Eurasian daughters of their brother officers grew in the early nineteenth century, chose them as wives. A few British officers, Captain Innes Munro was one, deplored the practice of taking Indian companions, condemning it as 'a singular (and I think an unnatural taste), preferring them to white women', but he was decidedly in the minority.[39] Many officers found their companions from the daughters of Indian soldiers under their command, so reinforcing the 'service family' as a self-contained unit.[40] Where they could, they sent their Eurasian daughters to the ladies' seminaries in the Presidency towns and to England to be 'finished'. When they returned they were married off to fellow officers, a process described in Charles D'Oyley's satirical poem 'Tom Raw', in which the aspiring Lieutenant Raw married his Colonel's 'dingy' daughter to advance his prospects of promotion.[41]

Whenever they could officers left capital or income to secure their daughters' futures. The wills of officers of the late eighteenth century show that junior officers frequently had little to leave. Captain Alexander Paterson left his daughter 2000 pagodas (about Rs 6–7000), in trust with the SPCK missionaries Schwartz and Gericke at Trinchinopoly.[42] Senior officers could do better for their daughters and leave them as substantial heiresses. Sarah, the daughter of Lieutenant-Colonel Humphrey Harper, who was born at Vellore in 1777, was left £5000.[43] A General, Sir John Pater for instance, could help his Eurasian daughter make an excellent match. Sapphira, his daughter by Arabella Robinson, was married to John Hawkey, a Captain in the Royal Navy. Pater, by his own account had set them up generously, for he left Sapphira all the plate, glass and furniture which had been loaned to them. Hawkey was forgiven the 10,750 pagodas which had been lent him by Pater.[44]

In the later years of the eighteenth century there were many Eurasian military daughters whose inherited wealth was a marked marital attraction. The contemporary novel 'Hartly House' refers to two Eurasian girls boarded at a ladies' school where they were to remain, 'until proposals are received for their change of condition, their fortunes are small (for Calcutta fortunes) twenty thousand rupees only'.[45] But, for every Eurasian heiress there were many more impoverished officers' daughters placed, after the death of their fathers, in the military orphanages which were founded towards the end of the eighteenth century. The future for these girls depended largely on finding a husband, at the monthly public dances – perhaps a civil servant, more often a military officer or merchant.

★

Many of the Eurasian boys and girls born to British military officers serving in India in the late eighteenth and early nineteenth century had some start in life. Upper class British fathers did all within their means to maintain the social status of their children as best they could, either sending them back to Britain, contributing to orphanage systems in India, seeking employment for the boys and suitable marriages for the girls. 'Class' counted in these childrens' favour, as it did against the children of the military rank and file. Their fathers came from the poorest and most disadvantaged sectors of society in Britain. 'Poor whites' had never been welcome to the Company in India, whose policy had invariably been to return to Britain any vagrants, sailors who had jumped ship, indeed any who were in India without their licence.[46] The need for a large military force to back the expansion of British territorial interests brought in its train rapid and alarming social consequences – military 'poor whites' were by the end of the eighteenth century the largest British social group stimulating a rapid acceleration in the population of 'poor Eurasian' children in India. As early as 1784 the SPCK reported that 700 Eurasian children were being born each year in the Madras Presidency alone, and that 'the fathers of these people being usually soldiers and the lower order of people, too often neglect their offspring and suffer them to follow the caste of their mothers'.[47]

Service as a soldier in India for a shilling a day appealed only to those with few prospects in Britain. Most recruits were drawn from distressed areas of Britain, Scotland, and the countryside of England where land enclosure policies at the end of the eighteenth century had ensured that 'the decay of the village poor had reached catastrophic proportions'.[48] Most of the Company's recruits at the end of the eighteenth century were agricultural labourers. Only a few were tradesmen or had been in 'white collar' occupations. Until they set out for India the furthest journey of the majority probably had been to their nearest market town.[49] When they embarked they were young – between 15 and 19, illiterate and often in very poor physical condition.[50] The Company's problem in recruitment of satisfactory soldiers is clear in the dismissive comment of Governor-General Cornwallis: 'The contemptible trash of which the Company's European force is composed makes me shudder'.[51] They, and the soldiers of the Royal Army in India, stood on the lowest rung of the British ladder, separated from the civil servants and their officers by an unbridgeable social gap.

The living conditions and life style of the men reflected their lack of status, carried over to their children, and provided a poor environment for their upbringing. Whilst a General would have his palatial house and often a zenana, junior officers their bungalows, the men made do in 'immensely long buildings, thatched, and almost entirely open on all sides like a tanner's drying house'.[52] They lived communally without privacy, save for the Sergeants in their separate rooms, surrounded by their women and children, servants and camp followers of all kinds. Once the daily duty of the parade ground was done, apart from the bazaar, there was nowhere to go and nothing to do. Drink provided one answer; an ever available supply of fiery spirits bought by the soldier from the bazaar or smuggled in, often by their women.[53]

The cheap indulgence helped alleviate the monotony, heat and discomfort of the soldier's daily life, but was also a major cause of disorder in the cantonment leading to sexual promiscuity, illness and consequent incapacity for military duty. Surgeons at Madras, reporting on the sick returns at the military hospital there in 1802, listed the most frequent illnesses as itches, fluxes, fevers and venereal disease, attributed to 'immoderate use of arrack' and 'sleeping out when in liquor'.[54] Theft and violence were commonplace in the barracks. At Chinsura, for example, a depot for acclimatising soldiers newly arrived from Britain, civil and military authority were frequently at loggerheads as soldiers sold their socks and shirts to pay for spirits, molested Indian women, and attacked the civil police.[55]

Military commanders, faced with the problem of maintaining discipline amongst their men, generally preferred them to be married.

> Every commanding officer with reference to the health, the morals, and the discipline of the men under his charge, will lead him to prefer these connexions [marriage], to a system of concubinage or still more to a promiscuous and hazardous intercourse with the women of the bazar (sic). For one of these alternatives it will hardly be denied he must chuse.[56]

There were, however, almost insuperable problems to the implementation of a policy of British marriage for soldiers – few British women and the cost to the soldier himself. No women came out with the Company's recruits and just a few with the Royal Army. The fleet which sailed from Britain in 1791 brought 2987 Royal Army other ranks, but only 117 women.[57] Company policy, which whilst it controlled residence in India, restricted as much as possible the entry of working class women. In consequence there were few British women whom their soldiers might marry.[58] Cost was a further deterrent to a soldier, for humble though his status was, manual work by him or his wife was thought to be racially demeaning.

> The pay of a soldier is insufficient to support a wife with any degree of credit to the Regiment in which he belongs especially

in this country where he cannot devote his leisure to manual labour, or convert her earnings towards her own support and that of his family.[59]

In the ban on work by soldiers' wives, who though low in the ranks of British society, were expected to uphold its racial position, lies a fundamental contrast between a soldier's life in colonial India and elsewhere. Much else, poor accommodation, harsh discipline, little pay, social subordination, was the British soldier's lot wherever he served. Strict regulations governed the lives of British solders and their wives. Soldiers had to seek their commanding officer's permission to marry, and the good character of the aspirant wife established first. What was *not* allowed in India, but was elsewhere, was the opportunity for soldiers' wives to earn money. The standing orders of the 10th Regiment of Infantry stationed at Palermo in 1815, for instance, gave Sergeants' wives the right to do the officers' washing, and the soldiers' wives to do the regiment's, for which they received washing money every month. The Quartermaster further undertook never 'to give any Needlework out of the Regiment which can be done in it'.[60]

Few soldiers in India of the late eighteenth and early nineteenth century married. Where they did it was as often to the Eurasian daughters of their fellows as to British women.[61] Most lived with local Indian women, a practice which military authority attempted to control. In Royal regiments a 'policy of attaching soldiers to native women' was in operation by 1810.[62] If regiments left for Europe, as the 66th and 78th did in 1817, their women were taken on by soldiers in other units.[63] Many other soldiers, neither married nor cohabiting, found female company in casual relationships, the consequences of which were unsuccessfully countered by the establishment of lock hospitals for women in the early nineteenth century.[64]

★

Although the permissive sexual behaviour of British males in India was tacitly condoned by the Company in London and its local government, it was never officially countenanced. The Company preferred at first to turn a blind eye to the inevitable emergence of a poor illegitimate Eurasian population than to take any practical measures which would have made it possible for their men to marry. But, from the later years of the eighteenth century, attitudes of disapproval towards cohabitation with Indian women began to be voiced, intensifying as the nineteenth century advanced. These were directly related to new ideas of British national identity, public behaviour, and a philosophy of colonial rule which developed in Britain and India at the same time. These ideas, prompted by the secular task of governing a distant and alien territorial empire, were buttressed by the moral concepts generated by a Protestant revival in Britain. In British India of the early nineteenth century Church linked with State as an evangelical force to underpin the colonial order. Together Church and State promoted public observance of Christian morality as an affirmation of British racial superiority over the character, religious beliefs and customs of India's peoples: 'A new moral racism came to confirm the vision of a disciplined Christian people'.[65]

With backing in Parliament and the Court of Directors, the evangelical movement provided the impetus for a hoped for moral regeneration amongst the British in India and the conversion to Christianity of Indians themselves.[66] Company chaplains and missionaries, the latter allowed into India officially from 1813, were the natural spearhead of an attack on the custom of liaisons between British men and Indian women as the most glaring contradiction between what should be expected of a disciplined Christian people and their actual behaviour. The protagonists of a new moral order were supported by ardent sympathisers, of whom Mary Sherwood was a most influential example. She was the wife of an army officer stationed at Cawnpore from 1808 to 1813, where she set up an elementary school and devoted herself to the rescue for Christianity of soldiers' children. Little remembered today, Mary Sherwood became a prolific and highly successful writer and is an important source in the study of changing attitudes towards liaisons between British men and Indian women. Sherwood was the author of many books, of which *The History of Little Henry and his Bearer* was the most popular. First published in 1815, it had reached its twentieth edition by 1823. New editions continued until 1884.[67]

Mary Sherwood's writings show a Christian compassion for the children of mixed race coupled with a profound aversion to the circumstances of their birth, strongly influenced by a quite unChristian view of the alleged moral depravity of their mothers. It is significant that, in most British comment of her time on the Eurasian population, the blame for their alleged moral shortcomings or personality defects was routinely placed upon the Indian mother rather than the British father.[68] In Sherwood's memoirs, she recalled the 'half-caste' children who came to be taught by her:

They were civil and well behaved externally, but so profoundly ignorant that they had never heard the name of Christ! These, and many such as these, are the daughters of Europeans, of Englishmen and English gentlemen – of men who have known what it is to have a tender, well educated Christian mother, and honourable and aimiable sisters.[69]

Sherwood felt that in the heathenism and depravity of Indian women lay the greatest threat to the moral character and future Christianity of their Eurasian children. The view was shared by many involved in early nineteenth century charitable activity. The Bible Society of Bombay, placed the blame in 1814 firmly on the shoulders of Indian mothers:

> The mother is often of no religion and seldom has any means of bestowing an acquaintance with even the first and plainest truths of religion – she is often profligate and more likely to corrupt those who are near her. There are instances of such mothers bringing up their children as Mohammedans and devoting them from their first years to prostitution.[70]

The History of George Desmond, Sherwood's cautionary novel, exemplifies the vehemence of the evangelical attack on Indo-British cohabitation. Every contemporary prejudice against Indian women is rehearsed in its account of the seduction of George Desmond, a young civil servant of good family, by the dancing-girl Amena. Her child, acknowledged by George, is proved to be by her Indian lover, neatly instancing a common concern amongst British men over the fidelity of their Indian companions.[71] George's forgiving wife, poisoned by the discarded Amena's servant, is presented as a saintly paradigm of British womanhood. The general view of many was echoed in the hapless George's reflections upon the wife whom he had lost:

> O what a contrast was there between the love of such a woman and that of Amena! By my attachment to Emily my character was refined and exalted – by my connexion with Amena, it was depressed and degraded.[72]

Although the rationale for the evangelical attack on cohabitation was ostensibly the illegitimacy of the resulting children, and the malign influence of the mothers on their upbringing, the evidence suggests that race, just as much as morality, was at the heart of the issue, particularly where the Company's covenanted civil servants were concerned. Assistant Surgeon Tracy, stationed at Dindigul in 1834, wrestled with a problem brought by his conversion to practising Christianity. Should he put away his long-term companion, Ventamina, or should he marry her? She was willing to convert to marry him, but Tracy was fearful of his father's reaction and the Company's response, since he had to have its permission to marry. In the event, marry her he did, but not before enquiring whether it could be done in secret.[73]

The suspicion that arguments based on morality cloaked an increasing public disapproval of *any* British relationships which sullied their racial purity is endorsed by the growing disapproval in the early nineteenth century of marriages amongst the British elite to Eurasian women. The public dances for the female wards of the Upper Military Academy, Calcutta, which had been attended so eagerly fifty years earlier had been discontinued by the 1830s.[74] It was thus harder for Eurasian girls to meet potential British husbands. Public argument against marriages to Eurasian women skirted the question of race and focussed on their social consequences. It was conceded that 'many of the half-cast ladies are the most aimiable companions, possess affectionate hearts and perform all the duties of good wives with tenderness and alacrity'.[75] But it was also argued that they did not mix well in British society; that they lacked education; were reluctant to leave India when their men retired; and – probably most important of all – would handicap the career of an ambitious husband.

★

It is hard to tell precisely how swiftly private behaviour responded to the vehement attack in the early nineteenth century on the propriety of Indo-British liaisons and marriages. Those who took public positions on the moral issue and advocated change were more likely to speak out than those who quietly continued to live their own lives as they thought best. There were always some who, privately at least, were prepared to excuse the old ways. Samuel Browne, a covenanted civil servant stationed near Delhi in the 1820s, was one. He, like so many of his contemporaries had a close Eurasian relative, a half-sister married to Lieutenant-Colonel Monier Williams, then Surveyor-General of Bombay. Writing to his mother in 1828 of one of his friends he urged her: 'Do not think with such horror of his living with a native woman . . . I do not say that the connection is a desirable one but it should not be considered as heinous as persons in England are inclined to think'.[76] Browne, who observed that those who lived with Indian women for any length of time never married a European, undoubtedly liked them for themselves, as many of his contemporaries and predecessors in India clearly did. Even the future Lord Metcalfe, who in the first years of the nineteenth century was one of Governor-General Wellesley's staff, did not practise what he preached. At first a vigorous protagonist of the new moral order, Metcalfe soon conformed to the old customs of the country, and had three sons by a Rajput lady with whom he lived for seven years.[77]

But by the 1830s the practice by the British elite in India of keeping an Indian companion, though by no means extinct, was much diminished. British wills in Bengal in 1830–2 record less than one in four bequests to Indian women and their children compared with almost two in five fifty years earlier.[78] The proportion of illegitimate births registered in the Bengal Presidency had dropped to one in ten in 1830 from the one in two recorded at St John's Church, Calcutta between 1767 and 1781.[79] Such a dramatic fall may perhaps be attributed in part to the possibility that fewer illegitimate children were baptised than fifty years earlier, although there is no evidence of this. Perhaps Indian women companions were under greater pressure to avoid childbirth in the 1830s than the 1780s. Even allowing for such possibilities it seems that upper class British men were at least publicly conforming to the social pressure which frowned ever more on public liaisons with Indian women. It does not follow, however, that private behaviour always matched public morality. The fashionable brothels of Calcutta, Mrs Maxwell's and Mother Brookes' to name two, were probably as well patronised as their counterparts in London of the day.[80]

If change was gradual, and its pace varied by British occupational group, it had much to do with the relative scarcity of British women and the cost of their maintenance. In 1810 it was reported that there were only 250 Englishwomen available as marriage partners in Bengal for some 4000 'respectable Englishmen', a ratio which probably still held true as late as 1830. To some extent this gap was filled by the increasing numbers of Eurasian daughters of covenanted civil servants and officers coming to maturity at the time. It was thought that in Calcutta alone there were more than 500 marriageable Eurasian girls in the 1820s. Their chance of a British marriage was enhanced by the great increase in numbers of young writers and military cadets coming out from Britain after 1813.[81] Many of them, for all the social disapproval, married Eurasian girls – so much so that in 1832 it was remarked that 'amongst the officers who held the highest situation on the staff of the Company's service in Calcutta, there is not at present one who is not married to a female of Indian descent'.[82]

The marriage at this time of Eurasian women back into the upper levels of British society had an important adverse effect on the standing and marital prospects of Eurasian males. The Eurasian daughter of a military officer might well marry back into her 'class'. Her brother, in contrast, after 1791 when covenanted service was effectively closed to him, could at best hope to be a government clerk and lost his 'gentlemanly' status. Young educated Eurasian men were not welcome at the public dances where many of their sisters met British husbands. Contemporary comment suggests that the sisters, 'conscious of their superior prospects, look down upon their male relatives with an undisguised disdain'.[83] Governor John Malcolm observed the effect on Eurasian men:

> The male part rarely marry the European women, and their connections with their own class, or with the native females of India, produce a race still darker than themselves . . . while, on the other hand, the children of females who have inter-married with Europeans, from being fairer, and belonging to another society, become in one or two generations, altogether separated from that race of natives from whom they are maternally descended.[84]

Change in social behaviour was naturally slowest among the military. As late as 1842 Captain Richard Burton recorded that 'there was hardly an officer in Baroda who was not morganatically married to a Hindi or Hindu woman'.[85] Yet many officers did marry, more often than not to the Eurasian daughters of their fellow officers. Least likely of all to marry, of all British males in India, were the military rank and file. By the 1820s little change was noticeable in their social behaviour. Most still lived unmarried with Indian or Portuguese women, and were responsible for the vast majority of the growing population of 'poor Eurasians'.[86] The desertion of many of these children, whether through the return of their fathers to Britain, their death, or other causes, increased the size of this socially vulnerable element in British society which had to depend upon official action for its education and subsequent employment.

Between 1773 and 1833 the Eurasian population of British stock in India had grown at what seemed an exponential rate. It was generally poor, with little prospect in future life, and a cause for concern to the rulers of British India. Its parentage flouted the norms of Christian behaviour now asserted and expected of the Company's servants. Yet its very existence exposed the ostrich like quality of the Company's policy which actively discouraged the admittance to India of the class of English women who might have provided the wives for the poorer in British society. The 'Eurasian problem' was one which Bishop Heber thought was substantially of the Company's own making:

> I never met with any public man connected with India, who did not lament the increase of the half-caste population as a great source of the present mischief and future danger to the tranquillity of the Colony. Why then forbid the introduction of a class of women to the white colonists; and so far, at least, diminish the evil of which they complain?[87]

The Company preferred, however, to transfer, as far as it could, the management of the problem for which its policy was ultimately responsible to British society in India which was expected to make suitable arrangements for the education and employment of its Eurasian children. But, it was a problem into which the Company was progressively and reluctantly to be drawn as the social claims of Eurasians outstripped the financial resources of British society in India to meet them.

2

Charity and Children in Care

One Sunday morning in February 1835 the elite of the British community in Bombay was gathered at St. Thomas's Church for the annual sermon on behalf of the Society for the Education of the Poor. The Governor of Bombay was the President of the Society. He sat closest to the pulpit with the other members of the British establishment, in strict order of precedence, ranged behind him.[1] Boys from the Society's orphanage sang in the choir. The other boys and girls were ranged around the walls of the church. At the end of the service the annual collection for the Society was taken, and the objects of that benevolence, the charity boys and girls, returned to the orphanage in the cart which had been bought for their transport.[2]

This occasion was a public demonstration of the responsibility accepted by the better off in British society in India for the welfare of the children of their poor. The Bombay Society was just one of a wide network of charity funds, free schools, and orphanages which existed by 1830 in British India. Organised charity aimed to relieve the growing problem of 'poor whites' – British men, their widows, and their British and Eurasian children who were unable to support themselves. Unlike Britain at the time, no Poor Law existed to regulate and order relief in the Company's Indian territories. Its place was taken by a network of voluntary agencies, military, civil, religious, which raised and dispensed local funds, and drew in Government moral and financial support to an ever increasing extent as the needy poor increased.

By the 1830s there were probably between two and three thousand children, many of them Eurasian, in the charitable institutions of the three main Presidency towns and elsewhere in British India. They were the fortunate ones. Extensive though the system was it nevertheless fell far short of the need. Throughout the late eighteenth century orphanage managements struggled for funds to meet the needs of those of British descent with a claim on society's protection. Their frequent appeals for additional income repeatedly stressed the waiting lists for children whom they could not afford to take in. As the Governors of the Calcutta Free School recorded in 1817, 'twenty or thirty deserving subjects are frequently rejected at a single meeting'. They were sure there were many more yet who would try and get in if they thought they had a chance.[3] For each Eurasian child who was accommodated there was another who could not be and who faced an adult life without education or training. In this inadequate provision lies one of the central reasons for the development of a large under-class of Eurasians whose existence was to cause such concern to British authority.

The need for some organised system of care for the orphans of 'poor whites' was recognised early in the eighteenth century. British communities in the Presidency towns established schools for which the Chaplain was chiefly responsible. By the middle of the century, however, it was becoming clear that the small scale establishments of earlier years were inadequate to meet a growing demand. The cause was two-fold; firstly more British men in India, secondly the high death rate amongst them. Of all the covenanted civil servants, the best-off amongst the British and most able to care for their health, who went out to India between 1762 and 1771 only one in ten had managed to return to Britain by 1784. Almost *half* had died in India.[4] Many of them died young and poor, leaving their children in need.

Many references at the time illustrate the widespread European poverty and distress to be found by the end of the eighteenth century in Presidency towns, an aspect of the British social state which perhaps has received less attention hitherto than it warrants. By 1800, for example, the Vestry of St. John's Church, Calcutta, had established a permanent fund for the 'relief of distressed Europeans and others'. Accidents, ill-health and business failure all added to the number of Britons and their descendants thrown on public charity. Despite public collections, handsome legacies from the estates of prominent men such as the rich Eurasian, Charles Weston, and grudging contributions from the Court of Directors in London, the resources of the fund were soon inadequate to the task of supporting an ever increasing number of beneficiaries. Many of them came from respectable walks of British non-official life: school-teachers, mariners, tradesmen, indigo cultivators and wives deserted by soldiers. By the 1820s the fund was supporting 573 Europeans and 734 Eurasians.[5]

★

The rapid expansion of the existing free school and orphanage system which took place in the forty years between 1780 and 1820 was a response to the increasing numbers of poor Britons and Eurasians. A few privileged Eurasians with wealthy fathers were sent back to Britain for their education or to the private schools which developed around 1780 to meet the need. But for the majority, those who were lucky enough even to find a place, the orphanage provided an institutional framework in which to begin life, receive food, clothing and protection, and an elementary education.

The institutional life to which these children were committed extended through to adult life, for orphanage managements implemented the way in which British society believed they should be brought up and the degree of education that it was felt proper that they should receive. The orphanage decided the future of their charges in adult life, either as soldiers, soldiers' wives, tradesmen or junior civil servants. For most Eurasian children to reach adulthood was merely to exchange one institution for another, and to continue life within a regulated framework – a process which played an inevitable part in developing the dependence of Eurasians on state employment for their place in European society.

The fully fledged orphanage system which existed by the 1820s gives the impression of being the consequence of deliberate policy and principles applied consistently in all three Presidencies. The regime was remarkably similar in each orphanage; the cost per child was very comparable between one and another; the standards of medical care and education very similar in each. Successful experience was indeed interchanged between institutions, such as the use of orphanage boys to carry out Government printing.[6] The development of the system was, however, more a pragmatic evolutionary process than the product of deliberate official policy. The initiative, in what was a piecemeal and reactive response to a growing social problem came primarily from the British community in India – officials, the military, and missionaries who saw the need at first hand. As the problem exceeded local financial resources they dragged an ever-reluctant Court of Directors in London into taking on an increasing share of the cost.

The development of a wide institutional response to the problem of increasing numbers of Eurasian children was spearheaded by the Company's Armies in Bengal and Madras who established their own orphanages in the 1780s, reflecting the nature of the 'service family' in which the care of the dependants of officers and men was a responsibility accepted by the military community. Officers were expected to finance the care of their own children themselves, and in 1783 the officers of the Bengal Army agreed to a monthly stoppage of pay to defray the cost.[7] Their original proposal was to send all officers' children back to Britain, educate them there, apprentice them to suitable careers, or, if suitable, return them as cadets to follow their fathers in India. This last provision, for reasons which are discussed later, was vetoed by the Court of Directors. Only those children who were legitimate and wholly British – a minority – were returned to England. The vast majority, Eurasian and illegitimate, stayed in India and were educated at the Upper Male and Female Orphanages at Calcutta.[8]

In the same year that the Upper Military Orphanage was founded, the Bengal Military Orphan Society proposed to the Company in London that it should take on the responsibility for the orphans of soldiers and non-commissioned officers in a separate institution. The Society was to manage the orphanage and the Company to pay the cost. Despite an initial dispute over the monthly allowance per child – the Company offered Rs 3, the Society asked for and got Rs 5 – the Lower Military Orphanage was established at Alipore in 1784 with separate accommodation for boys and girls.[9] At the other two Presidencies – Madras and Bombay – orphan provision was made, but not on the scale of Bengal. At Madras there were military orphanages for boys and girls by 1797, but children of officers were housed together with the children of other ranks. Bombay was the only Presidency of the three without a military orphanage, choosing instead to levy its officers, as in Bengal, and after 1817 to send their children to the Free School. There were far fewer officers in the Bombay Army in 1784, 268 compared with 931 in Bengal, which may well explain why officers in Bombay did not follow the example of the Bengal and Madras Presidencies in setting up a specifically military institution.[10]

Whilst the Company's Army took the initiative in dealing with their orphans in the late eighteenth century, the Royal Army in India had a different and less benevolent policy. The Company's Army did not discriminate between legitimate and illegitimate children, nor between Eurasian and Briton. All were eligible for care. In contrast there was *no* provision at all by the Royal Army for the care of the Eurasian children of soldiers even if their parents were married. Permission to marry, legitimacy, and British parentage on both sides were the touchstones of Royal Army policy as far as children were concerned. Only orphans who met these criteria might be return to the care of the Military Asylum at Chelsea. Neither was the Royal Army prepared to pay any costs for Eurasian children born 'off the strength' and left behind when Royal regiments were posted out of India. The official view was that 'the embarrassments attending the provision of orphans of soldiers by Native women and other children of the same description left in India upon the departure of a regiment for Europe grow out of the local habits incidental to the country'.[11]

It is to the Company's credit that it frequently stepped in where Royal Army children, British or Eurasian, were left abandoned. In consequence, although Eurasian children were in the majority at the Lower Military Orphanage at Alipore, there was always a substantial minority of children of wholly British birth – one in four in 1828.[12] Tension seems to have existed between the Eurasian and British children reflecting in reverse the attitudes of the adult world outside. An apocryphal story that one British girl – Sarah Abbot – was persecuted to death by Eurasian orphans went the rounds in 1815 and gave Mary Sherwood a reason to press for a separate asylum – the European Female Orphan Asylum – to be set up specifically for the British daughters of Royal Army soldiers. 'It was not right', [she argued] 'and an offence to propriety, to class the daughters of English women of good character with children which had been nurtured by Hindoo and Mussulman mothers of the lowest description'.[13]

★

At the same time as the military set up their systems of orphan relief civil authorities in the Presidency towns expanded their capacity. New institutions were grafted on to the orphanages and charity foundations of the early eighteenth century in an attempt to cope with a demand which always seemed to grow ahead of resources. A Free School at Calcutta was founded in 1789 and merged with the earlier Charity School in 1800. By 1818 it boarded 189 boys and 87 girls as well as educating 36 day boys.[14] Civil orphanages for boys and girls were opened in Madras in 1807 and 1810 respectively. At Bombay, the Society for the Education of the Poor was founded in 1815, expanding the capacity of the original Charity School. By 1817 it was educating 83 boys and 46 girls and had a 'long list of children waiting for admission as soon as the funds will allow'.[15]

All these schools were perennially short of funds, a circumstance which led to admission policies which discriminated against Eurasians. European children had first priority at the Calcutta Free School; then 'the next in preference are country-born children of mixed race, whose situation renders them objects of great pity'.[16] At Bombay and Madras the admission regulations placed illegitimate Eurasians in the lowest category of all.[17] Since not all applicants could be accommodated an admission policy was inevitable. But it was not *need* which determined priority, but the concept of those who were deemed the most *deserving*. They were the children of those parents who had observed the approved code of public behaviour – Christian marriage between British or European men and women. The penalty for non-observance of the code fell on the illegitimate, generally Eurasian child. In this manner public morality was upheld. Its consequence was that those children most in need were generally last in the queue, or excluded altogether.

For those children excluded from official civil relief the growing number of missionary schools in the early nineteenth century provided some possibility of education. Missionaries took all children, whatever their race, providing they were Christians. As early as the mid-eighteenth century the SPCK operating in the Madras Presidency were establishing schools and being paid by the Church Vestry to house and educate Eurasian children.[18] The Serampore Baptists, who set up the Benevolent Institution in Calcutta and sister organisations later in other parts of Bengal saw their role as 'a kind of auxiliary to the Free School, receiving into its bosom those which the other Institution is unable to accommodate'. By 1818, 238 children were under their instruction in Calcutta, 198 of whom were either Portuguese or Eurasian Christians. These were, however, but a small minority of the children whom the Baptists estimated were in need in the city alone.[19] Once missionaries were allowed free entry into India after 1813, their contribution to the education of the poor expanded rapidly. Whatever the denomination virtually the first activity at each new missionary post was to start a school, often supervised by the missionary's wife. By the 1830s wherever there was a substantial British station or settlement in India a missionary school was bound to be found as well.

The rapid expansion of a system of care for the children of the British poor in the late eighteenth and early nineteenth century was driven by two principal motives. The first was philanthropic, a recognition that there was a moral responsibility on the part of the better off in British society towards the poor. The second, a pragmatic motive, was fear that the social order might be threatened by large numbers of uneducated and unemployed descendants of British fathers. The threat was all the more real to a ruling elite which felt its security rested on the esteem in which it was held by the Indian ruled. 'It is', wrote Sir John Malcolm in 1826, 'upon their continued impression of the superiority of our character that our existence must depend'.[20]

British leaders in late eighteenth century India were undoubtedly influenced by the charitable movements of the time in Britain in which religious bodies – the Methodists and SPCK for example – were active in promoting what has been described as a 'tissue of conspicuous philanthropy'.[21] The European practice of establishing free schools in major towns was an argument advanced for the Calcutta Free School in 1796 and it is notable that in India the Company's senior officials were involved in the management of charity schools. The management of the Bombay Free School was a typical instance. The Governor of Bombay was the President and his Council its Vice-Presidents. The Bishop of Calcutta became its Patron, and the Archdeacon of Bombay acted as Chairman of the Committee of Management.[22] Records of individual charitable donations to orphanages and free schools show too a widespread and tangible commitment by the better off in the British community to their poor. Legacies were often substantial. A large bequest of Rs 6,000 from Mrs Eleanor Boyd in 1767 for the benefit of poor orphans later played a vital part in enlarging the Bombay Free School. It was first lodged in the Company's Treasury, forgotten, but rediscovered in 1808, by which time it had grown with interest added to Rs 26,000.[23]

If altruism was one important motive, self-interest within the British community was another. The military removed an encumbrance to its discipline and movements when, at the age of five *all* children, Eurasian or British, legitimate or illegitimate, orphaned or not, were sent down to the orphanage at Calcutta. Missionaries established a useful place in British society by running schools. Once the Serampore Baptists had gained official permission to set up the Benevolent Institution in Calcutta, despite the protests of the Managers of the Free School who probably felt that it might compete with them for donations, John Marshman commented to his parent society in Britain that it gave 'us [the Baptists] as its conductors the focus of an establishment in Calcutta'.[24] The rescue of Eurasian children was an essential preliminary to their greater aim of mass Indian conversion. Civil society in general saw a benefit in institutional care of children who otherwise would become 'burdensome to Society, the character and interest of which must be more affected by them as they gradually constitute a larger part of its mass'.[25]

The socialisation of this 'mass' was the primary aim of the orphanage and free school movement of the time. Once children were within the boundaries of the orphanage they could be held safe from the world outside. The development of their moral character and utility to British society could then be undertaken in Christian hands, away from the influence of their Hindu or Muslim mothers.[26] To those involved in the process the raw material taken into the orphanages seemed most unpromising. Many of the Eurasian children spoke little or no English. They brought with them into the orphanage and school the skills necessary for survival on the streets or in the cantonment. The Benevolent Institution noted their regrettable tendency to swear and to steal school property. Books, slates and penknives 'disappeared'. At Madras Dr. Bell, who took charge of the Male Military Orphanage in 1789 described his charges as, 'in general, stubborn perverse and obstinate: much given to lying and addicted to tricks and perversity'.[27]

The challenge to orphanage managers was to mould these children into useful members of society. There are striking similarities between the aims and practices in India and in Britain at the time. In Britain promoters of schooling for the poor argued that, 'it would teach godliness and subordination, drill them for work, impart craft skills, and ensure that the commonality would not be a drain upon, or a threat to, society'.[28] Society in India had the same objectives for its charity children. But, in India there was an additional dimension – the definition of their place within colonial society. 'Usefulness' in India was not simply a matter of creating industrious members of society who knew their own place, but how the product of the orphanage might benefit the colonial state and relate to the Indian population at large. The place assigned was to provide a 'linking role' between Briton and Indian. The Baptists described it as 'filling an intermediate station between the European employer and the native labourer'. Eurasians were to be humble assistants who understood Indian behaviour, could speak their languages as well as English, and who would be 'capable of sustaining the fierceness of the vertical sun'.[29] This utilitarian view was widely held in British thought of the early nineteenth century. Sir John Malcolm who, when Governor of Bombay in 1829, was active in promoting many schemes to widen Eurasian opportunity, saw the linking role as fundamental to the Eurasian place in British society. Whilst he would not concede Eurasian equality with British moral character and drive he nevertheless felt that 'their education and means of adding to their knowledge will generally give [them] many advantages over the natives in similar pursuits'.[30]

The rationalisation of the role of Eurasians in British society, whilst it prescribed a place, set clear upper limits. They should not presume to join the ruling race on their own ground and so their upbringing should be spartan and Christian. Their future role as adults was reflected in the moral and educational regime of the orphanage, and in their lifestyle, dress and diet. Instruction in the Christian faith took a prominent part in their daily routine. Children started the day at the orphan school at Tanjore run by the SPCK with prayers at half past six. Christian doctrine was explained to them during their breakfast. The day was full of constructive activity until five when they were allowed one hour's supervised activity. In the evening there was public prayer, supper and bed. On Sundays orphans attended church in the morning, learned the catechism during the day and had an evening service before bed.[31]

There seems to have been some relaxation in the austerity of earlier orphanage days by the 1830s. When gymnastic poles for children to use in the playground were introduced at the Free School, Calcutta in 1834, the Managers commented that, 'education was little understood, when it was thought proper to abridge the little pleasures of youth, and to uphold a stern discipline in that season of life, which is the most innocently sportive'. Yet, a moral benefit still seemed necessary to justify the pleasure of the boys. 'In a climate, like that of India, where the mind and body so naturally yield to indolence and sloth any device which has a contrary tendency is important'.[32]

The future place of orphanage wards in adult society was reflected too in what they wore, ate and learned. Lack of funds ensured that all was of the simplest. Orphanage managements, beset with claims on their resources, placed great emphasis on their frugality – generally spending around Rs 10 each month on each child. However, the social class of the children, the modest place sketched out for them in adult life, provided a handy justification for their simple and educationally basic upbringing.

> The charity boys [wrote Sir John Malcolm] should be clothed
> fed and altogether maintained at the lowest possible rate; not

only the economy of the establishment requires this, but the future success of these children, and their advancement as a class in the community. If educated with the habits of Europeans, they will . . . be certain to fail.[33]

Contemporary descriptions of the lives of orphanage children illustrate their spartan upbringing. At Madras they lived, worked and slept in large open buildings of the sort in which private soldiers of the Army were housed. Often the buildings were in poor repair and crowded. At the Free School, Calcutta, it was not until 1835 that it was possible to enlarge the dormitory accommodation for girls and allow them:

> To separate the cots a little space from one another, whereas they had formerly touched, and the consequent suffering of the children may be imagined in a climate like this, lying as they did, 120 of them in comparatively speaking a very small and confined room.[34]

The childrens' dress was European in style but just as simple as their accommodation. Boys wore long trousers and a shirt changed four times a week. When they went to church a waistcoat was worn and a leather cap. Older boys wore shoes, the younger went bare-foot. Girls wore plain dresses. Their clothing marked them as members of British society, but was appropriate to their humble station.

The largest single category of orphanage expense was food, typically accounting for around one-third of all expenditure.[35] The diet owed something to the West but more to India. Congee, kedgeree, bread and milk featured frequently, with half a pound of beef, bread and vegetable followed by plum pudding to mark the Sunday – all eaten by hand from a clay bowl.[36] The orphanage boy, William Webbe from Madras, recalled like Oliver Twist that, 'the boys, I am sure, as was often my case, could eat twice as much more as was given for a meal, but a second supply was never allowed'.[37]

Hard though the regime was the childrens' health was taken seriously. Each orphanage had its visiting surgeon, but epidemics could spread quickly amongst children living in close quarters. Many girls at Madras in 1794 who had been inoculated for smallpox caught measles and died.[38] The death rate amongst orphans was high – one in ten of the girls at Madras between 1787 and 1800 died in the orphanage, but the memory of William Webbe again, who remembered happily the comforts and attention of the sick bay suggests that the high rate of child deaths may be attributed more to the state of medical knowledge at the time, rather than to any lack of care on the part of orphanage managements.[39]

*

The general treatment of orphans seems to have been determined less by their racial origin and more by what was thought fitting for their class in British society. Not all orphans were equal. Most boys received an elementary education whilst girls were prepared for marriage or lives as ladies' maids; the latter practice was discontinued by the 1820s at Madras 'as it has generally been the means of their seduction'.[40] A minority – the children of officers and gentlemen housed at the Upper Military Asylum at Calcutta – were given a superior education. The boys were expected to be articled to trades or else to become junior civil servants. Their curriculum added astronomy, mechanics, and natural philosophy to the basics of English, Arithmetic, and Geometry. Probably the level of tuition was as good as was available at the private schools of Calcutta. It contrasts with what was thought appropriate for the sons of soldiers who did not progress beyond reading, spelling 'to the extent of six syllables', writing and basic arithmetic. However, even they were better educated than most of their fathers, who generally were illiterate.

Girls were thought to need far less of an academic education than boys. Once the daughters of soldiers had the rudiments of reading, writing and arithmetic they spent most of their time at needlework. The daughters of officers, like their brothers, received a rather better scholastic grounding but also learned needlework and embroidery. Social accomplishments were considered particularly important for these girls. Since they were expected to marry 'gentlemen', they were taught the arts of the ballroom.[41] European dancing masters were in great demand at all the girls' schools of Calcutta.

What public charity had clearly in mind was the rearing of boys who would make reliable employees, and girls who would make dutiful wives or support themselves by craft skills. Thus all the girls at the Bombay Free School were taught 'the whole work of a laundress' so that they would make better housewives, 'in that state of life in which it has pleased God to call them'.[42] The Benevolent Institution concentrated on needlework skills to provide, 'not only the means of being useful in their family circles, but of saving them from destitution'.[43]

Since funds were always in short supply and the demand greater than could be met orphanage managements felt their primary task was to get children off the street and to clothe and feed them. Only a small proportion of funds could be allocated to their education. This stimulated a search for the most economical way of teaching with as few schoolmasters as possible. The solution to the problem was pioneered by Dr. Alexander Bell who was the first Superintendent of the Military Male Asylum at Madras from 1797 to 1807. His system of using older boys to teach the younger was adopted widely in India and later in similar establishments in Britain. Senior pupils were paired off with juniors as 'tutors' and 'pupils'. The Headmaster took the top class and as each lesson was mastered by the seniors it was passed on by the boy assistant teachers. The Bell system had the virtue of extreme economy, and although there must be some doubt over the educational standards it achieved, it had the benefit that the school bred its own supply of teachers. By 1812 a number of Bell's 'old boys' at Madras were teachers at the school, pioneering what was later to become an important source of employment and contribution to society for many Eurasians.[44]

Little could be done in the orphanages to prepare their charges with trade skills for adult life. There seemed little need for the boys at the military orphanages who were destined to return to army life as drummers and bandsmen to be more than basically literate. For those to be employed as clerks in government and business offices a good grasp of reading, arithmetic and the ability to write with a fair hand were qualifications enough. There were, however, some sporadic attempts to provide a vocational training. The printing press introduced by Dr. Kerr at Madras in 1801, and later at Calcutta, was one which had the benefit of providing a future source of employment for many Eurasians.[45] The Bombay Free School tried – unsuccessfully – in the 1830's to teach boys shoemaking, tailoring and book binding.[46] Most orphanages, however, anxious to get their charges off their books as soon as possible, preferred to apprentice without rather than train within. As a policy it seems to have been reasonably successful, and orphanage managements often reported that demand for their boys exceeded supply; an explanation offered by the Lower Military Orphan School at Alipore to complaints in 1819 that they were not offering boys to become apprentices at the Botanical Gardens.[47] In 1812 only five of the 126 boys at the Madras Military Orphanage between 1789 and 1794 were out of work.[48]

★

The orphanages sent their children out into the adult world at a tender age, the boys with no skills save a basic education, the girls with even less learning but able to housekeep and to sew. But society saw the achievement in practical terms – the rescue of children from dangerous moral influence and their equipment for a worthy Christian life in the humbler walks of European society. If there often seems a touch of self congratulation in the annual reports of the orphanage managements perhaps it is pardonable, for, limited though their achievements were, they were real enough. Though many of the children of 'poor whites' slipped through the net, many others received support and education. The orphanages and free schools rescued many who 'would now have been wandering around the lanes of the metropolis, in the most wretched and forlorn condition', and gave them some start in life.[49]

The relatively better fortune of orphanage boys compared with the many excluded from the system, prompts consideration of what was a limited overall response to the social problem of an expanding under-class of Eurasian children. If British society was concerned, as indeed it was, at the threat which such a group could pose to good order and stability, why it may be asked was it that the solution was so inadequate to the scale of the problem? There seems no one comprehensive answer to the question. Provision was largely a pragmatic and always a belated response to the development of an unanticipated, costly, and always an unwelcome problem. The response of British society in India which saw the problem at first hand was reasonably positive, but the official attitude of the Company in London was more ambiguous, influenced both by considerations of cost and a belief that its servants in India, whose children the destitute were, should carry the primary responsibility. At first the Company's view was that all it should contribute to the orphanage movement was moral backing.[50] Furthermore it drew the line at support for children born to those who did not observe the conventions. In 1756 the Company wrote to its government at Bombay complaining that they had admitted 'bastards' to the orphanage there. In future, they requested, preference should be given to the children of 'Honest Parents'.[51]

By the end of the eighteenth century, as the Eurasian population began to rise dramatically, it became clear that the Company's official argument that relief was essentially the responsibility of the British community in India could no longer be sustained. As demand for support outstripped local ability to pay the Company was drawn ever more deeply into financing the growing system. It contributed in many ways – sometimes a monthly grant per child; agreement to allocate a proportion of the profits from official lotteries; donation of unclaimed prize money; and approval of schemes which gave shared benefits to the Government and orphanage, such as contracts for government printing. It needed, however, the banking failures in Calcutta of the 1830s to enmesh the Company fully into support of the system. As voluntary contributions to the Calcutta Free School fell and distressed parents applied for places for their children, the Bengal Government had to step in with a donation of Rs 9,600. By 1835 it was providing more than half of the school's funds.[52]

The Company, by the 1830s, had been forced to fulfil a quasi Poor Law function in its Indian territories and was committed to rising costs, a matter of concern in the context of its own financial difficulties from the late eighteenth century on. By 1829 the annual expense on the Lower Military Orphanage at Alipore alone had risen to Rs 211,267 a year, and most other institutions depended to some degree on Government money.[53] A determination to control the rising expense of its operations in India inhibited the Company from doing any more than seemed absolutely necessary and led to policies – described later – of discouraging the growth of a Eurasian population and of ensuring that it posed no real threat to the stability of the regime, rather than take on the impossibly expensive charge of educating all the needy descendants of the British in India.

Some of the Company's own officials in India themselves argued that a policy which educated Eurasians was mistaken. Sir Thomas Munro, Governor of Madras in 1824, was a vigorous exponent of the case for non-intervention. His view was that the best course would be to leave the Eurasian poor to find their own level, and that their best interests would be served by integration into Indian society rather than that they should 'remain dependant on us'. He saw them left to their own devices, employed as servants, mechanics, shopkeepers and merchants, with later generations 'forced to look for subsistence as Bullocksmen, Peons, Labourers and Rayets. This [he commented] is what happened to the descendants of the Portuguese on the West Coast, and there is no reason why the same thing should not happen to the descendants of European soldiers if it be not prevented by imprudent interference'.[54]

Though Munro's argument was placed in an Indian context, his views and those of like minded officials that the true interests of 'poor Eurasians' lay in the withdrawal of state support and an encouragement of individual self sufficiency reflected the contemporary utilitarian argument in Britain that, if the relief of the poor rates were removed, individuals would be forced to be self reliant and do better than ever they could on state support – an argument which strikes a chord to this day.[55] The limited extent of the Company's provision of care and education for the children of 'poor whites' in India needs then to be judged in the context of what was thought suitable for the education of the working classes in Britain of the time rather than by late twentieth century stand- ards. No general right to education for the poor existed in Britain, any more than it did in India. Class, perhaps more than racial considerations, governed the Company's policy towards the children of its 'poor whites'. As many as could reasonably be afforded and would be useful to society, were educated. Arguments of legitimacy proved a useful outer bound to the Company's responsibility, save in the case of the military, which clearly pre- sented a special case. The system left many children to fend for themselves, some of whom were rescued by the work of missionary associations.

The special problem of British India was that those in British society who filled the place of the working-class community in Britain were predominantly Eurasian. Thomas Munro's argument that they should be allowed to merge into the indigenous population posed particular problems for, as Christians, there was no place for them in Indian society, save at the lowest levels of subsistence – a problem itself for British racial prestige. It ignored the British self-identification of Eurasians themselves and the wish of their fathers that they should be treated as members of British society. Whether educated or not, the majority of the Eurasian population were both psychologically and economically dependant on British rule. Those educated in the orphanages of the time, reared in institutional care rather than in stable families, learned there the lessons of conformity and their proper place on the lower slopes of British society, and inevitably looked to that society to provide for their adult livelihood. Their opportunity lay in the need which an expanding British India had for them, a need which had important implications for their employment – the topic of the next chapter.

3

Eurasian Employment
A Limited Opportunity

As ever more Eurasian children became adults in the late eighteenth and early nineteenth centuries, so the question of how they might be employed became more pressing. British civil servants, army officers and professional men – if they lived to retirement – generally returned to Europe. Their Eurasian children, particularly those whose fathers were poor, were destined for the most part to begin and end their days in India. Since their parentage, religion, education, way of life and aspirations placed them within the broad framework of the British community, it was inevitable that they should look to this, rather than Indian society for their employment in adult life.

The society into which Eurasians were born was, in common with all European colonial regimes, an artificial implant within its host country. Typically a small cadre of European administrators and military men drawn from their mother country's bourgeoisie headed an expatriate society wherein official employment took the place of birth, wealth and land at home. Thus a marked feature of the transition period in British India from a trading role to paramountcy on the continent was the development by its governing cadre of civil servants of an ever closer sense of occupational identity and social exclusiveness. At the time the process drew critical comment:

> The service of the Company has certain ideas of rank and consequence attached to it, which often produces ludicrous effects on the intercourse of society. All persons in civil and military appointments affect a superiority over such as are not in the service.[1]

By the early nineteenth century British society in India had gone far to develop the social exclusiveness, rigidity, conformism and the intricate patterns of class distinction and uncodified norms of behaviour typically associated with its later history. The Governor-General stood the head of an 'aristocracy' of the Company's covenanted civil servants. British military officers ranked below with their own gradations of social exclusiveness. To be, for instance, a Royal Army officer in India was more socially acceptable than to be a Company officer.[2] Non-officials – typically business men – had a lower status yet, unless they were wealthy. When the Bengal Club was founded in 1827, the heads of the great Agency Houses in Calcutta were not at first thought acceptable for membership.[3] At the foot of British society the mass of the military rank and file had, of course, no pretensions to social acceptability whatever.

It was into a British social structure in which occupation determined status and whose artificiality largely precluded upward social movement that growing numbers of Eurasian men had to fit. The decision – the reasons for which are discussed later – to exclude Eurasians formally from the covenanted service of the Company in 1791 was therefore of momentous consequence to their educated sector. Its consequences were threefold. Eurasians were barred from the higher salaries of Government service; they lost social parity with the elite of British society in India; and they were separated in class from the official families from which many had come. Since occupation determined status a wide social gap divided Eurasians, when employed as clerks in Government service, from their half-brothers in covenanted employment. Though they were often educated together in Britain and treated there on an equal social basis, once in India strict colonial convention applied. As Frederick Shore put it, 'the distinction between them is almost as great as that of Brahmin and Pariah'.[4]

When the pattern of Eurasian employment which developed in the early nineteenth century is examined it is tempting at first to conclude from its uniformity a clearly defined British policy. But closer inspection reveals inconsistencies between overall policy and the pragmatic needs of British government. Policy, for example, decreed that Eurasians, officers or men, should not fill combatant roles in the Company's Army. Yet, many Eurasians were allowed to serve as officers in the irregular military units of the Company's Army. Again, at moments of perceived external danger, as in 1799, there was no hesitation in recruiting Eurasians into armed militia forces.[5] Expediency and utility often overrode policy. At times this worked to the benefit of Eurasians. The exclusion of Indians from almost all posts of government responsibility in the early nineteenth century favoured Eurasians who obtained a virtual monopoly of the lower reaches of the government administrative machine. To local British officials, rather than the Court of Directors in London, the employment of Eurasians in government service, albeit in junior functions, made good sense. Self-interest – the provision of employment for their own sons – and the needs of administration interlinked. The literate Eurasians who largely ran Government administration by the early nineteenth century supplemented an inadequate number of covenanted servants.

If in practice British officialdom took a pragmatic approach to the question of Eurasian employment a general view of the place which they should occupy, and the upper limits of responsibility which should be allowed them became more clearly apparent in British thinking in the early years of the nineteenth century. Whilst it was recognised that Eurasians could be helpful junior members of British society, it should not be at a level which might compromise the 'respect' which British rule sought to instil in its Indian subjects.[6]

The problems which faced the Eurasian elite in achieving remunerative occupation extended beyond exclusion from covenanted service in India. Various measures and actions made it hard for them to achieve success, high income or capital in non-official roles. A ban on land ownership was one of these. From 1790 Eurasians, as well as British subjects, were not allowed to own land save in exceptional cases. Originally it was probably not so much a measure directed against Eurasians as such, as an attempt to preclude British subjects – as John Maxwell did at Cawnpore – from evading the ban on land ownership by buying in the names of their Eurasian sons.[7] Yet, when the regulations were relaxed in 1831 and Eurasians were once again allowed to own land, their rights were often discouraged in practice as local officials tried to 'deter them as much as possible . . . as they have become 'troublesome' to the constituted authorities'.[8] Adam Maxwell, in whose name his father had bought his land, was one of the Eurasians whom the authorities found 'troublesome'. He was expropriated in 1831 for failure to pay his taxes, and six years later sentenced to six months imprisonment at Cawnpore on a flimsy charge of fraud.[9]

British competition limited Eurasian opportunity in other lucrative non-official roles – the professions, business and skilled trades. Once restrictions on British immigration to India were lifted in 1813 lawyers, headmasters, merchants, agents, indigo planters, and skilled craftsmen came out to India in greater numbers to compete with Eurasians for the best jobs in non-official British society. Although the policy of allowing British immigration was not specifically directed at limiting Eurasian opportunity, that was its effect. Insofar as Eurasians received any job protection from increasing non-official competition it was in terms of what was felt proper for their assigned and junior place in British society. The Court of Directors continued to refuse permits for British clerks in commercial houses, 'who would be competing with a half-caste or an Indian'.[10]

The limitation of opportunity for educated Eurasians to achieve wealth between 1773 and 1833 has much to do with the poverty which characterised the Anglo-Indian community of the later nineteenth and twentieth centuries in British India. There were very few Eurasian men of capital in the community's formative days. Those who succeeded against the odds often benefited from special situations: Charles Weston from winning the Calcutta Lottery; James Kyd from his inheritance and position as the Company's ship-builder in Calcutta; and Peter Carstairs from the clothing contract for the Army in Madras. Others started on their way to success from outside British territory: James Skinner first made his name in the service of the Mahratas and William Palmer at Hyderabad.[11] The scarcity of wealthy men amongst Eurasians by the 1830s prejudiced their community's future greatly. It reinforced a secondary and dependent perception in British eyes, reduced the capacity of the community to help itself, and lost it opportunities of improving its own public standing. In 1830, when the appointment of some Eurasians and Indians as honorary magistrates in Calcutta was first considered by the Governor-General, Lord William Bentinck, he was advised that though it would be hard to find suitably qualified Indians,

> Still more difficult is it to find these requisite qualifications among the Indo-British race. In their present state of advancement as to property, there is not one to put in comparison with the worthy and enlightened James Kyd.[12]

★

Within the limited range of employment open to Eurasians there was nevertheless a hierarchy of employment which reflected the social class of their fathers and their own level of education. Sons of Generals, those with strong British connections or inherited wealth, obtained the better jobs. The sons of the military rank and file got the least well paid. Social differences between Eurasians at birth were replicated in later life in their various occupations. Class counted as much as did race.

At the foot of the Eurasian class structure stood the Eurasian sons of soldiers. The destiny of most was to exchange the institu- tional life of the orphanage for that of the army in which their fathers had served. Their sisters too were sent from the military orphanage to become soldiers' wives. Only a small minority married civilians.[13] As soldiers' wives Eurasian girls faced a pre- carious future. They were given little choice in whom they married. On the death of their husbands or, if left behind when soldiers of Royal regiments returned to Europe, they and their children joined the destitutes of European society, working as servants, living by their wits, or depending on inadequate charity. Their plight did not go unrecognised though by the military 'family' in whose interest the Directors in London were strongly lobbied by local military authority. 'There is not', the Commander-in-Chief, Bengal, observed in 1818, 'any branch of the community more deserving of consideration than the young women in question, after they quit the Orphan School'.[14]

The boys returned to military life as early as the age of ten, but mostly at twelve to thirteen, to serve as drummers, fifers and trumpeters, an occupation specifically reserved to them and which took the majority of military orphans. The remaining few were apprenticed, sent to sea, or given a start as writers.[15] As bandsmen Eurasian boys illustrate most vividly the ambiguity of the Eurasian position, poised midway between the European and Indian. Although readmitted to the 'service family' in which they had been born they were, unlike the children of British parents, not officially permitted to enlist as soldiers once they reached the age of fifteen – a regulation to which a blind eye may sometimes have been turned in practice. Bandsmen were paid by the officers, not the Government. In Indian regiments they were tried by Indian officers at courts-martial, but when posted to the Company's European regiments, they were tried by British officers.[16] Even their uniforms marked them out as singular, as being within the regiment but not fully of it. The material was of European rather than Indian quality, but the jacket facings were of a different colour to the rest of the regiment. Hats were an uneasy compromise between an Indian turban and a British grenadier cap.[17] In addition to their musical duties, bandsmen acted as orderlies, messengers, stretcher-bearers, and officers' servants.

Although the essential difference between a British soldier and a Eurasian bandsman was that one was a combatant and the other not, the Army treated both even-handedly. A bandsman could serve all his life before retirement to a colony of military veterans. John Doherty died at Sylhet in 1853, aged 50, but still serving as a musician. Promotion to non-commissioned rank could come early. Thomas Evans was a Bandmaster in 1829 at 26 and James Kingsbury Drum-Major of the 59th Native Infantry in 1827 at the same age. Though most bandsmen stayed as bandsmen some, such as James Hammerdinger, later became writers. Others were found minor supervisory posts later in life. At his death in 1846 Patrick Coyle was Inspector of Peons at the General Post Office, Calcutta.[18] The Army went further yet in guaranteeing an education and future employment to their bandsmen's sons, just as they did to those of their soldiers. Eurasian or British, they were all entitled to go to the Lower Military Orphanage at Calcutta where, in 1828, one in three children were second or third generation Eurasians.[19] The sons of Eurasian bandsmen followed their fathers back into the army again as musicians, and the daughters were married off to soldiers as their mothers had been. Class, rather than racial discrimination, was the touchstone of the Army system for its soldiers and bandsmen.

Though army service provided a mainstay of adult employment for poor Eurasians this in itself was insufficient to absorb the growing population. Consequently official policy sought to place boys wherever they could in a variety of useful employments, of which surveying, medical service, printing, and seafaring are a representative selection. In creating jobs of this sort Government and British society looked for a return of benefit from Eurasian employment. The formation, for instance, of the Carnatic Corps of Artificers at Madras in 1821 illustrates the twin objectives of providing for Eurasian employment. Nearly thirty years later the Corps still existed, but its state of demoralisation was symptomatic of the consequences of an equivocal attitude by the authorities towards poor Eurasians. The artificers were enlisted on European pay scales, but no career structure was put in place, and no promotion on merit countenanced. Furthermore, as their Superintendent reported in 1849, their status within the military was as ambiguous as that of Eurasian bandsmen. Although they were enlisted as Europeans and subject to full military discipline, they were still classed as 'native camp followers'.[20]

Such measures, though they provided a subsistence existence for many working class Eurasians, were quite inadequate to a rapidly increasing demand for employment. There is no firm data for Eurasian unemployment in the early nineteenth century, but anecdotal evidence suggests it was already considerable. William Huggins, who had been an indigo planter at Tirhoot, argued that a solution was the wholesale employment of Eurasians as soldiers. In this way, he thought that they would provide a valuable counterbalance to the predominance of Indians in the Company's Army and overcome the very visible problem of Eurasian unemployment for, 'Many young men, who are begging on the streets of Calcutta, or starving would be rescued from poverty and rendered serviceable to their country, instead of being in misery and degradation'.[21] A human face to the problems of the Eurasian poor, little educated and generally unskilled, is given by the 'Humble Petition' of Jonathan Seville to the magistrate at Tullyghur, in which he reported that he was an unemployed country-born from the Lower Orphan School with a wife and two small daughters, and pleaded for a 'small trifle' to help him get them to Benares where he had a brother.[22] Many such as he formed the population of the urban slums on the fringes of the urban residential areas of Calcutta and whose deaths appear in the burial records of the time throughout British India listed simply as 'a Eurasian pauper'.

★

At the foot of the social scale the Eurasian poor were trapped, as were 'poor whites', by the limited opportunities accorded them in a rigid colonial class system. But for those born higher in the social scale the administrative demands of a larger and more complex government machine in the early nineteenth century with a growing need for a relatively inexpensive, literate, and English-speaking work force brought opportunity. This opened careers in Government service for educated Eurasians as clerical workers, engineers, surveyors and apothecaries. Indigo cultivation in up country Bengal offered employment outside Government service as supervisors, and many Eurasians found civil and military employment further afield outside British India in the territories of independent Indian states.

No employment open to educated Eurasians in British India at the time was more desired than clerical employment in Government service. Since £500 per annum (approximately Rs 500 a month) was after 1793 the upper limit which might be paid to a 'Native of India', a clerkship was perforce the apex of Eurasian aspiration. The success by the 1830s of Eurasians in monopolising the better paid jobs in Government offices was fundamental to their place in British society. It provided a commonality of interest amongst educated Eurasians and provided a transient sense of security until a change in British policy favouring the development of a Western-educated Indian middle class began to threaten the Eurasian status quo.

For some fifty years from the 1780s the interests of British Government in India coincided with those of the British fathers of Eurasian sons, and of the sons themselves. Educated Eurasians offered Government a reliable work force to supplement a small covenanted service facing an ever increasing work load. There were just 374 covenanted civil servants in Bengal in 1810. Thirteen years later there were still only 370, of whom 15 were on leave and 131 employed as judges.[23] Just as patronage for the covenanted civil service was jealously guarded by the Court of Directors in London, so local government patronage was used by Company officials in India for the benefit of their Eurasian sons.

Two main reasons made a career in Government service particularly attractive to the Eurasian elite, for all that the capacity assigned to them was subordinate. Firstly, it afforded reasonable security (despite the recurrent attempts at retrenchment in Government expenditure from the late eighteenth century on) and the prospect of an ex gratia pension on retirement. Secondly, Government service carried status. Even though a clear social distinction was made between covenanted and uncovenanted servants the latter were at the centre of Government affairs, and Eurasians in the service were at the least junior members of the governing elite which rated itself at the forefront of British society.

Hours of work were not onerous, generally from 10 a.m. to 4 p.m.. In the office Eurasian officials worked alongside British covenanted servants and developed personal friendships which surmounted problems of public status. Patrick Sutherland, for instance, the head assistant (Register) of the Military Board at Calcutta, prominent in the affairs of the Calcutta Free School, left his son Henry 'a pair of silver claret jugs' which had been sent to him from England, 'as a token from the children of my dear and ever to be lamented friend the late Colonel Thomas Alexander Cobbe'.[24] Senior uncovenanted servants such as Willoughby Da Costa, foreman of the Company's Mint at Calcutta, or William Benjamin Kirkpatrick, one time Baptist missionary, but later in a diverse career Deputy Register at the Sadr Diwani Adalat, ranked themselves as 'gentlemen' and described themselves as such. The libraries, wardrobes, furniture and carriages that senior uncovenanted officials left at death suggest that, though they lived on narrow salaries in British terms, they enjoyed a comfortable European lifestyle.[25] If not a part of fashionable British society, they had a definite standing within its middle class circles.

The development of an uncovenanted service which became so vital to the prospects of educated Eurasians traces back to the earliest days of a British presence in India when writers were hired on a monthly ad hoc basis to help out in the counting houses, offices and stores in the laborious business of keeping and transcribing accounts and records, and of copying letters to and from the Company in London. From about the mid-eighteenth century the hiring of monthly writers on a casual basis began to move towards the establishment, unofficially at first, of a permanent administrative service. These local appointments were a recognised route for the entry of Eurasians into covenanted posts, until their debarment in 1791. Fathers in the service naturally tried to use their influence to advance the prospects of their Eurasian sons. Herbert Pyefinch, for instance, the Company's cooper at Calcutta petitioned the Court in 1779 for the appointment of his Eurasian son Solomon. The application was backed by glowing references from the Government in Calcutta. Solomon was accepted as a covenanted writer, although he does not seem to have taken up his post.[26]

At first the Company in London was highly opposed to the establishment of an uncovenanted service, for it clearly threatened their patronage and control of posts in India. In 1774 the Government of Bengal was instructed never again to employ any European without permission. The Court wrote again on the subject in 1782, for clearly Bengal had taken no notice at all of their previous instructions. Once again they demanded explicit obedience to their orders. They were not to receive it. Instead they were sent a detailed review of the numbers and salaries of the uncovenanted servants at the Presidency offices, and an argument that any change in current practice would be more expensive, and less efficient.[27] The argument carried the day: for, except in the Salt Department, uncovenanted servants kept their posts and thereafter the existence of the service was implicitly recognised by the Company in London.

The review is itself a valuable source for knowledge of the numbers, pay and duties of the government administrative staff at the end of the eighteenth century. It emphasised the capability and special qualifications of the Eurasians who held such posts. Important issues such as Eurasian acclimatisation and facility with Indian languages were highlighted. British rule in India needed both at the time. In commending F. LeBlanc, at the time Examiner at the Customs House, his departmental head pointed out that he spoke not only 'the language of the country but also Malabar, Coromandel, Portuguese and French'. He was indispensable, for 'during the hours of office there may be from 50 to 200 people, Merchants included, so that few European constitutions could hold out so long to write in the middle of such a crowd'.[28]

The value of Eurasians to Government business was not limited to a knowledge of Indian languages and an ability to work well in hot and humid offices – in which it has been suggested that it was a Eurasian clerk who first invented the swinging fan. The review showed that many were extremely good at their jobs. Fledgling covenanted writers new to India could hardly take the place of a highly experienced official like Thomas Ivory who had served for nine years and drew Rs 300 a month for his work in the Treasury and a further Rs 200 in the Accountant General's office. He was recommended by the Treasurer for a covenanted appointment, which it seemed he did not get, with the argument that, 'Money requires the Assistance of a person of that accuracy and steadiness which Mr. Ivory possesses, nor could I with safety to myself or the public, intrust [sic] any part of it but to a person of his regularity and assiduity'.[29]

By the 1780s a hierarchy had already developed in the uncovenanted service. Temporary writers and apprentices were at its foot. Above them were junior assistants paid around Rs 100 a month, who rose in time to be examiners and in due time head assistants in their departments. At this the highest level, until the uncovenanted were allowed to become junior civil court judges and deputy collectors in the 1820s, pay was Rs 300 a month. Many spent a lifetime in their departments, slowly climbing the ladder of responsibility, just as in the covenanted service or army. Periods of twenty or thirty years were not uncommon, although few, if any, could match Charles Cornelius's record. He was first employed in 1769 and served sixty years at the Board of Trade, of which he was the senior uncovenanted assistant at the time of his death in 1829.[30] Such exceptional lengths of service may be attributed to a lack of formal pension arrangements at the time, although pensions were often paid to those with considerable service or retired through disability. They ended, however, with the death of the husband leaving their wives to plead for some allowance. The Company's Government in Bengal was frequently in trouble with its masters in

London for granting pensions which were considered too generous.[31] By 1810 uncovenanted servants in Bombay had managed to establish a pension fund of their own to which each contributed 4 percent of his salary. But twenty-five years later their fellows in Bengal were still petitioning to do the same.[32]

By the 1830s Eurasians had achieved a near monopoly on the jobs open to Europeans in the uncovenanted service, which were paid at a much higher rate than those performed by Indians. European pay could range up to Rs 400 whilst the Indian scale started at a much lower rate and peaked at Rs 200.[33] At Calcutta in 1831 four out of five 'European' jobs were held by Eurasians, and of the eighteen serving Registers – the most senior post open – fifteen were Eurasians and two British. One cannot be placed as either British or Eurasian, but none were Indian.[34] The situation at Madras was much the same, though this did not stop the Eurasians there petitioning in 1833 for an even larger proportion; a request which was rejected since they already held over half the higher paid uncovenanted appointments.[35]

*

A positive policy of patronage operated in the interests of educated Eurasians in the most coveted jobs in Government offices. It extended to a further range of official appointments outside the Presidency towns. With territories to be mapped, revenue assessments to be made, hospitals to be administered, roads and public buildings to be constructed, the need for Eurasian employment met with a Government requirement for an intermediate class of official able to supervise the labour of a largely Indian work force. Increasing numbers of Eurasians were trained from the late eighteenth century as surveyors, medical assistants and mechanical engineers. Experienced officials assumed quite considerable responsibility, but there was an upper limit to their aspirations since even the most senior answered to a covenanted servant, however junior.

The need for a cadre of surveyor's assistants was evident from the end of the eighteenth century when the first surveying school, which trained boys from the Madras Military Orphanage, was opened in 1799. Its graduates served in all three Presidencies. At the school the young apprentices were given a basic training in draughtsmanship, writing and arithmetic before being sent into the field for practical experience, equipped with theodolites and plane tables. Once they were qualified, young assistant surveyors were either employed in copying maps or else posted to out-stations.

British ideas of class and status carried through into the arrangements for orphanages for the Eurasian children of the East India Company's Bengal army. The children of officers were housed separately (*above, North-East View of the Military Orphan House, near Calcutta, for the Children of Officers, 1794, P63*), from the children of the rank and file (*below, Military Orphan School, opposite Calcutta, for the Children of Private Soldiers, 1794, P57*).

The children of private soldiers, mainly Eurasians, were taken from their mothers at the age of five and sent down country to the orphan school to receive a spartan but wholesome Christian education. Boys and girls went back in due course to the army as non-combatants and soldiers' wives respectively.

The orphan children of officers were sent back to England, if both their parents had been born British. Eurasians, the great majority, were retained in India, destined for clerkships in government offices or marriage to British officers and civilians. (*By permission of the British Library*)

Anne Jennings' Sampler, (c. 1790) Anne's sampler was completed under the supervision of Mistress Parker at the Orphan School, Calcutta. A fine example of the work undertaken by the wards of orphanages which combined the tuition of needlework skills with the encouragement of Christian virtues, twin objectives of the system. The purpose was to prepare young girls for the role of dutiful wives or to enable them to support themselves in later life as milliners and seamstresses.

Nothing, at present, is known for certain of Anne's later life. *(Courtesy of Mrs. C.J. Jarrett, Witney Antiques)*

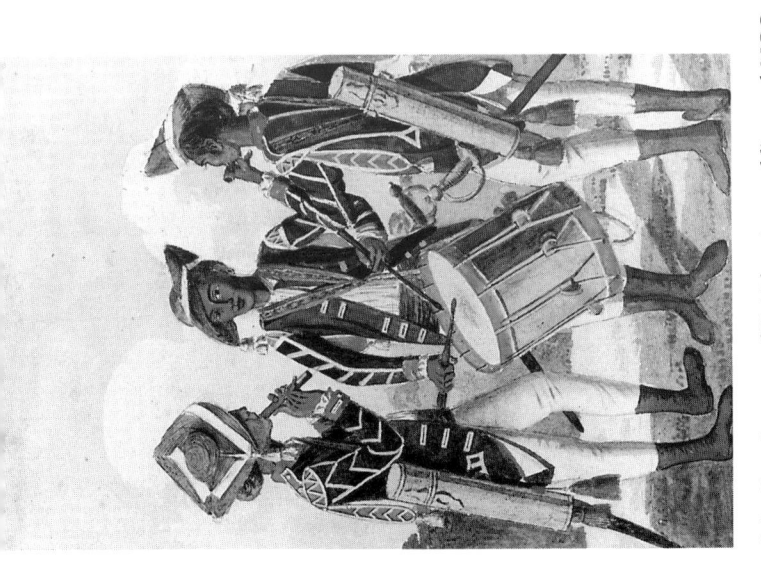

Most of the Eurasian sons of British private soldiers and NCOs left their orphanages at the age of between twelve to thirteen to become military bandsmen and musicians, an employment reserved exclusively for them (*above, Sepoy drum and fifers neg. no. 67709*). Their uniforms were extremely fanciful. (*below, Bandmaster and Musician, Madras Army, 1846 photo no. 7585*). Many remained bandsmen all their working life, with the post of bandmaster as their highest aspiration. (*Courtesy of the Director, National Army Museum*)

Rev. Andrew Bell (1753–1852), educationalist. Previously a teacher in America and curate at Cookham, Berkshire, Bell arrived at Madras in 1787 as an adventurer with no income. He found many opportunities of clerical advancement, was chaplain to the 4th European regiment at Arcot together with several other deputy chaplaincies, as well becoming junior chaplain at Fort St. David. As the first Superintendent of the Military Male Orphan Asylum he introduced a system whereby the older boys taught the younger, an economical plan followed in most other orphanages in British India. Ten years later he returned to Britain with a fortune of £25,000.

By the time of his death Bell had made over £120,000 to trustees to endow benevolent and educational work. Of this £50,000 was earmarked to found Madras College at St. Andrews. (*P1418, by permission of the British Library*)

Apothecary, First Class, c. 1840. The highest rank to which a Eurasian might rise in the medical service of the East India Company's army. Boys entered the service as apprentices from orphanages, and might in due time rise to the rank of Apothecary. They appear to have ranked as warrant officers, and were familiarly called 'Black Pots' by British soldiers.

Even as late as the 1930s Eurasian doctors in the Indian Army Medical Department, the so-called 'darkie-docs', were ranked as warrant officers, first class, although commissions were granted them in the second world war. (*Author's collection*)

Lieutenant-Colonel James Skinner, C.B., (1778–1841) in later life, by Ghulam Husayn Khan. As rich as celebrated for his military prowess, Skinner was the most respected Eurasian of his day. He entered British service reluctantly in 1804 after serving as a Maratha officer, and pioneered the development of irregular cavalry regiments to support the regular army of the East India Company. Displays of the mounted prowess of his 'Yellow Boys', in which Skinner himself excelled, invariably impressed visiting dignitaries, whose patronage advanced his career and wealth. (*E 108, by permission of the British Library*)

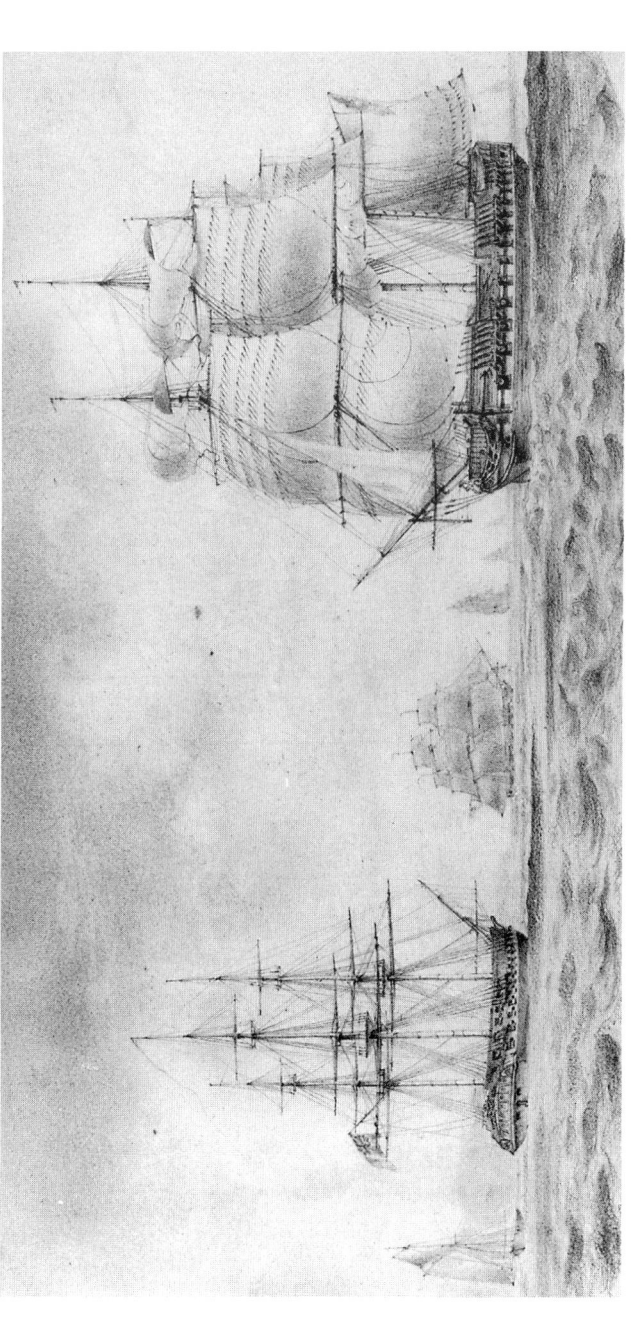

The General Kyd, (above right, in full sail) was launched in November 1813; the largest ship built at the Kidderpore dockyard of James Kyd (1786–1836), the East India Company's master ship builder at Calcutta. She displaced 1200 tons, and her launching was attended by the Governor-General and his wife, together with 400 guests – 'almost all the beauty, rank and fashion of Calcutta'.

James Kyd sailed in her to England in 1818 and received a silver plate from the Admiralty in recognition of his skill in saving a naval frigate which had been given up for lost after a collision with an East Indiaman, off St. Helena. Kyd left a painting of *The General Kyd* in his will to Thomas Boulting 'who had so great a share in the construction of the ship'. *(PU 6394, by permission of the National Maritime Museum)*

The British Residency at Hyderabad c. 1810. Built between 1803–6 by the Resident, James Achilles Kirkpatrick, whose civil marriage to Khair un Nissa was described by Governor-General Lord Wellesley as 'an outrage on the general principles of morality'.

The Residency housed the office from which the Eurasian entrepreneur William Palmer, (1780–1867), started his banking business in 1810, which collapsed in 1824 after prodigious early success. Notwithstanding accusations of illegality levelled at Palmer for his dealings with the Nizam, two of his four sons were commissioned into the Company's Madras Army, whilst the other two served in the Nizam's army, which also provided husbands for all three of his daughters. (*WD 1712, by permission of the British Library*)

There, under the direction of the Collector and their Surveyor, generally a military officer, they prepared maps either for general use or for revenue assessments.[36] As with their contemporaries in Government offices, surveyors climbed a ladder of promotion from Apprentice to Third, Second and ultimately First Class Assistant Surveyor. At this post they were paid Rs 159 a month plus a horse, tent and a baggage allowance when on survey, raising the total to Rs 291.[37]

A fairly similar career pattern applied to Eurasians in the medical service. In early British days in India Company surgeons had employed Eurasians and Indians, often at their own cost, as dressers and assistants. By the end of the eighteenth century a more formally structured subordinate medical service began to emerge. Boys, often from the Bengal Military Orphanage, were trained as dressers and compounders with the eventual prospect of promotion to sub-assistant surgeons at a salary of Rs 100 a month. By 1812 there was a formal hierarchy in place whereby a pupil would advance to a dresser, then to a medical apprentice, and like Surveyors through from Third to Second, and then to Apothecary, First Class.[38] Their numbers were substantial, 200 in the Madras Presidency alone where they set up their own Benevolent Fund in 1831.[39] Their pay scale ranged up from Rs 55 a month for the most junior to Rs 145 a month for the most senior on field service. These held positions of considerable responsibility heading in military hospitals a team of assistants, apprentices, dressers and compounders responsible directly to the surgeon in charge. Perhaps chief nursing officer would be the closest contemporary role description. The status and authority of an Apothecary, First Class was reflected in his uniform of scarlet coat, peaked cap with gold lace band, white gloves, black silk stock and white trousers.[40]

In theory it was possible for an Apothecary to rise to the rank of assistant or full surgeon, and there is evidence in Bengal that one or two did although they were not even then granted covenanted status.[41] But for almost all Apothecary, First Class was the ceiling. Even then practice varied by Presidency. Eurasian medical entrants seemed to have done better in Bengal and Madras than in Bombay where in 1823 only 'qualified European doctors' were appointed to the post of sub-assistant surgeons which Eurasians might expect to hold elsewhere.[42]

Opportunities for Eurasians in a subordinate engineering service opened up rather later than in surveying and medicine. A subordinate branch of the Bengal Public Works Department was open in 1829 to 'Europeans, Eurasians, Hindoos and Mohammedans' with salaries up to Rs 145 a month. Eurasians had a clear advantage in this role, since it was stipulated that candidates needed a 'sufficient knowledge of English and Accounts', as well as to 'know the native language fluently'.[43] In the same year an Engineer Institution at Bombay trained fifteen 'European half-caste' and sixty-four Indian students. Eurasians received Rs 15 a month whilst in training; Indians Rs 5. Once a Eurasian had graduated from the Institute, he became an apprentice and moved up – as in the subordinate surveying and medical service – by grades to Assistant Engineer, First Class. His pay at the top level was Rs 185 a month with an extra Rs 85 when in the field, where he was provided with a subaltern's tent, to mark his European status out to the Indian workers under his command.[44]

★

Government employment was the single most important source of employment for Eurasians of the early nineteenth century, whether as non-combatants in the army for the sons of soldiers, or as minor officials for the sons of the better off British. But many Eurasians were engaged in other 'European' occupations, in professions, the arts or business concerns. A few were seafarers. A general picture of the occupational profile of educated Eurasians in the early 1830s can be drawn by analysing the lists of Eurasian and non-official British residents of Calcutta and Bengal which were published in *The Calcutta Annual Register and Directory* for 1831. Even with allowance for the fact that the data only covers Bengal, a profile can be constructed in broad terms of the variety of Eurasian employment which can be compared with that of the non-official British, who outnumbered 'respectable' Eurasians two to one.

Clerical and administrative employment was the stronghold for Eurasians, not only in Government service but in business houses too. Twice as many Eurasians were employed in this way as were British, the only major category in which Eurasians accounted for a proportion of jobs in excess of their share of European population. There were numbers of Eurasians employed in the professions at the time, either as advocates, doctors, missionaries and schoolmasters, but in all these they met strong competition from British professionals who arrived in increasing numbers from 1813 onwards. For example, seventy-eight British lawyers were licensed to practise in Bengal between 1813 and 1831, and in 1831 only six out of the sixty-two practising there were Eurasian.[45]

Table 1 Analysis of Occupations of Eurasians and Non-Official Europeans in Bengal, 1831[46]

Occupation	Eurasians	Europeans	Total	Eurasian percentage
Clerical/Admin.	659	386	1045	63
Professional	56	186	242	23
City Officials	–	47	47	–
Arts	31	32	63	49
Trades	36	161	197	18
Marine	4	158	162	3
Indigo	83	560	643	13
Commercial	119	330	449	27
Unclassified	2	18	20	10
Pensioners	18	18	36	50
Total Occupations	1008	1896	2904	35

It was difficult too for Eurasians to establish successful medical practices. In 1831 there were twenty doctors practising privately in Calcutta, but only four of them were Eurasian. Numerical competition was one important factor in the underrepresentation of Eurasians in potentially lucrative non-official careers. But other factors operated as well. To be a doctor or a lawyer required a university education. By the 1820s first or second generation Eurasians generally could not afford the great expense of sending their sons to study in Europe. Indeed there was no advanced education whatever open to Eurasians in India, save for those few who studied for the Church at Bishop's College, Calcutta.[47] The final factor – vital to the establishment of a successful legal or medical practice – was the question of Eurasian social acceptability. Britons preferred to brief or be treated by British lawyers and doctors. One Eurasian doctor at least, Dr. Paris Dick, educated and qualified in Britain, returned there discouraged by his exclusion from polite society in Calcutta.[48] Patronage and social acceptance mattered too in the business of portrait painting, where local Eurasian artists competed with a stream of fashionable (and talented) British painters. The Eurasian Charles Pote's ability – he was trained in Britain – was not enough for him to make a living by his art. He joined the uncovenanted civil service before finishing his life as a schoolmaster at Dacca.[49]

British newcomers to India, even in more modest professional careers, received preference over Eurasian residents. Lack of university degrees proved a handicap to most Eurasians in an expanding teaching profession, though it was a natural career opportunity for boys who had been monitors at charity schools. Eurasians contributed a significant number of assistant teachers in the early 1830s paid at between Rs 50 and Rs 150 a month, but most headmasters were brought in from Britain. There were some exceptions. The Parental Academy, set up in 1823 by Eurasians specifically for their community, counted Eurasians and domiciled Britons amongst its early headmasters, but eventually imported headmasters from Britain. Some private schools too in Calcutta were owned by Eurasians. Frederick Linstedt's was one of these, although even he found it necessary to bring in a Scottish partner in 1821.[50]

Least financially rewarding of all amongst professions, the missionary movement gave employment to Eurasians but once again British expatriates were generally preferred. Nearly 200 licences were granted to British missionaries between 1814 and 1831. Eurasians were a minority amongst ministers in every missionary society, generally working their way up from the ranks of catechists and teachers. Only seven Eurasians can be identified amongst the seventy-seven missionaries appointed by the London Missionary Society in India between 1814 and 1831.[51] Yet, Eurasians often won praise for their devotion to duty, and had the great advantage over many of their British colleagues of being able to preach fluently in the languages of their Indian congregations. A visiting deputation of the LMS commented in 1827 of a Mr. Walton, the Eurasian assistant missionary at Bellary:

> On Lord's days he preaches in Malabar on the Mission premises. On Mondays in Canarese in the Pettah or town, also on Wednesdays in the evening in the School Rooms – Thursdays in the Fort in Tamil – Friday mornings at a village in Canarese – on Saturdays in the Town again in Telegoo.[52]

The Wesleyans also used locally recruited missionaries in Ceylon and South India but none was allowed to have full responsibility for a mission station.[53] Of all missionary societies only the Baptists had a positive policy towards the employment of Eurasians as missionaries, with eleven known Eurasians and a further nine 'probables' amongst their missionaries in India up until 1830.[54]

They drew them without distinction from the well-educated and the poor. John Ricketts and William Kirkpatrick were examples of the well-educated, whilst William Buckingham, the son of a soldier brought up at the Lower Orphan School, was one of those recruited from a humble social background.[55] The Baptist policy of local recruitment had much to do with the scarcity of their funds. Their establishment of a college at Serampore to provide a flow of catechists was motivated by 'the necessity of preparing missionaries in this country and thus of avoiding the almost overwhelming expenses of missionaries educated in Europe'.[56] Eurasians were an attractive economic proposition at the usual Baptist salary of about Rs 60 a month compared to the Rs 250 customarily paid by the LMS or USPG to their British missionaries.

Outside government service and the professions there were opportunities for educated Eurasians in trade and commerce but these also were dominated by the non-official British in the 1830s. Indigo farming was, of all the commercial opportunities, best favoured by well off British fathers looking for employment for their Eurasian sons. Social acceptance was easier for Eurasians up country than in the formal society of Calcutta. The writer Emma Roberts referred to the many Eurasians in indigo of up country Bengal, observing that they were, 'generally speaking, intelligent, well-formed men, ever ready to contribute to any proposed amusement, and opening their doors readily at all times for the reception of guests'.[57] Amongst their numbers were the sons of wealthy men. Two of Colonel Henry Imlach's three Eurasian sons, Alexander and Henry, were settled at Purneah, where Henry was murdered in 1825. Also at Purneah were two of Lieutenant-General Palmer's grandsons backed by the wealth of their British uncle, John Palmer, Calcutta's 'Prince of Merchants'.[58] But most Eurasians in indigo did not possess the capital to become proprietors. Once again their role was subsidiary as factory managers, on salaries of between Rs 150 and Rs 250 a month.

A striking aspect of the Eurasian employment profile by the early 1830s was their underrepresentation in crafts and trades. There were no substantial Eurasian shopkeepers, livery stable owners, bakers or cabinet makers in Calcutta of the early 1830s, although Eurasians do feature amongst lists of musicians, organists, carvers and gilders and numbers were silversmiths in Madras. Some Eurasians did however make a living as merchants, traders and agents; men like Cornelius Hoff who made cigars at Chinsurah and the hotel keeper J. Shoreham at Serampore. Thomas Wodin was a boat builder and agent at Dacca, whilst T. Black owned the *Asiatic Press* and George Stuart Dick was in partnership with William Crump as a wine merchant. A few agency houses in Calcutta had Eurasian partners but, apart from Barretto's, none could be considered in the first rank.

Whilst it is clear that a significant minority of the early nineteenth century Eurasian elite contributed to the commercial and professional life of British India at the time, their general place in non-official British society was by the 1830s as secondary as in the conduct of Government. William Huggins summed the picture up:

> Some have got property; and are merchants and tradesmen; so that among the diversified population of Calcutta, you meet them in great numbers, sometimes in respectable but generally in low situations.[59]

As access for non-officials to India, many of whom were merchants, planters and agents, became easier after 1813 Eurasians tended to be crowded out of commercial life. If they were craftsmen the new British arrivals had better training than to be found in India's small European society. Businessmen were often better educated and trained than was possible for Eurasians who had not been educated in Britain. The British who came to India to do business had moreover access to better contacts, capital and financial backing from Britain than could be available to Eurasians brought up in India and effectively separated from the main stream of their fathers' families. Strong though the competition was, Eurasians themselves did not compete with any great enthusiasm, influenced without doubt by the general British notion that a life in trade was an ungentlemanly occupation. A correspondent to the *Bengal Hurkaru*, a leading Calcutta newspaper, who was himself in trade, put the problem of the attitudes of educated Eurasians succinctly:

> Raise tradesmen in the estimation of your youth and you will soon find a desire in them to become one; but while the distinction exists by which respectable Tradesmen are thrown into the background of society, never hope for your youths to follow what they are almost instructed to consider a name of degradation.[60]

Even John Shore, a civil servant himself and the son of a former Governor-General, a man sympathetic to what he saw as British disinterest in the predicament of educated Eurasians, argued that an important aspect of the problem was the attitudes of Eurasians themselves and their obsession with gentlemanly status, whatever their rank at birth.[61] He saw the Eurasian problem as one of class rather than race or colour. But educated Eurasians saw the maintenance of such class standing as they had in British society as best to be obtained through occupations regarded as *gentlemanly* in British colonial society – Government service, not trade or commerce.

The jobs which Eurasians held and what they earned by them determined where they fitted into the social spectrum of British India. Even at their poorest, as paupers and recipients of charity, they had a place. There were after all many British born in the same predicament. The more they earned, the nearer they moved towards the hub of British society. The very few who were wealthy – Charles Weston, James Kyd and William Palmer, for instance, were close to and widely accepted in the most select British cadres. The Eurasian problem was that so *few* were wealthy. At the lowest level of employment a drummer might expect Rs 11 a month. A little higher up the scale the Baptists hoped to get their charges Rs 20, a sum which 'though trifling to Europeans, is found fully adequate to the wants of these youths in their low sphere of life; and in some cases it enables them to support a destitute mother, and perhaps an orphan brother or sister'.[62] Of the educated Eurasians, particularly those who worked in Government offices, only a handful earned more than Rs 250 a month, and the few who did could not expect to do so until late in their working lives.[63] Indeed the *most* that an Eurasian might earn in Government service was set at the *least* a young and newly-arrived covenanted civil servant received. Their prospects soon took them far beyond any Eurasian expectation. A covenanted Assistant's pay started at Rs 400 and rose to Rs 3,000 once the Collector of a district. If appointed as a Resident to an Indian court his salary rose to Rs 5,500 a month, with appropriate expenses.[64]

Eurasians were determined nevertheless to maintain a European life style in public even if it caused hardship in private, the display of which was noted by one observer in 1832:

> A writer on a salary of forty to fifty rupees a month, will be seen driving on the course in his buggey, with his raven hair frizzed out in the most exquisite manner, without a hat, in all the style and appearance of a first-rate civilian – yet follow him home as I have done, and you will find him in half an hour seated in front of a small crazy bungalow with nothing on but a shirt and a pair of dirty chintz pijammahs.[65]

The consequences of this attempt to keep up with Europeans on much higher incomes show clearly in the records of estates left by the better paid Eurasians. Only a very few left substantial capital. Most senior uncovenanted officials clearly enjoyed a moderately comfortable lifestyle – the extensive wardrobes, libraries, furniture, musical instruments, coaches and horses which they left show that. But they lived up to their incomes and left little money or property to their wives and children. Sarah, the wife of John Ricketts who had reached the rank of a junior civil court judge, lived after his death on the interest from Rs 5,500 raised by John's friends, and a Government pension of Rs 50 a month. By the time of her death in 1848, she had pawned all her jewels and plate.[66]

The financial problems and lack of capital amongst the Eurasian population naturally became more pronounced as it moved into its second and later generations. The mass of the poor had in any case no money to inherit or to leave, and little opportunity to earning much. The better off Eurasians kept up a European life style but, unlike their fathers, few could leave capital to their children. The savings which they had were vulnerable to bank failures, such as those which occurred in Calcutta in the early 1830s, and were obviously harder for them to replace than for the better paid British.[67]

The lack of earning potential and capital at the apex of Eurasian society, coupled with the determination to keep up European appearances as far as possible, precluded the formation of wealth and enhanced the relative security and status of official employment to Eurasian parents. They used their local influence and connections to form official families which paralleled, at a much lower economic level, British family patronage from London. Nine members of the Madge family were uncovenanted servants at Calcutta in 1831, six from the Cornelius family. Many other families had three or four relatives in Government offices.[68]

This commitment to salaried official employment from father to son shaped the attitudes of educated Eurasians, and deepened the psychological dependence of the Eurasian elite on the state for their living. Their vulnerability was to be exposed when their hitherto protected near monopoly on the better paid posts in official administration met in the 1830s the inevitable challenge of a new educated Indian middle class which could write and speak in English.

4

Eurasians in the Official Eye

The sixty years between 1773 and 1833 have been identified by Anglo-Indian chroniclers of their country's history as the decisive phase in which official policy specifically singled out the Eurasian population of British India for discrimination and discouragement. 'At certain periods of our history, our treatment by the British was not only deliberately but advisedly repressive and unnaturally cruel'.[1] The period is contrasted with the years up until the last quarter of the eighteenth century – a so-called Anglo-Indian 'golden age' in which the 'Anglo-Indian' community 'rapidly grew in numbers, wealth, power and prestige'.[2] No date is more important in marking the change in perceived British policy than the 19th April 1791 when the Court of Directors in London voted to reject the Eurasian John Turing, who came from a family long in the service in the Company, as a candidate writer for Fort St. George and minuted that no 'Natives of India' should henceforth be allowed to serve them as covenanted civil or military officers.[3] Thereafter exceptions to the rule were few and far between, as Eurasians were classified with the vast majority of the Indian ruled rather than the British rulers – the crucial issue to educated Eurasians of the time and of deep resentment to the later Anglo-Indian community.

It cannot be denied that there was discrimination against Eurasians on the grounds of their race and birth, although British policy makers of the time were prepared to defend their decision *not* to treat them as British subjects on rational, legal and pragmatic grounds, and indeed to modify policy under pressure or when circumstances dictated. Policy, it will be seen in examining the evidence, was less discriminatory, at least in theory, in the 1820s and 1830s than at the end of the eighteenth century. To Eurasians themselves *any* measure which seemed to affect their own interests, left them less opportunity, or marked them out as a class with civil disabilities, helped build a picture in their own mind of a coherent official policy directed specifically against them. In reality Eurasians were often almost inadvertent casualties of far wider political issues and British modes of thought concerning their stance in relation to their rapidly growing Indian territories, and of the complexities and dangers of the British transition from trade to rule between 1773 and 1833. It was, paradoxical as it may seem, *because* they were of British paternal descent that it became expedient to deny Eurasians full British status, for experience showed all colonial powers the vital necessity of retaining the key levers of political control of subject territories in the hands of their own nationals and out of those of the indigenous populations of western descent.

Until the 1780s there are few traces of official discrimination against Eurasians as a category, although there is no evidence that any Eurasians had ever risen to head any of the three British Presidencies. Once, however, the Regulating Act of 1773 had established the concepts of the 'British Subject' and the 'Native of India' the question of whether Eurasians were British subjects or not became open to interpretation, for the act was silent on the question of their status. For a while, although their status was unclear, the Company seemed to accept Eurasians as British subjects. Charles Weston and at least one other Eurasian, for instance, sat together with British subjects on the jury which tried and convicted the Maharaja Nuncomar in 1775.[4] The Eurasian sons of Company officials continued for a while to be put forward for covenanted employment. Henry Powney recommended his nephew, George, for employment as a writer at Madras in 1776 referring to him as a 'Native of the Place'.[5] Indeed, even as late as 1789, Major Robert Kelly gained a cadetship for his Eurasian son, Robert.[6] But a study of the applications to the Company for employment suggests that by the 1780s Eurasian applications were already few and far between. Those accepted were more likely to receive military cadetships than the much more desirable writerships.

The first signs that a formal official policy inimical to Eurasian interests was developing in London were seen in 1784 when the Managers of the Bengal Military Orphan Society proposed that they would send, at their own expense *all* the orphans of officers, boys and girls, British and Eurasian, back to Britain for their education. They hoped, in accordance with former practice whereby sons were appointed 'minor cadets' almost at birth and followed their fathers into the military, that those wards who were thought suitable would return to India in due course as cadets. The plan was vetoed by the Company, although the establishment of the orphanage was approved. Of particular significance in the Company's response was that henceforth the return to Britain of any officer's children was forbidden, unless they 'were legitimate children where both parents were European'. The ruling applied to the children of officers legally married to Indian Christian or Eurasian women, as well as those who were illegitimate. Legitimacy was not the test. Racial origin was.[7]

It was no coincidence that the formation of an official policy towards Eurasians is first discerned in the 1780s and was most discriminatory in the thirty years which followed. In the first place the rapid acceleration of Eurasian numbers rendered them an increasingly visible population group to policy makers. Since the entry of British non official residents to India was restricted by the Company, British born Eurasians threatened to become the largest civilian population group of European descent in British India, a position that they had certainly attained by the 1830s. Indeed Eurasians in British India filled to a large extent the position occupied by creole populations in the colonial territories of British and other Western powers in South East Asia, the Americas and West Indies. The rise of Eurasians in British India coincided too with wider issues abroad, the loss of the British North American colonies to descendants of the British themselves, and the outbreak of war in Europe with republican France whose interests in India continued to provide British authority with grounds for concern.

These developments bore directly on Eurasians in India although the effects on their position were incidental to the wider issues facing British policy makers. The arrival in 1786 of Lord Cornwallis as Governor-General who had surrendered to the American colonists at Yorktown five years earlier, marked the break with the old merchant days in which the Company's Governors had risen to their positions on the basis of long service in India. Thereafter – with the exception of the brief tenure of John Shore – Governors-General were political appointees. Cornwallis and Lord Wellesley after 1798 were to be the agents of a decisive shift in British policy towards their Indian possessions in which official ideology stressed the superiority of British moral virtue over a generalised belief in native depravity.[8] In the years of momentous change in the nature, extent and theory of British Government in India at the end of the eighteenth and the start of the nineteenth centuries, official policy for the first time took some serious note of Eurasians as a specific and identifiable racial category.

The measures which affected Eurasians adversely – exclusion from covenanted service, a ban on land ownership, disqualification from jury service, recall from the military service of Indian states, and financial disincentives to marriages between British officials, high or low, and Eurasians and Indian Christians – were first implemented under the rule of Cornwallis and Wellesley. It was a time when British security of tenure in India was far from assured and a new philosophy of British rule was in its early stages of development. This philosophy which legitimised, to British satisfaction at least, their new role as territorial rulers stressed British racial qualities. It sought to rationalise these in terms of an inherent superiority in the British character, military prowess, religious beliefs and probity, and a general capacity to govern fairly and well. The best safeguard for its aspirations was believed to be in the maintenance of a wide behavioural and social distance from all things and peoples Eastern, and the firm British control of all significant positions of civil and military power to the exclusion of Natives of India. Thus it was believed that the respect, if not the love, of the Indian population would be obtained, and dangers of moral contamination from Eastern beliefs, practices and customs be avoided. The Court of Directors at this time was explicit on how it expected its servants to behave:

> To preserve the ascendancy which our National Character has acquired over the minds of the Natives of India must ever be of importance to the maintenance of the Political Power we possess in the East, and we are well persuaded that the end is not to be served by a disregard of the external observation of religion, or by any assimilation of Eastern manners and opinion, but rather by retaining all the distinctions of our National principles, character and usages.[9]

The days in which it could be remarked of Madras that 'there is a good church with an organ, tho' a little prayer goes a long way with the British here' , and that the contrast between weekdays and Sundays at Calcutta was that, 'if any indeed any difference was made, it was only to commit sin the more greatly', no longer conformed to a vision of rule in which a British moral code inherently superior to the 'heathen' beliefs of their subjects became an integral element of British self-perception.[10] Church legitimised State, a symbiosis well expressed by a newly appointed chaplain, Claudius Buchanan, in 1800. Preaching before Governor-General Wellesley, he declared that:

> It is an eternal truth, that the Christian religion is the rock on which rests our existence as a civilized [sic] nation, on which rests our social blessings, and our individual happiness. Take away this rock and you give your country to convulsion and endless disgrace.[11]

The message was one that Wellesley wanted to hear. The sermon was printed by government order, and won Buchanan his temporal reward of appointment as Vice-Principal of the College at Fort William, on which Wellesley rested his hopes of a new breed of public official, uncontaminated by the temptations of the country which they were to govern.

*

Although the doctrine of British moral ascendancy which sustained its rule was evolved with the Indian population at large in mind, the maternal ancestry of Eurasians swept them into the orbit of the new thinking. The increasing emphasis on a British national character raised the question to the British as to the degree in which Eurasians shared in it. A further question mark over the Eurasian character was posed by the general British belief that Europeans who settled in the tropics degenerated physically and mentally. The thesis that a population of mixed race would inevitably become racially inferior to one of pure European stock appeared to the British of the day borne out by the miserable condition of the descendants of the Portuguese in India, a heterogeneous population in which it was difficult to distinguish those with some claim to Portuguese blood from the majority who were the descendants of Indian Christian converts. Their poverty and alleged depravity were much commented upon at the time.[12]

In contemporary explanation of the measures which began to discriminate against Eurasians the issue of the illegitimacy of many, the argument that Indians did not respect them because of the low caste of their mothers, and that they lacked British moral and physical qualities through their infusion of Indian blood, were frequently advanced. Of illegitimacy it may be remarked that it seemed to matter far more to British public opinion where Eurasians were concerned, than to their own kind. Company patronage was not withheld from the illegitimate sons of the British peerage of whom John Mordaunt, the natural son of the Earl of Peterborough, and a Mr Ray, the son of Lord Sandwich by the notorious actress Mrs Ray, were but two examples.[13]

The questions which began to be voiced concerning the Eurasian character were the public face of the deeper issue which raised the Eurasian question from the simply social to the political. The problem was the extent to which a large and rapidly growing mixed race population in British India could be accommodated within a new philosophy which argued that the Briton was inherently superior to the Indian. It may be speculated that had the Eurasians of British stock remained, as hitherto, few in number then they would have continued to be relatively easily absorbed into the framework of British rule. But Eurasians were numerous. For the most part they were children of 'poor whites', and by the beginning of the nineteenth century they formed a substantial population of British paternal descent which seemed sure to grow much larger.

The evidence is fragmentary but enough to conclude that British policy had decided by the end of the eighteenth century that Eurasians, unless they had their own means, would not be allowed to return to Britain as British subjects were, and indeed expected to do. Lord Valentia, a well connected visitor to India much exercised by the apparent risk to colonial stability of a large population of part Western descent, argued in 1809 that the problem could be solved by their repatriation to Britain, a policy which found no favour.[14] Instead, the ruling of 1784 that the illegitimate children of the Company's officers could not be returned to Britain for education effectively ensured that they had to make India their home. Similarly, the practice that only those British soldiers who had married European women were allowed to take their wives and children back to Britain with them dictated that most of their children were left in India. The question was tested in 1817 at Fort St. George when the Commander-in-Chief asked the Advocate General to rule under what authority was it prohibited for soldiers to take back their Eurasian or Indian wives and children. The answer was that there was no such ruling, but the local government made it clear that it had no intention of abandoning long existing usage.[15]

It may perhaps be that a fear of racial 'contamination' in Britain, argued so vehemently by Captain Innes Munro as likely 'to give a sallow tinge to the complexion of Britons', was one of the reasons for a policy of confining the lives of poor Eurasians to India. Perhaps Munro's argument that life for Eurasians in the land of their birth would 'be more conducive to their real happiness' was genuinely believed, although some scepticism of altruistic motives would be understandable.[16] A more pragmatic explanation, other than Eurasian happiness or the arrival of thousands in Britain, is that the Company was unwilling to accommodate so many 'free' passengers in its shipping. Whatever the reasons for the policy its consequence – a large population of British paternal descent living in India – raised the key question of how far it should be accepted as British when in India, and whether, as with creole communities in other lands, it might pose an internal political risk to British rule in India.

The dangers of European colonisation in India were deeply grounded in British thinking at the time at which Eurasian numbers in India began to grow. The influential Charles Grant warned that extensive British settlement would lead to settlers becoming 'very bold and assuming to our government there'.[17] It was argued furthermore that if, as was likely, such settlers came from the British lower classes who were 'addicted to excesses disgusting to the natives', this might strike a fundamental blow at the code of behaviour upon which colonial rule was now to be based:

> Colonization [sic], and even a large indiscriminate resort of British settlers to India, by gradually lessening the deference and respect in which Europeans are held, tend to shake the opinion entertained by the natives of the superiority of our character, and might excite them to an effort for the subversion and utter extinction of our power'.[18]

The Company was furthermore never entirely sure of the long term trustworthiness of its own military officers. A threat by them to withdraw their service in protest against a cut in their field allowances was quickly brought under control in 1766, but their grievances over slow promotion and poor pay remained very real thereafter. There was continuing apprehension lest they might form a politically unreliable military caste in India. Governor-General Warren Hastings minuted that one of the arguments for putting the Company's army under Royal control was 'to prevent the danger of military independence'.[19] Lord Cornwallis, who succeeded him, favoured the move and felt it was dangerous to British interests for army officers to be allowed to settle in India after retirement lest they, 'might have it in their power to create serious embarrassment to the Government'.[20]

Whilst the Company was able to control the inflow of British subjects into India and to keep the number of non officials resident there at a level unlikely to pose any risk of a settler class arising, Eurasians as 'Natives of India' had a right to live in India. Those

Eurasians, fortunate enough to have been sent to Britain for education and who wished to return to India were entitled to do so, provided they could prove that they were *not* British subjects.[21] What concerned the Company particularly was that the social profile of the Eurasian population in British India matched the very groups who were so unwelcome as colonists. Most were the children of 'poor whites', felt so inappropriate to the maintenance of British prestige. Those who were educated were predominantly the sons of those very Company officers whose loyalty could not necessarily be taken for granted. The clear risk of the development of a hereditary military officer caste in British India would be the more grave were it to comprise a significant Eurasian element with the legal right to residence there.

The evidence points firmly to a conclusion that British policy makers considered that Eurasians, should they be well led or politically organised, might pose a serious risk to British security in India. Conversely the perceived risk could be used as a justification for the exclusion of Eurasians from any positions of significant civil or military power. Any organised action by Eurasians brought the concern to the fore, as in 1818 when a petition for the redress of their grievances brought no action save the observation:

> The Court cannot but perceive among the memorialists indications of a spirit which, were it supported by numbers of their own description sufficient to form a strong physical force of themselves, or by power and influence to command an adequate physical force of aboriginal natives, might give birth to events which cannot be contemplated without alarm.[22]

*

The decision in 1791 to exclude Eurasians, as 'Natives of India', from covenanted civil and military service was followed by orders in Bengal which barred any Eurasians from military combatant service in the Company's regular army. A variety of reasons were brought forward at the time and subsequently to explain the motives for the Company's decision. Perhaps the most ingenuous and comforting to British self-esteem was that they were measures forced upon the British by Indian opinion.

> It cannot be [wrote Emma Roberts] too strongly impressed upon the reader's mind that these exclusions originated in the prejudices of the natives, who, while professing their willingness to be governed by Europeans, absolutely refused to submit to

Eurasians in the Official Eye

persons springing from outcast females. Hence the impossibility of admitting half-castes into the Company's Army.[23]

By the 1830s this was an often repeated post hoc rationalisation accepted without question to this day, although vigorously and naturally enough rebutted by Eurasians themselves. They saw the prime cause of any adverse Indian opinion as the direct consequence of the distinction made between them and British subjects. They argued that before their exclusion Eurasian covenanted officials were 'particularly respected by the Natives, who, from the circumstances of their being born in the country, reposed in them the greatest confidence'.[24] The difficulty in accepting the British proposition that it was in deference to Indian opinion that Eurasians were initially excluded lies firstly in the general British indifference at the time to Indian opinion, a behavioural pattern well documented by many contemporary commentators.[25] It lies secondly, and most convincingly, with the careers of many Eurasian officers in the early nineteenth century who, though debarred from the Company's covenanted service, successfully commanded Indian soldiers in the Company's irregular units and in the armies of independent Indian states. The problem lay not in Eurasian fitness to command but an unwillingness to let them occupy positions of responsibility.

A further explanation for the exclusion of Eurasians in 1791 has been that their continued appointment would have been at the expense of the much prized individual control of patronage by individual directors of the Company for 'their own relatives, friends and political allies'.[26] Since that was also the view taken by the knowledgeable Captain Williamson, writing in 1810, it bears examination. The evidence, however, is that it no more stands up to scrutiny than the assertion that Indians were unwilling to serve under Eurasians. After the exclusion of 1791 the Company's directors continued to favour the sons of their servants in India as before – so long as they could prove that their parents were both Europeans and that they were not illegitimate. Remarkably, though John Turing was rejected on the grounds that he was a Native of India, his namesake and relative John Turing – who *was* legitimate and a British subject – was appointed a writer to Fort St. George and served there from 1795 onwards.[27] In the years which followed the British sons of Company servants continued to supply an important proportion of successful applicants – 819 of the 5,925 writers and cadets appointed between 1813 and 1833.[28] The Company's policy of the beneficial use of patronage for their servants' sons did not change, it was merely that Eurasian sons were henceforth officially excluded from consideration.

When the Directors took their decision to exclude Eurasians in 1791 they minuted no explanatory reasons and have left it to posterity to deduce their motives. The weight of evidence, however, suggests that an apprehension of future danger from a growing population of European descent made it politic to ensure that Eurasians were effectively demilitarised. The decision in 1795 to exclude *all* Eurasians from combatant roles in Bengal embraced the Eurasian sons of the British rank and file as well as the officer class. It was first argued by the near contemporary, Viscount Valentia, that the decision was triggered by the creole settler revolt in French San Domingo of 1791, a view repeated in the 1930s by H. A. Stark.[29] A problem with this interpretation is that the Court's decision in 1791 was taken in April, whilst it was not until May that the French Revolutionary National Assembly voted that free persons of colour in their colonies should be enfranchised. It was even later in the year that the bloody uprisings which engulfed creole settlers, those of mixed race, and eventually the slaves of San Domingo broke out.[30]

What seems more likely is that in 1791 the Court belatedly came into line with a policy which had already been implemented for several years by their Governor-General in India, Lord Cornwallis, who had had the humiliating experience in America of surrendering to a colonists' revolt. Cornwallis not only believed in the Europeanisation of all key points of civil and military control in India but was a vigorous protagonist of plans to bring the Company's Army in India under Royal Army control. He had no powers over the Company's patronage, but since he was Commander-in-Chief as well as Governor-General, had direct authority over the Royal Army in India. Well before the Company decided to exclude Eurasians from their army Cornwallis was carrying the policy out within the Royal Army. In 1789 he wrote to the War Office to explain his policy of Eurasian exclusion was based on, 'the injuries which could accrue to the Discipline and Reputation of H.M.'s troops employed in India, from the admission of Persons as officers, or even as soldiers, who are born of Black women, natives of the Country'. The War Office gave entire approval of his conduct. The next year, preceding the Court's own decision on the matter, the War Office issued an order, described as 'invariable and absolute', forbidding the employment of any as officers or soldiers who could not prove that both parents were Europeans, 'without any mixture of the blood of natives of India'.[31]

One further Company decision, taken in the year following the exclusion of Eurasians in India, supports the argument that a concern over the political reliability of indigenous populations of Western descent was the fundamental issue rather than colour or legitimacy, incidental though they may have been. In 1792 the Court resolved that at another of their possessions, the island of St. Helena, no native of the island should be allowed to act as a Councillor, nor should he 'be capable of holding or possessing the military command'.[32] The regulation for St. Helena did not go as far as that for India, but its intent was just as clear – to counter any possibility of military or civil independence of action by the descendants of colonists.

*

The exclusion of Eurasians in India was strictly enforced after 1791. When James Playdell could not produce his baptismal certificate or an affidavit to prove his British birth in 1794, his appointment as a Bengal cadet was revoked.[33] Captain Henry Haldane, at one time an aide-de-camp to Cornwallis, had the application for his eldest and Eurasian son Henry rejected in 1793, though both his younger sons, born after his marriage to Maria Helm, were granted cadetships.[34] Even directors of the Company were unable to bend the rules. David Scott, a future Chairman, trying in 1796 to help the son of a friend found that, 'from his being of an Indian mother I find great difficulty in it'.[35] Nor could a former Governor-General, Sir John Shore, arrange an appointment for his Eurasian son, though his legitimate son, Frederick John, was admitted.

There were nevertheless a few exceptions to the general rule. The Directors suspended their own regulations in 1792 for the benefit of Charles Holloway, the son of one of their merchants. But the appointment was to the unhealthy and politically unimportant station of Bencoolen in Sumatra where his father had died.[36] The regulations were enforced less rigidly when the candidate was legitimate, and not a first generation Eurasian. Frederick Mullins, who was appointed in 1818 and in time rose to command the 12th Bengal Native Infantry, was the country born son of a British merchant and his Portuguese wife.[37] But the rarity of exceptions – the appointment of Sir Charles Metcalfe's illegitimate son, James, in 1836 was one such – serve only to confirm that after 1791 virtually no first generation Eurasians, and only a few of second and later were appointed. When they were it was as military officers not as civil servants.[38]

It has been claimed that in 1791 not only were Eurasians excluded for the future but those already in office were dismissed.[39] The case of John Nairne is cited as an instance. He had already made two trips to India as a sworn officer of the Company's fleet before 1791. His application to make a third in 1795 was turned down by the Court but he was allowed to return to India as a free mariner.[40] This seems to have been the *only* recorded instance where an Eurasian, already in service in 1791, was debarred for the future. Far from dismissing Eurasians already serving, the Company allowed them to continue, presumably because their political reliability was already proved and accepted. There seems to have been no discrimination, either social or professional, against such officers: the 'gallant' Major Nairne, renowned for his bravery and much admired by his Commander-in-Chief, General Lake, was killed at Kachaura in 1803. Robert Stevenson rose to command as a Major-General at Cawnpore, and was a founder member of the Bengal Club in 1827. Lieutenant-General Richard Jones, for all that he was described as 'dark complexioned', commanded the Bombay Army against the Marathas. James Auchmuty rose to General officer rank, whilst his brothers Richard and John continued in the Bengal Civil Service until 1808 and 1827 respectively.[41]

★

The focus of historical attention on official policy towards Eurasians has invariably centred on the exclusion of educated males from the Company's covenanted service. Scant attention has been paid to the development of official policy towards the marriage of British males to Eurasian or Indian women at the start of the nineteenth century. If one primary objective of British policy was to neutralise Eurasians as a political force, the second was to check the rise in a Eurasian population which inevitably blurred the clear line between rulers and ruled which overall British policy sought now to draw.

An acrimonious debate in 1804 over which dependants should benefit from a new charitable fund for the widows and dependants of Bengal civil servants, well illustrates the degree to which the opinion of the 'new moralists' of British society had triumphed over the more relaxed social attitudes of earlier days. All the civil servants were agreed on the need for a fund for their dependants, but were fundamentally divided over who should be allowed to have a claim on it. The older civil servants naturally wanted their unofficial Indian 'wives' and Eurasian children to be able to claim. They were opposed by the younger civil servants, especially those who were graduates from the College of Fort William, the creation of Governor-General Wellesley. They insisted that Indian 'wives' and Eurasian children should be excluded from benefit, save for the return of any contributions which had been made by the deceased contributor.

As the controversy raged the Rev. Claudius Buchanan commented that, 'the junior servants who are now or have been in college almost without voice exclaim against a measure which they conceive would have a tendency to sanction vice, and countenance an illicit connection with native women'.[42] He praised the young Charles Metcalfe, than a rising star in the Governor-General's private office, as the leader of the party for exclusion. Metcalfe urged the need for the British to stand aloof from the Indian population, and linked the countenancing of illegitimate children to 'the destruction of public principles, to the overthrow of established and sacred institutions, to the disgrace of the character of the settlement and to the injury of our country'.[43] He had the support of the Governor-General and of the Court of Directors who in approval voted £2500 a year to augment the fund's voluntary contributions.

The line taken over the Bengal Civil Fund was followed in the regulations for the Military Funds which were set up soon after by Company officers in all three Presidencies and by the Marine in Bombay. Their regulations defined the criteria for deciding who was eligible. *Any* claimant, wife or child, was required to have been born of married European parents, 'four removes from an Asiatic or African being considered as European blood'.[44] The issue debated so fiercely had ostensibly been one of public morality – of 'illicit relations' and illegitimacy. But the true objection revealed in the regulations of the funds was to *any* intermixing of British and Indian blood and consequent increase in the Eurasian proportion of the British community in India. Those excluded were not only Indian partners and their illegitimate children. They were *also* the legally married Christian Indian or Eurasian wives and their legitimate Eurasian children.

The use of financial sanctions to discourage the Company's servants from marriage or cohabitation with Indian or Eurasian women was applied to the lowest as well as to the highest in rank.

By 1793 the Eurasian and Indian wives and widows of non-commissioned officers and soldiers, even when legally married, had been excluded from the benefits of Lord Clive's Fund. Pensions from the fund were paid to officers and their wives in London but, since many widows of the Company's rank and file were born in India and stayed there after their husband's death, they were allowed at first to draw their pensions in India. After 1793 no widows were allowed benefit in India, unless their marriage lines proved they were Europeans and not 'Natives of India'.[45] Since soldiers returning to Britain were not allowed, nor could afford, to take even their legally married wives back with them, the problem of providing for wives in illness and old age was forced on to local charity. The injustice of this was voiced by the Vestry of St. Mary's Madras, reporting in 1805 that:

> Many relicts of soldiers, whose husbands were equally distinguished for bravery and length of service, have been disappointed in their expectation of obtaining the Bounty. Some of these through age and infirmity, unable to provide for their own subsistence, have been rescued from a state of beggary.[46]

The Company's reply was that the matter was merely one of cost and not principle.[47] It is hard, however, to take this at face value since the cost, at around 2d a day for each widow, was an inconsiderable drain on the fund. Again cost might have been advanced as a justification for a further disincentive to the marriage of British soldiers to Eurasian or Indian women – the refusal after 1810 of soldiers' marriage allowances save only to wives of British birth. But the Commander-in-Chief, Bengal was quite clear on the true motive. It was, he thought, 'meant to prevent an encouragement to Europeans for marrying women, natives of the East Indies'.[48]

★

From around 1820 a relaxation in the official policy which had so adversely affected Eurasian interests in the last years of the eighteenth and the very early years of the nineteenth centuries began to be apparent. Grounds for any real concern over Eurasian potential for political mischief were gone. The war with France in Europe was over and her threat to British interests in India dispelled. Successful campaigns against Mysore, Nepal, the Marathas, the Pindaris and into Burma had secured British paramountcy in India itself. British Residents at the courts of remaining independent states safeguarded the Company's interests. It had become clear too that the policy of restricting the size of the Eurasian population through financial discouragement had failed and that its social consequences were becoming painfully apparent in increasing Eurasian destitution. Although the main thrust of official policy, that first-generation Eurasians were 'Natives of India' was not to change, the stringency of the policies which had disadvantaged Eurasians were relaxed. If a sceptical interpretation were to be placed on the shift it would be that there was now little to fear from a largely poor Eurasian community save its potential embarrassment to the prestige of British rule. However, such a conclusion should be tempered by recognition of humanitarian motives, expressed particularly by the military 'service family', of a need to ameliorate the Eurasian situation.

It is clear that even the early years of the nineteenth century local officials often dissented from the hard line towards Eurasians of the Company in London. Lieutenant-General Cradock, for instance, when commanding at Fort St. George in 1805, continued to grant pensions in contravention of official policy to the Eurasian widows of soldiers in need.[49] The exclusion of Eurasian wives from the marriage allowances paid to the British wives of the Company's soldiers was argued by military officials to the Company at home to be a disruptive issue within its army. It differentiated between the wives of their soldiers causing resentment amongst them. Worse yet it encouraged the smuggling by wives of arrack into camp to earn some money. The problem was worst:

> amongst those half cast and Native females in the Regiment who have no legitimate means of support, but the soldier's nett pay, and amongst whom illicit means of support is actually in full trade. This class of people are the most numerous and have the largest families without any allowance from Government, and are consequently in a wretched state of poverty and misery.[50]

Not all local opinion, however, was agreed on the desirability of restoring marriage allowances to the Eurasian wives of British soldiers. Thomas Munro, Governor at Madras, minuted in 1824 that the inevitable consequence of such a step would be to accelerate the growth of a Eurasian population 'who we shall have taught by indulgence not to provide for themselves'. Whilst his objection was ostensibly humanitarian, his projections of the numbers of Eurasian children who might be born as a result – 'in twenty years in place of the wives and families of twelve thousand we shall have those of twenty or thirty thousand' – suggests that his real concern was the eventual size of the Eurasian population.[51]

Despite Munro's opposition marriage allowances were restored to Eurasian, though not to Indian Christian wives, in 1824 but at half the rate for British wives. The justification was that, 'born in India and habituated to live chiefly on rice the wants and wishes of the Half-Caste are much more confined than those of European women'.[52] Also in that year the Court reversed its previous policy and directed that the Indian or Eurasian widows of soldiers should once again, provided they were legally married, be entitled to pensions from Lord Clive's Fund.[53] Munro's dire prediction, incidentally, proved grossly exaggerated. The Eurasian population did continue to increase in the later 1820s, but rather than one in three soldiers marrying in India (on which he had based his Eurasian population projections) the actual was only one in ten – even after the allowances had been restored. Nor did the measure prove extremely costly. The 403 Eurasian wives of Bengal British soldiers drew a mere Rs 19,000 between them in 1829.[54]

There were comparable improvements in the financial position of many Eurasian wives of Company officers in the 1820s. Local Governments disregarded Company instructions and often paid them pensions on their husband's death. In Bengal when the Government there heard that officers' Eurasian wives were again to benefit from Lord Clive's Fund, their comment was, that was what they were doing already. At Madras half-pensions had been paid to the Eurasian widows of officers since 1815 on an ex gratia basis. From 1826 they received them as of right. The most dramatic improvement in their position came early in the 1830s and, most surprisingly, was initiated by the Company's Directors in London despite opposition from military officers. By 1833 all the civil and military funds had agreed to readmit Eurasian wives and their children to the benefits from which they had been excluded in the early nineteenth century. The Bengal civil and military funds led the way in removing the exclusion which the Directors freely admitted had been imposed in the first instance to deter the marriage of British covenanted servants to Eurasian women. By the early 1830s, urged on by a Eurasian petition which argued that it was unjust to penalise officers' wives just because they had been born illegitimate, the Court put pressure on their Army officers in Bombay and Madras who had repeatedly voted to retain the bar on benefit to Eurasian widows and their children. Once the Directors had threatened to withdraw their contributions to the funds, they too came reluctantly into line.[55]

There was a logic in the Directors reversal of earlier policy, for in 1827 they had reinterpreted the categories of Eurasians who were excluded from covenanted civil and military service as 'Natives of India'. From then on only *first* generation Eurasians were to be excluded, a decision strongly welcomed by the English language press of Calcutta.[56] The reasons for the relaxation cannot be determined with certainty for, as with the decision to exclude all Eurasians in 1791, the official record gives no details. But it is reasonable to surmise, since most of the Company's senior military officers at the time were said to be married to Eurasian women, that they had pressed successfully for a dispensation which would benefit the chances of military commissions for their sons. If that were so, though some second generation Eurasians did serve as officers in the Company's Army and even the Indian Navy thereafter, the numbers who benefited from the Company's patronage were too few to materially affect the status of educated Eurasians in British India. Indeed, since many of those Eurasians who achieved some wealth, men like Peter Carstairs or General Jones for instance, chose to retire like their British counterparts to Britain, and since the Eurasian wives of British officers also returned with their husbands, such wealth as there was within the resident Eurasian population in India was always subject to attrition. Those who were too poor to go to England had to stay in India.

When examining the Company's official policy towards Eurasians in the critical years between 1773 and 1833 there is some danger in concluding, particularly as far as the Company in London was concerned, that it was an active policy, and that Eurasians were continually high on the agenda of political issues. That is the interpretation which later generations of the Anglo-Indian community have tended to put on the exclusion of Eurasians from covenanted service in 1791 and the general lack of encouragement they received in their ambitions to be accepted on a basis of equality of treatment and opportunity as British subjects. This is an understandable perspective from the Anglo-Indian viewpoint but does not do justice to the essentially pragmatic and responsive nature of British policy during the period. Whilst Eurasian numbers were small and the British territorial stake in India minimal no official policies were needed. It was only when Eurasian numbers grew rapidly and they became significant within the population of British descent in India that policies emerged, both social and political. It is no coincidence that Eurasians became a matter for political attention in the 1780s and 1790s as British policy makers considered their essential interest – the continuation of their colonial rule. In the key decision to exclude Eurasians from covenanted service, the evidence suggests that considerations of internal security were paramount, and that Eurasians fell victim to a political theory which saw the best route to British security in excluding all of Indian descent from civil and military authority. The real concerns in the 1790s that Eurasians might emerge as a political force had long been discounted by the 1830s, but events in the territories of other colonial powers, those of Spanish America in particular, ensured that doubt over Eurasian political reliability was never quite dispelled.

Until Eurasians forced themselves onto the public political agenda with their Petition to Parliament in 1830 – whose aims, objectives, and achievements are discussed later – there is little evidence that the Company's Directors gave more than cursory attention to the Eurasian question. But the relaxation of the rules governing covenanted employment of Eurasians, the new eligibility of Eurasian women to the benefits of civil and military funds, and the restoration of marriage allowances to the Eurasian wives of British soldiers suggest that the real concern felt by the Company in London at the political potential of the Eurasian population to disturb its security at the end of the eighteenth century had much abated by the 1830s. It seems too that London was responsive to the views and representations of their local Governments in India on whom the responsibility for carrying out policy largely devolved. It is not to be doubted that these officials generally subscribed to and implemented with little misgiving the doctrines of British national ascendancy which emerged at the end of the eighteenth century. But, as far as Eurasians were concerned, a paternalistic interest often tempered local interpretation of policy. It was more visible amongst senior officers of the Company's army, concerned publicly for even-handed treatment for the Eurasian as well as the British wives of their men, and personally for the career opportunities for their sons.

5

Towards a Reluctant Community

The tentative emergence in the 1820s of an embryo Eurasian community in British India was predicated largely by British policy towards educated Eurasians. Since the 1790s they had been relegated to inferior roles in Government upon which as a group they were to a large degree economically dependant. The narrow limits of opportunity open or acceptable to the Eurasian elite, and the rising rhetoric of British social and racial prejudice in the early nineteenth century, prompted the discovery of a communal self interest amongst Eurasians which led in the 1820s to an agenda of educational, occupational and political initiative. Its aims were to counter the apparent marginalisation of Eurasians within the British community in India. For the first time individual Eurasians became articulate and active in promoting the shared interests of their social class. It has been argued that, 'The Anglo-Indian community was forced, through British rejection to form themselves into a cohesive unit'.[1] In accepting the broad argument that Eurasian community consciousness was forced upon them, the essential unwillingness of Eurasians to become a community is underlined, a point which will be developed later.

But, to speak in the 1820s of 'Eurasians' as if they were an homogeneous society, or of them as a 'cohesive' unit, is to oversimplify and anticipate time by far. Indeed, to regard them at that time as a 'community' in any *structured* sense is also premature. Most questionable of all is to infer from the Eurasian communal activities of the 1820s the existence of an accepted ethnic self identity. Certainly official policy and social distancing tended to promote a *British* concept of a discrete Eurasian racial identity from the end of the eighteenth century onwards. The British view was not, however, accepted or shared by educated Eurasians whose objectives were quite the reverse of a desire to forge an ethnic identity. Their aim was to lessen, as far as might be achieved, the social and occupational gap which was beginning to separate them from the main stream of British society in India.

Indeed, if ever a community could have wished for its own corporate dissolution, and for complete integration with its paternal society, it would have been the educated Eurasians of early nineteenth century India. Their rhetoric and actions suggest more the emergence of a social and political pressure group amongst an educated elite, than the establishment of an ethnic 'community' in a real or desired sense. If a sense of 'belonging' is accepted as an essential attribute of a true community, the predicament of Eurasians was that they sought to belong to the British community, rather than to one another. The emergence of a Eurasian 'community' as such in British India was occasioned by the establishment by British policy and opinion of occupational, social, racial and political boundaries within which Eurasians were to be confined.

It has been well observed that 'class' was a key element within the structure of British society in India, an aspect replicated within its Eurasian sector. Eurasian bandsmen, at its foot, were far removed economically and socially from those employed in the senior grades of the uncovenanted service. They in their turn might have little in common, save their racial origin, with the few wealthy or famous Eurasians, such as Lieutenant-Colonel Skinner. Thus the overwhelming impression, in examining the awakening of Eurasian self-interest in the 1820s, is of a minority group of urban Eurasians – mainly in Calcutta – who believed that, by birth and education, they had a natural right to be treated on a par with British officials. Eurasian activity was more a 'middle class' phenomenon than a popular movement. The aspirations of the emergent Eurasian community were 'class' based – an attempt by educated Eurasians to overcome the occupational as well as the racial barriers which excluded them from full membership of the British official family. The dilemma was that, the more pressing the Eurasian claim, the more they focused British attention on themselves. Their grievances brought to the fore historic fears of their political reliability. Their request for admission to covenanted service and to exemption from the Company's judicial system, open only to British subjects, raised in British minds the question of Eurasian presumption beyond their appointed place in the class, as well as the racial, structure of British society in India.

A still born attempt by Calcutta's Eurasians, which interested their counterparts in Madras and Bombay, to set up a gentleman's club exclusively for themselves in 1825 illustrates well the Eurasian dilemma and British reaction to what was seen as their social pretension.[2] The plan was, as so often in Eurasian public activity, a reaction against exclusion from the upper circles of British society. They hoped, in establishing their club, to provide a milieu which they could call their own and to which they could invite members of the British community on equal terms. Innocuous as the aims of the proposed club may now appear – it seems to have met only once – the plan fuelled fears in British circles that it might become, 'a radical institution fraught with danger in a political point of view, to the interests of the Honourable Company'.[3] In public debate some supported the project – although one Eurasian woman bemoaned the fact that it was a male only institution – but others strongly criticised the projected club as divisive, and contrary to the true interest of each Eurasian, 'that his body should amalgamate with the body of the Europeans'.[4]

British credentials were vital to the self perception of educated Eurasians. These necessarily required a repudiation of their Indian maternal ancestry, for British rejection of all things Indian naturally influenced a Eurasian elite seeking to conform to British codes and beliefs. Moreover there was little inherently attractive to educated Eurasians in identification with Indian society at large. The upper reaches of that society offered no place for educated Eurasians, a position well understood by Governor-General William Bentinck who minuted in 1829 that language, habits and religion linked them to their fathers' community rather than that of their mothers where, 'if Hindus they must hold the lowest rank, and by whom, if Mussulmans, they are little likely to be respected'.[5]

Many Eurasians from lower social backgrounds eventually either merged back into Indian society, or more typically formed a part of a growing poor Christian Indian society. But, better off Eurasians strove mightily to minimise recognition of their maternal ancestry, even to dissociating themselves from the languages of their native country.

> It is a mortifying fact [the Managers of the Eurasian Parental Academy complained in 1831] that East Indians [Eurasians] know little or nothing of the language, literature, manners and customs of the country in which they were born, and equally true it is that few are fit for useful employment, wherever the knowledge of the native language is considered a qualification.[6]

Upper income Eurasian parents often went so far, in their desire to emphasise that they were British, as to keep Indian children out of the private schools at which their children were educated.[7]

*

The encounter from the early nineteenth century with an ever more closely knit British official society aggravated problems of social acceptability for educated Eurasians. The British who made up official society were often educated at the same schools, had comparable social backgrounds, followed similar career paths, and were deeply conscious of their status as 'gentlemen'. Observers of the homogeneity of white colonial society have drawn attention to 'class' as an integral element in a social structure which was governed by accepted codes of behaviour, exclusive, and remarkably conformist in nature.[8] These tendencies, common enough in Britain itself, were magnified in the artificiality of the colonial context. British society in India depended essentially on the acceptance by the ruled of an 'inherent' superiority in their rulers (or so thought the British of the time), and a determination on their part that 'nothing was to be done which could create an impression of weakness or fallibility, and undermine the belief'.[9] British thinking assigned to itself its own place in India, generally kept to it, and expected others to do likewise.

Eurasian claims to a place in that ever more delineated and 'gentlemanly' British society in India – particularly by those who were the sons and daughters of covenanted officials – were social and cultural. With only few exceptions British fathers of rank had their Eurasian children baptised as Protestants and educated as Europeans. Language, dress and social behaviour emphasised the close cultural relation of Eurasian to Briton. But to the British of the day, differences were more important than similarities in determining the Eurasian position within their society. The most obvious signal to all of Eurasian difference was the colour of their skin. It placed them across the ever more rigidly drawn line of ruler and ruled. As a racial discriminator colour has, of course, a history which antedates the British arrival in India and was not confined to them alone. The traveller François Bernier reported of the Mughals in the seventeenth century that they chose their wives from the Kashmiris for their fairness and looks, and that 'children of the third and fourth generation, who have the brown com- plexion, and the languid manner of this country of their nativity, are held in much less respect than newcomers'.[10] The Indian women whom Alfonso de Albuquerque encouraged his Portuguese to wed in 1510 were, not the 'black' women of the Malabar but lighter skinned Muslims.[11] Even amongst the French of Pondicherry, popularly supposed to have taken a more relaxed view of colour than the British, a light skinned Eurasian was thought more likely to be successful in life.[12]

Skin colour became more important as a discriminator in British society as the nineteenth century progressed. Yet its importance antedated the concepts of British racial supremacy and the heyday of imperial rule. As early as 1758 a Mrs. Kindersley, visiting the Calcutta area, remarked that colour was seen by Eurasian women as a barrier to full acceptance into British polite society. If they were pretty, she commented, they often married Europeans but 'their children, being another remove from black, do not like to have their descent remembered'.[13]

As late as the 1780s, although notice was taken of colour, British attitudes were by no means consistently adverse, particularly where eligible Eurasian women were concerned. As long as they met British social class criteria, they seem to have been generally accepted in the upper reaches of British polite society. The author of 'Hartly House', a Calcutta novel of the 1780s, describes a theatre scene in which 'several country-born women figured away in the boxes, and by candlelight had absolutely the advantage of the Europeans'.[14] Up country at Baghlipore in 1807 a visit to a Doctor 'G' by the author Mary Sherwood suggests that upper-class Eurasian women had a better chance of integration into British society than their brothers. Doctor 'G' lived 'like a Nabob' with his seven Eurasian children. The boys, she noted, were considered unpresentable in polite society, but the girls 'had every advantage of countenance and education'.[15]

Despite popular rhetoric British colonial society, up until the 1830s at least, valued Eurasian women on account of their potential as wives. Consequently it was easier for them to be accepted as British rather than Indian. Maria Carey, the Eurasian wife of the sailor John Carey, who according to Holwell's contemporary narrative, survived her imprisonment in the Black Hole of Calcutta in 1756, received a recognition perhaps unique to Eurasian women –acceptance as a British heroine and a Government memorial to her memory placed in Calcutta's Roman Catholic Cathedral.[16] Eurasian men rarely married British women. When they did their wives were apt to be cold-shouldered by British polite society. But it was equally unacceptable that a Eurasian woman of birth should marry an Indian, however high his rank.[17] An attempt by the King of Oudh in 1830 to 'seduce' a Lieutenant-Colonel Simpson's daughter into his zenana was reported to Governor-General William Bentinck by the British Resident at Lucknow who felt that 'to prevent any degradation of our national character is I conceive an important part of my duty here'.[18] Even in the sad world of the European Lunatic Asylum at Bhowanipore, class rather than race determined the treatment of Eurasian women. Two classes of accommodation were provided, the first for ladies and gentlemen, the second for the lower classes. Amongst the patients there in 1834 were a Miss Purvis and a Mrs. Hutchinson. Both were listed as paupers but housed in the first class with their own furnished apartments and washing room. As the daughters of 'gentlemen' they kept their status despite their lunacy and poverty.[19]

As for Eurasian boys, the fairer they were the better. One British officer thought himself, 'extremely lucky my boy being as fair as I am, and having white hair'.[20] Colour was important by the late eighteenth century in deciding whether a boy should be sent back to England for education or not. Of the three Imhoff children, one died in infancy. The elder of the surviving two who was described as being fairer than most Eurasians was sent to England. His brother 'so dark, that if his mother is not absolutely black, he can scarcely be J's son though he was acknowledged', was educated at Calcutta.[21]

By the 1820s, when Bishop Heber reflected on the significance of colour and concluded that, 'European vanity leads us astray in supposing that our own is the primitive complexion', he was out of step with British thinking of his day. Even if some had agreed privately, none would have supported publicly his conclusion that the colour of Indians 'was perhaps the most agreable to the eye'.[22] The rhetoric of the 1820s and 1830s suggests that skin colour was becoming a more important social discriminator than hitherto. By the 1840s, when more British women came to India to live, colour placed even the well born Eurasian woman outside the pale of society. Social ostracism at Benares was the lot of one army officer who married a wealthy Eurasian, described by a contemporary as a 'nigger half caste woman'.[23] The regimental colonels who preferred their officers to keep Indian mistresses than to marry Eurasian women suggest that once the supply of eligible British women increased in India Eurasian women, as their brothers before them, began to be pushed away from the centres of British upper class society.

★

By the early nineteenth century an increasing proportion of the Eurasian population in British India was of second, third, or later generations. Their connections with contemporary Britain were necessarily increasingly tenuous. Though some Eurasians still were sent to Britain for their education, for the majority knowledge of British domestic behaviour and custom was at second hand. As Eurasian links with the land of their forefathers diminished, their claim to it as 'home' became a matter of ridicule to the British in India. An apocryphal 'Mrs. Colonel Yellowly' was for instance satirised, 'for the manufacture of Chutnee and Doppiajah curry; talking a great deal of a certain 'terra Incognita' called "home" '.[24]

Beyond the accidents of colour and part Indian ancestry factors of culture and class contributed to the distancing of British polite society from Eurasians. Differences in two areas which both shared – dress and accent – affected the British perception of Eurasians adversely. The Western dress of Eurasian women attracted critical comment from British observers of the social scene. Eurasian dress was often portrayed as outdated in fashion, and even worse – colourful and gaudy – with a liking for materials and jewellery considered typically Indian. Eurasian women were thought to look far better in Indian than Western costume and were criticised for wearing outmoded fashions, 'caring little about the date of their construction, providing the style be European'.[25] By the late 1820s a Mrs. Fenton was advised that it was 'the extremity of bad taste to appear in anything of Indian manufacture'. If she did buy any Indian material, 'I must not be seen in it, as none but half castes ever wear them'.[26] As for Eurasian men, their imitation of British fashion clearly irritated –

> Many a young Bond Street dandy struts with inconceivable self-satisfaction, and the youthful British, Portuguese, and French half-cast, with tawny face, and neck stiffened almost to suffocation, jumps from the sublime to the ridiculous in attempts at imitation.[27]

Since Western dress was the mark of the ruling race, the Eurasian variation upon it seemed to be an unwelcome, if unconscious, parody which might invite ridicule and so diminish British standing in Indian eyes.

Accent was a second factor which, to the upper class Briton, marked out the Eurasian. Little is heard on the development of a distinctive accent and idiom by Eurasians until the 1820s and 1830s when comment became frequent. Then it was described as a 'singular variety of the Anglo-Saxon tongue called the Cheechee language (Hindustani idiom Englished)', disagreeable to the ear, faulty in idiom, and with accents placed on the wrong syllable.[28] Amongst the poorest of Eurasians many spoke very little English at all.[29] It was generally believed by the British that, once acquired, the accent could not be lost – a compelling argument for sending their children back to Britain for their education. An imperfect command of the English language, grating on the sensitive British ear, once again marked out the Eurasian in British polite society.

Such peripheral issues as proper dress and accent were nonetheless integral elements of class recognition within the British code of 'gentlemanly' behaviour. Some British argued that, provided Eurasians conformed to what has been described as an 'unspoken code' of British life, they were welcome in British society.[30] The reality for most Eurasians by the 1820s was that they were not. Certainly some *did* meet the criteria. One such was Major-General Stevenson, whose rank outweighed his Eurasian descent. Another was Lieutenant-Colonel Skinner, whose military fame and generous hospitality overcame his faulty English. But they and others were exceptions for most educated Eurasians, by reason of their occupations, failed the gentlemanly test. Receptions at Government House were an important mark of social standing. Admittance differentiated the ruler from the ruled, the 'respectable' European from he who was not. Once Eurasians were excluded from covenanted service they lost the right to admission. Eurasian women were excluded, no matter the rank of their fathers or husband.[31] In justification it was argued that, since Indians of high rank were excluded, they would be affronted by the admission of Eurasians descended on their maternal side from, 'the lowest or least virtuous class of society'. This convenient rationalisation masked the true reason – a wish to discourage the marriage of the official British elite to Eurasians. 'Anglo-Indians' [the name by which British residents in India were popularly described at the time], it was argued, 'who choose to associate with the half caste children of the soil, forfeited their claims to mix among their equals'.[32]

Some Governors-General, such as Lord Hastings, took a more relaxed view. Prompted by his wife, he noted in his private diary that, 'Till Lady Loudon gave a private hint that colour would never be noticed, half caste ladies, though of the best education and conduct, were not admitted to Government House'.[33] An exceptional Eurasian of such prominence and public standing as James Kyd could not realistically be excluded, as Hastings recognised. 'Mr. Kyd was held in high esteem by the Marquis of Hastings who paid him considerable respect in society'.[34] But Kyd was one of all too few Eurasians of wealth and consequent social acceptability at the apex of British society in India. There is some evidence that the freer approach encouraged by Hastings survived him into the later 1820s, but a decade later Eurasians were once more to be excluded.

*

It has been justly observed of colonial societies in general that both rulers and ruled were typecast in stereotyped roles and attitudes which make it hard to penetrate 'ethnic role taking and discern the individual behind them'.[35] The general observation is amply supported by the evolution of a Eurasian stereotype in the early nineteenth century. In assigning particular personality, moral, intellectual and class characteristics a boundary was set to the place assigned to Eurasians in British society. There they were expected to remain, and not to aspire beyond.

The Eurasian stereotype was unflattering. It seems to have been rooted in the British assumption that degeneration of the national character was an inevitable consequence of long term residence in India. There, a robust British character was exposed to physical toll from the climate, and worse still, to moral risk from contact with Indian mores. Official acceptance of popular prejudice was recognised in the aim of Governor-General Wellesley's College at Fort William for young British officials. It was to provide:

> Solid foundations of industry, prudence, integrity, and religion, as should effectively guard against those temptations and corruptions with which the nature of the climate, and the particular depravity of the people of India, will surround them in every station, especially on their first arrival in India.[36]

Eurasians were seen to be doubly at risk. They were exposed to the direct influence of their Indian mothers, and they spent all their lives in India. Indolence and a loss of vigour, commonly attributed to Indians, was one important aspect of the Eurasian stereotype, male or female. Even sensible behaviour during the day-time heat brought adverse comment, such as:

> The indolent disposition of the daughters of Indo-Britons who instead of performing those duties which naturally devolve on them sit in a listless state of ennui during the interval that elapses between the morning and evening drives, or, what is worse, slumber on the hall sofas.[37]

Of more fundamental importance though was the development by the 1830s of an argument of Eurasian genetic inferiority to the British. It was prompted particularly by the efforts of educated Eurasians to challenge the boundaries prescribed for them by British society. '. . . It is a general theory,' [remarked the *Asiatic Journal* in 1838 of Eurasian ambitions to be treated on a par with British subjects] 'which has received the sanction of the oldest residents in British India, that the intermixture of blood has limited both the corporeal and the intellectual status of the race, whom it is the fashion of the day to regard with commiseration'.[38]

What was said in public of the Eurasian stereotype was, it appears, generally felt in private. The records of the London Missionary Society which employed a small number of Eurasian missionaries in early nineteenth century India contain correspondence on an issue debated in the late 1820s and early 1830s – should ordained Eurasian missionaries be paid as much as their British colleagues? The correspondence between the LMS headquarters in London and their British missionaries in the field on the question, [the Eurasian missionaries were not asked *their* views] was in confidence. Thus it may reasonably be assumed that what was said by individual missionaries about their Eurasian colleagues was what they really thought rather than what was expected to be said.

Back in 1827 it had been agreed within the LMS that all missionaries were equal, and there should be no discrimination over levels of pay on racial grounds. Nevertheless, the issue was debated again in 1831 when London asked their British missionaries in India for their views.[39] As far as the Society in London was concerned there seems no reason to suspect more than a desire to save costs if possible. British missionaries and their wives were expensive to ship out and maintain in India. Many died early leaving widows and children to be supported by the Society. Those who survived had children to educate and needed provision for their old age. Eurasians, as the Baptists had found, provided a more cost effective alternative.

The consensus of opinion amongst the British missionaries was that Eurasians needed less to live on than they did. It is in the content of the individual replies that the British concept of the Eurasian place in their society can be clearly seen. One argument was that Eurasians needed to be paid less since they were accustomed to the climate and so did not need to buy 'those means of sustenance (beer and wine etc.) which are very expensive in this country'. Eurasian difficulties of social acceptance were emphasised.

> Association with European residents and visitors . . . from which country born missionaries are for the most part exempted, renders it necessary that the furniture and the dress of European missionaries be somewhat better than they would think it their duty in other circumstances to use.[40]

Perhaps the missionaries may be suspected of justifying their own life style, for a visiting LMS delegation in 1827 reported that their Eurasian missionary and his wife at Cuddapah were, 'greatly respected by the English Gentlemen in the neighbourhood, who show them every kind attention'.[41]

Some missionaries argued that Eurasians were inherently attracted to the fripperies of life and to pay them more than they really needed for a basic existence was dangerous.[42] One, the Rev. W. Campbell, stationed at Bangalore, went further yet and argued that a European missionary who had been in India for only a year was better qualified to vote at District Meetings than an Eurasian who had five or six years experience.[43] He evidently shared the prevailing view, first heard as early as the start of the nineteenth century, that Eurasians had an 'evident inferiority' in mental and moral qualities to Europeans.[44]

To their credit there were those in British society in India of the 1820s and 1830s who did not share in, and were prepared to speak out against the stereotyping of Eurasians. The Rev. W. Miller at Nagercoil was one who opposed paying Eurasian missionaries less than Europeans. He asked,

> Why should we simply on account of their race, or colour, or education, create a distinction which in the present state of society in this country will inevitably cause them to be looked on as an inferior order of men?[45]

There were others too who did not subscribe to a belief in inherent Eurasian inferiority. The Rev. John Statham, a Baptist minister, defended the intellectual capability of Eurasian boys. Drawing on his wide experience as a teacher, he pointed out that, 'the first boys of all classes in the different schools of Calcutta were invariably Indo-

Britons'.[46] The indigo planter, William Huggins, dismissed the argument that the mixture of Indian and European blood produced Eurasian inferiority as one which was, 'only productive of animosity and subverts the harmony of society'.[47] There was consistent public support too in the 1820s for a more liberal attitude to Eurasians from the *Bengal Hurkaru*, a leading Calcutta English language newspaper of the time. Its retired editor, James Sutherland, commended Eurasian ability, capacity, and fitness for greater responsibilities to the 1832 Parliamentary Select Committee.[48]

Though such men spoke up they were little heeded in the development of the Eurasian stereotype and the establishment of the social boundaries thought proper by British opinion. By 1838, when the *Confessions of an Eurasian* was published this social boundary, beyond which but a few Eurasians might pass, was firmly established and the stereotype well-formed. *The Confessions*, which purported to be the self account of a wealthy Eurasian's experiences in India and Britain parade every prejudice. They summarised and satirised all aspects of the Eurasian stereotype in British eyes – idle, gullible, timid, ill educated, inarticulate, and above all, deeply presumptuous in aspiring to the status of a British 'gentleman'.[49] The Briton had his stereotype too in his own mind – 'Energetic and active, courageous and speculative', all that Eurasians were held not to be.[50]

★

The progressive exclusion of educated Eurasians from the upper reaches of British society in early nineteenth century India naturally fostered a spirit of resentment and common cause amongst them. They became in consequence more articulate at what they conceived to be their unfair treatment in British society. Social snubs were taken seriously, and presumed even when they did not exist. Thus a Eurasian as distinguished as James Skinner, who had many British friends and admirers, was bitterly mortified when he was eventually granted a Royal military commission in 1828. The Company had refused to give him one in its Army and its military establishment in Bengal was reluctant to promulgate his eventual Royal commission which outranked the Company equivalent. Skinner was sure that it was all a matter of racial discrimination. But the true reason was *not* that he was a Eurasian but that his new rank as a Royal Lieutenant-Colonel gave him precedence over *all* Company regulars of the same rank. The Company over ruled the Bengal military, but to Skinner, sensitive to any slight, the matter rankled deeply.[51]

Sometimes Eurasian feelings of resentment brought farcical consequences. Two of the teachers at the Calcutta Grammar School were bound over in 1824, and a third was imprisoned for a month. They had been convicted of assaulting their Eurasian Headmaster, R. Halifax. In their defence they argued that 'he had broken out all of a sudden saying that he condemned, abhorred, and detested all Englishmen, and the English nation'.[52] Every slight added to a feeling of rejection, and drove Eurasians with any claim to social standing within the British community towards each other.

Protestant Christianity was a second bond which linked most British Eurasians and was central to their claim to membership of the wider British community in India. As other forms of social contact diminished outside the work place attendance at religious worship provided a bridge between Eurasians and Britons and, as members of church and chapel congregations, Eurasians had a standing in their own right. The education of many Eurasians depended on the schools of missionary societies, which gave some opportunities in adult life as catechists, schoolmasters and missionaries. Most educated Eurasians of British descent were Protestant, whereas the Portuguese were principally Roman Catholic. Where Eurasians of Portuguese descent were accepted into British Eurasian circles, such as Willoughby Da Costa and the Derozio family, they too were Protestants.[53]

The fault lines of social and religious demarcation in British society were replicated in the world of Protestantism in India. Though it provided a common bond, social standing was reflected to a great, if not absolute, degree in church and chapel congregations. The Anglican churches of the Presidency towns, raised to cathedral status following the establishment of an episcopal hierarchy in India in 1813, were the natural place of worship for the British hierarchy and congregations of the well to do. But many Eurasians, often from the poorest in society, worshipped there and at the Anglican churches at military stations. Bishop Heber was well aware in 1824 of the numerical importance of Eurasians amongst his flock, observing that, 'From these a considerable proportion of my congregation in Calcutta is made up, and of these, 235 young persons whom I confirmed there yesterday, chiefly consisted'.[54]

Yet, though the Anglican Church welcomed Eurasians among the laity, they were excluded from the ranks of the clergy, for the appointment of chaplains was a part of the Company patronage exercised in London. When Thomas Middleton, the first Bishop of Calcutta, arrived at his see in 1815 he found that he was not allowed to ordain 'Natives of India', whether Indians or Eurasians. The establishment of Bishop's College at Calcutta in 1820 provided Middleton with a way to overcome this restriction on his powers. Its statutes allowed Indians, Britons, and Eurasians to be admitted, all of whom might eventually be ordained.[55] But progress was slow. Fourteen years after its foundation there were only eight students at the College which had been built to take seventy.[56] There were difficulties also with the seminary set up by the USPG at Madras – few candidates and many who dropped out. Even those few Eurasians who were ordained were speedily disillusioned when the USPG decided on lower pay rates for Eurasian than for British born clergy.[57]

The missionary organisations, whose role expanded after they were formally allowed to enter India from 1813, saw Eurasians as far more important to their activity than did the established Anglican Church. In turn educated Eurasians seemed to identify more easily with Protestant Dissenters. Albeit that the missions were directed from London, they found a larger place and a greater opportunity for active Eurasian participation. The large numbers of 'poor whites' and Eurasians in Presidency towns gave a natural base for establishing Christian non conformist congregations, an early instance of which was the Old Mission Church, Calcutta, founded by the Lutheran missionary John Kiernander in 1770. Many of its early converts were Portuguese Roman Catholics.[58] The Serampore Baptists chose the Lal Bazaar, a major centre of Eurasian population, as the site for their first church in Calcutta. They were encouraged by the Company's Chaplain in Calcutta, who felt the need for a place of Christian worship for those, 'who though bearing the Christian name, were too low in the scale of society to intrude on the patrician congregations of the Mission and Presidency churches'.[59] Missionary churches met the needs of Eurasians in Madras as well as Calcutta. 'Tucker's Chapel', popularly named after its pastor for fifteen years, opened in Black Town, Madras in 1820 specifically for Eurasians.

Missionary churches attracted 'poor whites' and Eurasians but many evangelically inclined Britons came too. By 1838 there were so many attending 'Tucker's Chapel' at Madras that, 'those for whom the chapel was built are kept out in consequence'.[60] The Baptist Lal Bazaar chapel, and after the break of the Serampore missionaries from their parent British society, their church in the Lower Circular Road, attracted congregations from a diverse social base. Indians in the congregation were far outnumbered by

Eurasians and British officers and other ranks.[61] At the Old Mission Church, Calcutta the original congregations of the very poor were joined in the early nineteenth century by better off Eurasians and even officials of the British covenanted service. Members of Council, including the Governor-General, John Shore, worshipped there. Leading Eurasians, such as Wale Byrn [who is still commemorated in the church], the Madge family, G.S. Hutteman and James Sheriff played important roles in the church's activities.[62]

Eurasians seemed to offer missionaries a useful route through to their ultimate goal – mass conversion of Hindus and Muslims. The Rev. J. Statham considered that Eurasians 'will be the most effective means of evangelising India at a future not remote period'.[63] Societies mobilised Eurasian youth for the task. The Calcutta Baptist Juvenile Society held lectures, devotional exercises and Sunday Schools, directed at Indians and Portuguese Roman Catholics. The link between the Serampore Baptists and leading Eurasians in Calcutta of the 1820s was especially close. John Ricketts, who became the prime mover in Eurasian affairs, was first a missionary though his service was cut short by illness. He was a committee member of the Baptist Missionary Society in Calcutta for many years. His wife helped the cause by raising funds. Many other Eurasians made donations and provided support in various ways.[64] Baptist backing for Eurasian aspirations was shown in the use of their press to publish a full account of their petition to Parliament in 1830.

*

A shared Christian faith linked many of the educated Eurasian community particularly in Calcutta, the focus of a developing Eurasian identity in the 1820s. Other factors – similarity of occupation, intermarriage, and domicile – also brought Eurasians together. The predominance of clerical occupation in Government service promoted its own strong sense of identity, 'in so much that one would imagine our East Indians [Eurasians] have got into an element totally impregnated with pen, ink, and paper'.[65] Indeed, by the late 1820s the probability of life for educated Eurasians as clerks caused a correspondent of the *Bengal Hurkaru* to observe that, 'by an irrevocable law of nature, they and their offspring are born and designed for nothing else than *keraneeships*, in the City of Palaces'.[66]

Marriage ties formed further bonds between Eurasian 'official' families. Although many Britons married Eurasian women, the marriage of Eurasian men to British women was rare indeed. Social prejudice apart, few Eurasian men could compete in financial prospects with British civil servants and military officers. Thus the choice of educated Eurasians tended to be limited to Eurasian women of similar background. John Ricketts, for instance, married Sarah Gardiner the daughter of a Company surgeon who had been educated at the Upper Military Academy, Calcutta.[67] Further down the social scale Eurasian men as well as British soldiers married Indian Christians or the Eurasian daughters of the British military rank and file.

Within the Presidency towns most Eurasians tended to live in the same neighbourhoods beyond the fashionable areas of British residence.[68] There were indeed no hard and fast lines of residential demarcation between Eurasian and Briton. Where they lived depended on wealth and social standing rather than race per se. Affluent Eurasians such as John Brightman, head of an Agency House, the Madges, Wale Byrn, James Kyd and the merchant George Dick, lived in the 1830s in the fashionable area of Chowringhee, Calcutta where, 'there were paved streets, and handsome squares of town houses in the neo-classical style, with white stucco colonnades and green venetian blinds'.[69] But most educated Eurasians lived further away from the more salubrious districts of central Calcutta. They clustered in the poorer areas of Dhurrumtollah and Bow Bazaar, described in 1822 as being 'the most densely inhabited part of Calcutta, as well as [having] a great number of Country-born Christians'.[70] Further away yet from the town centre, around the Circular Road, described as being an area of 'morasses and wildernesses . . . seldom visited by the fashionable quarter of the community' there were more Eurasian than British homes.[71]

The further from the centre of Calcutta, the higher the ratio of Eurasians to British, and the worse the living conditions. Most Eurasians lived in areas notorious for public squalor and high health risk. Not for them the paved roads of Chowringhee or the open spaces of Garden Reach, but the Circular Road and further yet – 'surrounded by broad ditches of stagnant water, filthy to an extreme degree'.[72] Their problem was where else to live? Most Eurasians simply could not afford the high rents of the central and healthier districts. The Eurasian social state was mirrored in where they lived, on the fringes of the British society to which they aspired. Eurasians, forced by economic necessity into close proximity in undesirable residential areas, naturally identified with each other in their common situation. Yet again necessity and exterior force, rather than any desire for ethnic identification, impelled them to a sense of community.

Towards a Reluctant Community

★

The reluctant emergence of a Eurasian sense of community in British India of the 1820s was reflected in the search for a suitable name by which they might describe themselves. By the end of the decade *East Indian* was generally and officially accepted, at least in Calcutta. Later in the nineteenth century *Eurasian* took its place until the official acceptance of *Anglo-Indian* as the community name in 1911. Many alternatives were considered in the search, which has led to the suggestion that this reflected a crisis of identity amongst Eurasians themselves, a view which does not stand up to closer inspection. The early history of the search for a name acceptable to Eurasians themselves, and which would be recognised in British official circles was a reaction to the popular (and meaningless) term *half caste* popularly applied to them. This had largely replaced the term *country born*, which was widely used up until the end of the eighteenth century. *Half caste* with its Indian connotation, ran entirely counter to the self-identification by Eurasians as British, and was deeply resented.[73]

Eurasians sought to replace an unwanted racial by a geographic term which would identify them as British in India. The search for a suitable name, which provoked much debate in the 1820s, reflected the embryo state of the community itself. Thus when nearly 200 Eurasians petitioned the Madras Government in 1827 to abolish the use of *half caste* in official documents, the organisers of the petition admitted that there was 'dissension and difference' over what should replace it. Some wanted *Eurasian*, others *Anglo-Asian*, *Indo-Briton*, *East Indian*, *Asiatick Briton*, or *Anglo-Indian*.[74]

Of the many alternatives canvassed, three had the widest currency: *Eurasian*, *Indo-Briton*, and *East Indian*, and each was at times in simultaneous use. *Eurasian* was the first to gain a measure of popular acceptance. It seems to have originated in the Calcutta Petition to Governor-General Lord Hastings of 1818, which asked him inter alia, 'to abrogate the degrading term of "half caste" from the Public Record of Government', and to use *Eurasian* instead.[75] The invention of the term was claimed by John Ricketts some years later and used by him in his first, and unsuccessful, attempt in 1821 to set up a school at Calcutta specifically for Eurasian boys – he intended to call it the 'Eurasian College'.

Although *Eurasian* was the first name to win popular support, *Indo-Briton*, with its overt British connotation, was also in use by 1822. In 1827, two years after the Eurasians of Calcutta had adopted

East Indian, Indo-Briton was adopted as an official designation by the authorities at Madras and continued in use there until well into the 1840s.[76] The decisive moment for the adoption of the third designation *East Indian* took place at a meeting at the Calcutta Town Hall in 1825 when a review of all the alternatives was made. *East Indian* was chosen by Calcutta Eurasians because it was argued to be 'the most common and familiar in England'. Perhaps its connotation with the East India Company itself decided the issue.[77]

Since only a few Eurasians – seventeen – attended the meeting in 1825, the decision to adopt *East Indian* can hardly be seen as an expression of community will, but nevertheless it rapidly overtook other designations and in the 1820s and 1830s became the official term of reference. Probably it was the unqualified support of the Eurasian activist John Ricketts which established it so firmly for a time. Yet, for all the efforts of Eurasians to avoid it, the abhorred term *half caste* continued in popular British use, as it does to this day.

★

The emergence of a leadership in the 1820s committed to betterment of Eurasian conditions in India and their treatment on a parity with British subjects was the catalyst which placed India's mixed race population firmly on the British political agenda. The framework within which a sense of common interest amongst Eurasians developed owed most to the external pressures of British attitudes and behaviour towards them, and to a reactive grievance at the exclusion from British mainstream society of their educated element. Leadership provided the momentum for action, for an attempt to improve social, educational, occupational and political prospects for Eurasians. That leadership was informal in character and largely dependant on the commitment and activity of relatively few. It was not always united in its actions, nor fully supported by all educated Eurasians, but sufficient numbers of them were prepared to articulate their grievances for their arguments to require the attention of British authority in India and in London.

Calcutta, where the greatest numbers of educated Eurasians lived, provided the leadership. Most of those who played prominent parts were well known to each other. They had often been to the same private or charity schools. Many were active in church affairs. As the sons or grandsons of British military or civil officers their backgrounds were similar. They were linked by friendship and often by membership of the various masonic lodges of Calcutta.[78] They were a cross section of the European middle class community of

Calcutta. Wale Byrn, Charles Linstedt, Willoughby Da Costa, and – most prominent of all – John Ricketts, were senior uncovenanted civil servants. Edward Brightman, George Stuart Dick, Alexander Imlach were businessmen. William Kirkpatrick, George Linstedt and H.L.V. Derozio were teachers. George Imlach was a surgeon, Henry Martindell – the grandson of a General -an attorney, and Charles Pote a painter.[79]

All made a contribution to Eurasian activities in the 1820s. But one, John William Ricketts, stood above all in his indefatigable pursuit and variety of endeavour to the advancement of Eurasian interests. He came the nearest to popular acceptance as an acknowledged leader, although the wealth and contacts of James Kyd gave him an unrivalled social pre-eminence. It was not to be until a century later, again at a time of renewed crisis for Eurasians in British India, that the then Anglo-Indian community found in Sir Henry Gidney, a spokesman of similar single mindedness and dedication to Eurasian interests as John Ricketts gave in the 1820s.

In his background and subsequent career Ricketts was typical of the Eurasian elite. His father, John Henry, the elder son of a British surgeon, came out to India in 1782 as an Engineer officer in the Company's army, was employed in survey work in Bengal, and is believed to have died at the siege of Seringapatam in 1792. His mother, Bibi Zeenut Ricketts lived until 1824 in Calcutta. His uncle, Robert Tristram, had a distinguished career in the British navy. John William was born in 1791, a year before his father's death, and brought up at the Upper Military Orphanage, Calcutta together with the other Eurasian sons of the Company's military officers.[80] He began his official career with a posting to Amboyna as an uncovenanted clerk. There he met Jabez Carey – the son of the Serampore missionary, William Carey – on the arrival of Jabez as Inspector of Schools in 1814. Jabez recorded that the Resident at Amboyna, Mr. Martin, 'recommended me to take accommodation with Mr. Ricketts of whom he gave a very high character', albeit Ricketts had fathered an illegitimate daughter two years earlier. By 1814, however, he was the Secretary of the local Bible Society.[81] His subsequent career, save for a brief spell as a Baptist missionary and his visit to England as the spokesman for the East Indian Petition to Parliament in 1830, followed a conventional pattern. Ricketts rose through the levels of the uncovenanted civil service in the Board of Customs to Deputy Register, and in 1833 was appointed a civil court judge (Sadr Amin) in the Jungle Mahals before promotion to Principal Sadr Amin at Gaya, near Patna. He died there in 1835.[82]

There are difficulties, since none of Ricketts' private correspondence is known to have survived, in examining the motives of the private man behind the public figure who threw himself so wholeheartedly into the Eurasian cause. But enough it known to make some assessment. His involvement in nearly every Eurasian social, educational and occupational initiative in the 1820s marks him as an activist – a man of tenacity and determination, despite the ill health which dogged him all his adult life. At his death his friend, the Rev. John Marshman, praised him for 'his spirit and perseverance', whilst admitting that his achievements owed more to 'his earnest honesty of purpose and his matter-of-fact sort of argument', than to any charismatic qualities or skills as an advocate.[83]

Ricketts had a self appointed mission to improve the social and political standing of educated Eurasians in British India. It was fuelled by a fervent Christian commitment encouraged by the Baptist missionaries of Serampore. At first he wanted to be a missionary. Jabez wrote to his father William Carey from Amboyna to tell him that, 'He [Ricketts] seems determined to leave all and follow Christ by openly possessing him by baptism and engaging in his work'.[84] Ricketts did indeed throw up his career and for a short time, until ill health drove him back to Calcutta, was a missionary at Murshidabad. As he followed his later career and redirected his energies to the affairs of his fellow Eurasians, he continued to be an active member of the Baptist congregations in the city.[85] The sense of injustice felt by so many educated Eurasians of the time at the lack of opportunity open to them in British society was fully shared by Ricketts. He was well educated and widely read – at his death he left little money but an extensive library. He lived as the 'gentleman' he felt himself to be. His house was well furnished, with much plate, cutlery and glass. His personal wardrobe was ample and, as befitting a civil court judge, he owned a horse and buggy.[86] Although more successful than many of his peers he felt that his personal potential had been frustrated by the Company's policy towards Eurasians. Had it not been, he wrote in a pamphlet printed and sold at his own cost in 1828, for the exclusion of Eurasians, 'I for one might now have been a Major, or a Colonel, in the service of the East India Company'. Instead he was an uncovenanted Government servant, paid far less, and with little opportunity for personal achievement. His work for Eurasians gave him a purpose – 'a public cause requiring much energy and perseverance', and a personal outlet for his frustrated ambition.[87]

6

Eurasians Up Country and in the Indian States

Most educated Eurasians at the end of the eighteenth and start of the nineteenth century lived in the three main Presidency towns of Calcutta, Madras and Bombay. This urban polarisation of Eurasian society in India persisted until the last years of British rule in India, when one in two of all Eurasians lived still in three main cities.[1] Many of the traditional spheres of Eurasian employment, clerical and government work, were to be found there. But, from the later years of the eighteenth century a significant minority of Eurasians lived either in up country Bengal or in the many independent Indian states. In Bengal a town such as Cawnpore, with its extensive military cantonments, provided opportunities for commercial employment. Indigo manufacture employed many educated Eurasians, if as overseers rather than as owners. The spread of missionary work took Eurasian missionaries into the country and lands outside direct British control. The careers of Revv. J.T. Thompson at Delhi and R.C. Fink at Chittagong are two illustrative examples of Baptist missionaries working in the early nineteenth century far from the traditional centres of Eurasian employment.[2] Government employment – as surveyors; with the Company's military as officers in command of irregular forces; or as clerical staff to British Residencies at the capitals of Indian states, provided further opportunity yet. And beyond the formal limits of British territory Eurasians were in demand in the military service and the civil employment of Indian rulers, large and small.

Without attention to the many Eurasians who lived outside the British Presidency towns, and particularly those who served the Indian princes – a hitherto unexamined sector – the picture is incomplete. Furthermore, their experience suggests that there was often more scope for Eurasians outside rather than within the urban centres of British territory. Educated Eurasians in particular, debarred after 1791 from the Company's military and civil service, found military and civil roles of considerable responsibility in Indian states throughout India. In consequence there is a more positive note to their achievements than those of their fellows in British towns. Eurasians were welcome in Indian states and often successful there whether in military or civil roles. Once away from the social conformism and restricted opportunity of British Presidency towns the distinction between British or Eurasian descent seems to have been of far less moment. It is clear too that the oft repeated British axiom, that Indians did not 'respect' Eurasians, carried little weight with the rulers and ministers of Indian states. The performance of Eurasians as army officers, whether in commanding the troops of Indian states, or in the development of a substantial corps of irregular units in the Company's own army, is in itself a powerful rebuttal of the axiom. It challenges the British stereotype of the Eurasian as unambitious and not suitable for positions of real responsibility.

*

The wealth of Indian rulers, the chance of service and gain, attracted European adventurers from the earliest days of Western involvement in India. They came from many countries eager to take mercenary pay wherever opportunity beckoned, irrespective of the official interests of their own nations. Western military specialists, especially those skilled in using cannon, were first in demand. François Bernier reported in the 1660s European mercenaries in the Mughal army. He noted they came from many races and were paid highly for their skills.[3] A century later John Grose remarked of the Marathas that they had many Europeans in their employ, 'mainly deserters and men of desperate fortunes'.[4]

The employment of European military skills by Indian rulers expanded rapidly at the end of the eighteenth century. The earliest need had been for specialists, but once Indian states began to organise their troops on European lines, they sought officers who could raise, train, and command infantry and cavalry units. When the Maratha leader, Mahadji Sindhia, employed the experienced Savoyard, Benoit de Boigne, in 1791 to develop a European style army for him, he pioneered a trend which, by the end of the century, saw his example followed by Arcot, Jaipur, Oudh, Hyderabad, and the Maratha states. Even in Nepal Gurkhas were dressed in a 'quaint imitation of the Company's uniform', and taught English words of command.[5] It has been estimated that as early as 1792 there were as many as 1500 European officers serving in the armies of Indian states.[6] Many were Eurasians, employed alongside a wide variety of European nationals in the so called 'free' companies [who sold their services to the highest bidder], as well as in the regular armies of Indian states.

Eurasians often officered 'free' companies such as that of George Thomas who, in a colourful career, served several Indian states before setting up his own military autocracy at Hariana. Both of his leading lieutenants, George Hopkins and Hyder Hearsey, were the Eurasian sons of Company officers. Hopkins was killed in action when Thomas was defeated at Georgegarh, but Hearsey eventually entered British service, bringing his own troops with him.[7] The day of the 'free' companies was over shortly after the start of the nineteenth century, but Eurasians continued to serve in the armies of Indian states. Soldiering for the Marathas gave an opportunity to many, some of whom served the British with distinction after the conclusion of the Maratha war of 1803/4. Both the Skinner brothers, Hyder Hearsey and Henry Foster – all of whom subsequently commanded British irregular cavalry units - were among the thirteen Eurasian officers known to be serving the Marathas in 1803.[8] In the Hyderabad state army at the same time a half, eleven out of twenty one officers, were Eurasians. The British Assistant Resident to Hyderabad clearly thought little of them, describing them as, 'low Europeans who would engage in any service which would afford a subsistence and half castes distinguished from natives merely by wearing a hat' – a description which certainly did not fit the well born William Palmer, who was one of them.[9] Thirty years later Hyderabad's number of European officers had increased fourfold, and though a half were by then British officers who held the most senior positions, the other half were recruited locally with Eurasians still allowed to exercise corps command.[10] At Oudh in the 1830s, where treaty provisions forbade the employment of British subjects by the King, the entire officer corps of a brigade of the state army under their commander, a son of a Company officer, General Roberts, was Eurasian.[11] Even the rulers of smaller Indian states employed Eurasians as their military officers. Captain Nicholas Willard was Captain Commandant of the Nawab of Banda's army in 1836, paid Rs 600 a month (part by the state and part by the Company). His second-in-command Charles Green was paid Rs 560, and Lewis Groves, who had been a drummer with the 73rd NI, was Sergeant-Major at Rs 29.[12]

Though most of the Indian states in whose armies Eurasians continued to serve after the conclusion of the Maratha war of 1803/4 were allied to the Company by subsidiary treaty, and thus subject to British influence, the Punjab was not. Many Eurasians served up until the 1840s in the formidable and well-equipped army built up by its ruler, Ranjit Singh. His chief generals were experienced soldiers from the Napoleonic armies, but two Eurasians – John Holmes and Gordon (alias Carron) – commanded battalions. Both were believed to have deserted the Bengal Horse Artillery in which they had once served as trumpeters. Three others – Jacob, a son of George Thomas; William Campbell, who later commanded the Afghan Army; and Henry Van Cortlandt, who ended his career as a British Lieutenant-Colonel – held senior appointments. There were Eurasians too amongst the Punjab's junior officers. Even the army's bandmasters were Eurasian.[13]

Eurasians of the early nineteenth century benefited too from the development of Company 'irregular' units. Raised first on a temporary basis as light cavalry in the Maratha campaign, most units were disbanded in 1805 after its end. But, by the 1820s these units had become a sizeable and permanent feature of the Company's Army. Naturally enough, units which were raised by Eurasians – Skinner, Hearsey and Foster – were officered by their appointees, generally their relatives and sons.

The importance to educated Eurasians of the rapid expansion of military employment, first in the service of Indian states and then in the Company's own irregular units cannot be over estimated. Before the formal ban on covenanted military service in the Company's army, mercenary employment had been a useful source of 'gentlemanly' employment for those Eurasians whose fathers lacked the London patronage to have them accepted in the Company's Army. After 1791 mercenary service was the *only* avenue for Eurasians to follow their fathers as officers and gentlemen. These appointments inevitably became a valuable element in the network of local Company patronage as fathers used their influence to have their sons accepted in Indian state armies and the Company's local irregular units. In illustration, John Doveton, who was later to be the most significant benefactor to the cause of Eurasian education, owed his start in the service of Hyderabad to a relative who had commanded a British contingent there. James Skinner was helped to join the Maratha Army by a military friend of his father. Hyder Hearsey placed his three sons in the army of Oudh. Even a Governor-General, Lord William Bentinck, was prepared to use his influence to have one of James Skinner's sons placed at Hyderabad. The reprimand which Colonel Van Cortlandt, a Royal army officer, received 'for having presented himself at a native court with the object of advancing his son's interests' – he gained Henry a place in the Punjab army – was exceptional.[14] Van Cortlandt had probably bypassed the normal machinery of patronage, for in their private capacities British officials used their connections as best they could to the advantage of their Eurasian sons.

*

There was, however, a marked contrast between the private behaviour of Company officials on behalf of their sons and the Company's official attitude to the presence on its borders of Indian armies organised on European lines – even if their military capacities were generally dismissed as inferior. The officers of Indian armies owed no allegiance to British interests, and by the last years of the eighteenth century had become the objects of official British suspicion. 'I much fear', wrote Governor-General Wellesley in 1798, 'that many British subjects might be found in India whose spirit of adventure would rather direct them to seek a new order of things, than to contribute to the maintenance of our power'.[15] He shared the concerns of Governor-General Cornwallis before him, which had influenced the decision to exclude Eurasians from military service in the Royal and Company armies in India.

Wellesley did not, however, initiate the British policy of controlling the employment of Europeans by the rulers of Indian states. As early as 1765 the Company's treaty with the Nawab of Bengal had stipulated that he would 'allow no Europeans whatever to be entertained'. Similar clauses were agreed with Tanjore in 1771 and Mysore in 1799.[16] Whether Eurasians were or not to be considered Europeans was not defined. With Oudh, however, in 1798 it was clear that the prohibition was restricted to British Subjects, and that Eurasians as Natives of India were to be allowed. The later treaty with Mahadji Sindhia in 1803 was more restrictive as far as Eurasians were concerned. Sindhia was prohibited from taking any Frenchman or subject of a European power or 'any British subject, whether European or native', without permission from the Company.[17] Eurasians were clearly included in this definition. The likely reason was Wellesley's determination that Sindhia should not rehire the Eurasian officers who had been recalled at the start of hostilities and pensioned off by the British, nor any others of his previous officer corps whether French, British, or from any other European country. It was a matter of practical British politics, rather than directed specifically at Eurasians as a racial category, as has been subsequently suggested.

Although military employment brought the prime opportunity for Eurasian employment in Indian states, there was civil employment also to be had in cities such as Lucknow and Hyderabad, either in the ruler's direct employ or in serving the needs of the European communities there. Just as Company policy sought to control the employment of British subjects as military officers in Indian states, so it aimed to hold the British civilian population in check. Licences were needed for British subjects to live more than ten miles from Presidency towns, and army commanders were ordered to turn back Europeans arriving at Oudh without the necessary permission.[18] Governor-General Wellesley took an even stronger line in 1798 in refusing *any* licences at all for Oudh and threatened to force all British subjects living there to return to Bengal.[19] In the event Wellesley did not carry out his threat and from the early years of the nineteenth century the European community at Lucknow continued to grow steadily. Once the impossibility of halting its growth became apparent policy switched tacitly to the control of British communities in Indian states. Residents monitored the observation of treaty restrictions on British employment by rulers, and returned annual lists of the numbers of British subjects in state employment.[20]

These controls favoured Eurasians, who were admitted to have a right to residence in Indian states, providing they were acceptable to the state itself and could prove to the British Resident that they were *not* British subjects. Even a Eurasian as undesirable in British eyes as George Walters, could not be denied his right to set up a 'Europe Shop' at Lucknow in 1812. By the 1830s many civilian Eurasians had found state employment, not only in the major states of Hyderabad and Oudh, but with lesser Indian governments. The states of Mysore, Cochin, Travancore and Tanjore between them employed numbers of Eurasians as apothecaries, bandmasters, judges, writers, translators, tailors, craftsmen, and even a dog doctor and a director of jails. At Mysore Sam Hayes was paid Rs 126 a month as Head Coachman with his son, Sam Hayes II, as his assistant. George Irmin was a revenue official to the Rajah of Adjigurh, and Alexander Rennick the surgeon to the Nawab of Banda.[21]

The Eurasians who lived in Indian cities saw advantages in British supervision of the European populations living there. At Lucknow, strictly speaking, the Resident's powers were restricted by treaty to his staff and their dependants. This limitation was at least one of the reasons for the early attempt to discourage the growth of European communities in Indian states, for it had been ruled in 1791 that the Resident could not interfere with the jurisdiction of the Court of Oudh in civil and criminal matters where the individuals concerned were not British subjects.[22] Forty years later when the Resident at Lucknow reported that he might 'almost be said to share with the King the sovereignty in his own capital', it is clear that the scope of Residency protection had increased considerably, and that it was extended to British subject and Eurasian alike.[23] The Resident at Gwalior sent, for instance, Mr. Lindsay, a Eurasian clerk at the Residency who had embezzled Rs 19,000, under armed guard to Agra in 1831 to stand trial.[24] At Lucknow the Resident administered a trust fund set up by the European community for the eight children of James Walters (the brother of George), who had arrived back there in 1818 penniless.[25] When George himself was sued in the Vizier's Court by a Lieutenant Courtayne over an inheritance, the Resident interceded on his behalf, referring to him incorrectly as a 'British Subject'.[26] Eurasians seem to have generally been treated as British subjects when in the states of Indian princes. The maintenance of British prestige in a foreign, though friendly state, was the issue at stake. As the Resident at Lucknow put it when arguing in 1836 that *all* Europeans should be under his authority, the aim was 'more fully to have them under control and save that degradation of character which would arise from liability to be summoned before native courts'.[27]

*

Control – the object of British policy in its own dominions, and through treaty and influence in neighbouring Indian states, was exercised informally as well as officially. British approval and patronage was indispensable to Europeans who hoped for business success on any major scale in Indian states, an issue well illustrated in the life of the Frenchman, Claude Martin, who enjoyed the confidence of the rulers of Oudh and the Company alike in amassing his huge fortune.[28] British backing was as vital to Eurasians as to any other European, for all that, as Natives of India, they were technically exempt from the restrictions attached to British subjects.

The career of Lieutenant-Colonel James Skinner as a businessman is far less well known than his fame as a soldier, employed first by the

Marathas and subsequently as the commander of Skinner's Horse, the first of the irregular cavalry units attached to the Company's army. He was able, by marrying the advantage of his legal status as a Native of India to high level British patronage, to achieve a considerable business fortune. Throughout his life, once he had exchanged the service of the Marathas for the Company's, Skinner enjoyed the backing of senior British officials. His personal generosity and easy open handed manner, coupled with his military renown, removed the social barriers which in general separated Eurasian from Briton, for all that Henry Fane described him as 'one of the darkest I ever saw'.[29] To Samuel Browne, a civil servant stationed near Delhi, the personal virtues of his 'old friend' Colonel Skinner transcended the accidents of colour and race. 'He is', Browne wrote home, 'a man of singular character, singular, I mean for simplicity and nobleness of heart and shrewdness of intellect – a rare man of opposite qualities'.[30] Skinner, who was never slow to complain at inadequate recognition of his own merits, benefited from high level patronage at every stage of his military and business career.

He owed to the Commander-in-Chief, General Lake, his first employment in 1803 by the British when he had been dismissed from the Maratha service and, after the conflict was over, the retention of his unit, albeit on a reduced scale, when all others were disbanded in 1805. Lake obtained for him too a Colonel's pension – although he ranked only as a Captain – in recognition of his merits, and backed his application to commute the pension for land.[31] The proposal was rejected at first on the erroneous grounds that Skinner was a British subject, a decision reversed in 1808 when his status as a Native of India was accepted by the Court in London. The situation was further improved in 1815 when the jaghirs he and his brother Robert held for life in the Aligarh district were granted to them and their descendants in perpetuity as an exceptional reward.[32] They were to prove remarkably more profitable to the Skinners than the monetary pensions which they replaced.

In mid career Skinner found in Lord Hastings a Governor-General who, recognising his military value, was deeply concerned that if he did not receive exceptional treatment he might be tempted once again into Maratha service. Hastings acted at once, despite opposition from the local military establishment to promote Skinner to the honorary rank of local Lieutenant-Colonel, ranking him ahead of all Company regular captains and subalterns when in the field.[33] Later on in his career Skinner enjoyed the friendship of the Commander-in-Chief, Lord

Combermere. Skinner entertained him with his customary open-handedness in 1828 at his camp at Balaspore, a 'fine little village belonging to Colonel James Skinner where he has a neat small fort and indigo factory'.[34] Skinner was indebted to Combermere and other supporters in England for his belated royal commission and decoration, as well as for his introduction to the newly arrived Governor-General, William Bentinck, whose 'attention [to Skinner] during my stay at the Presidency was highly flattering and gratifying to my feelings'.[35]

The support which Skinner received from successive British Residents at Delhi was of the greatest value to his public credit and developing business interests. Archibald Seton, the Resident there befriended Skinner, and when he was succeeded by Charles Metcalfe the support continued.[36] The rewards of this political backing were lands in perpetuity, indigo and trading interests on an extensive scale. Skinner's profits in 1820 alone were Rs 40,000, plus Rs 11,000 from selling hides, Rs 15,000 from the sale of ghee, as well as the proceeds from selling 2,000 bullocks.[37] Had Skinner not been an Eurasian such opportunities would not have legally been open to him. Equally, had he not retained the friendship and support of many influential British officials, he could not have made his personal fortune.

*

The career in Hyderabad of Skinner's contemporary and fellow Eurasian, William Palmer, illustrates as dramatically as Skinner's the extent of British influence in the internal affairs of independent Indian states at the time, the rewards which an individual might reap from British support – and the penalties of its withdrawal. A study of Palmer's career, its amazing early success and later catastrophic failure underlines the ambiguity of the Eurasian position in Indian states. Palmer would have been prohibited from starting his banking business at Hyderabad were he a British subject. He lost it when the restrictions applying to them were applied to him though a Native of India. Palmer's career suggests that in British society in India of the time 'class' and 'connection' might still surmount the negative of 'race'. A Eurasian of birth and education, of charm and talent, of ambition backed with powerful connections – as was William Palmer – could succeed despite the odds. But it demonstrates too the power of British influence which could be brought to bear on Eurasians living in Indian states. Once Palmer had lost his British patrons - Skinner never did – the local confidence on which his business depended was destroyed and the House of Palmer fell. In his time Palmer was a controversial person, and ill-regarded in historical retrospect, tainted with accusations of sharp trading and deceit, as vigorously rebutted as they were advanced. Whatever conclusions which may be drawn from the rise and fall of the House of Palmer in Hyderabad, one conclusion is sure. Palmer's career challenged the British stereotype of Eurasian lack of entrepreneurial spirit. William Palmer ventured, gained, and lost all.

Palmer was born in India in 1780, the first son by the second marriage of his father Lieutenant-General Palmer, to Faissan Nissa Begum. He was fortunate in his birth on two counts. The first that his father, who had been military and private secretary to Governor-General Warren Hastings, was a wealthy man. When Resident at the Court of the Peshwa his salary and allowances were said to have been £22,000 a year. William was sent to England for his education by his father who set out to use his wealth and contacts to secure the future of his children, whether natural or legitimate.[38] The second was that John, his elder British half brother, achieved a pre-eminence and contacts without compare in the commercial community of Calcutta. John Palmer, the 'Prince of Merchants', lived in style. 'No stranger arrived in Calcutta without dining at John Palmer's house', for all that it was in the unfashionable area of the Lal Bazaar. Any who arrived for dinner wearing silk stockings could never forget 'the torture they suffered under the table' from the bites of mosquitoes with which the area abounded.[39] The House of Palmer dominated the commercial scene of Calcutta until its own collapse in the banking crisis of 1830.[40] The powerful political influence which John could command, in particular that of Governor-General Lord Hastings, was at the service of his younger half brother, and was to be a vital factor in his early commercial success at Hyderabad.

William's career was based on his ability to relate British political backing for his projects to his influence with the Government of Hyderabad. His father's contacts had placed him in the army of Hyderabad in 1799, where by 1810 he commanded a battalion, and was in charge of revenue collection for several districts. The post paid Rs 1,000 a month and a percentage of the taxes raised.[41] Palmer later claimed to have behaved with considerable credit in his military career, putting down a rebellion against the Nizam, and that this justified the very substantial pensions paid to him and his family. The claim was dismissed by his political adversary, Charles

Metcalfe, who observed that 'his pretensions on this ground are totally without foundation'.[42] But this was not a view shared by the Nizam, who appointed him Commander of his bodyguard, and on the trust reposed in him Palmer commenced his commercial and banking career at Hyderabad.

In its early years between 1810 and 1814, with the support and covert investment of Henry Russell, then Resident at Hyderabad, Palmer set out to promote the cotton and opium trade of the Deccan, to develop a timber business on the river Godaveri and to set up a ship-building business at Masulipatam. Less publicly Palmer began to lend money to the Nizam's Government. By 1814 the business had achieved considerable success. Palmer's office was in the Residency compound where, according to the ingenuous claim of Henry Russell, 'the business was run so quietly that he was not aware of its existence'.[43] In these early years Palmer tested out the formula which he was later to use on a far wider scale. All depended on the confidence of the Nizam's Chief Minister, Chandu Lal, and the tacit support of British officials of the Bengal government, in providing financial loans to the government of Hyderabad. By 1814 Hyderabad was reckoned to owe nine lakhs of rupees to the House of Palmer.

The temporary withdrawal of Henry Russell from his secret and illegal involvement in the partnership after a dispute in 1814, led Palmer to bring in new partners for the next, and most successful phase, which lasted until 1820. Hans Sotheby, then the Second Assistant at the Residency, was added as a secret partner, which led ultimately to his dismissal by the Company. In two moves which were later to prove critical, Palmer placed his banking operation within the sphere of British official control. Firstly, he recruited a British subject, Sir William Rumbold, publicly into the partnership. Rumbold, who had come out to India in Governor-General Hastings' entourage, was married to his ward, Lady Harriet Rancliffe. Hastings appointed him a magistrate at Calcutta, and Rumbold provided William Palmer with direct access to the Governor-General. Since Rumbold was a British subject his entry into the partnership raised what was to prove the critical legal issue on which the partnership eventually foundered – the Usury Act of 1797.[44] The Act provided that twelve percent was the maximum legal rate for loans, and forbade British subjects to lend money without the approval of the Court of Directors or, but only in exceptional circumstances, the Governor-General in Council, to Indian princes. The aim of the Act was, 'after the experience we have had, both in Oude and the Carnatic, of the dreadful abuses which result from pecuniary dealings of British subjects with Native Princes', to put a stop either to individual British subjects achieving excessive power at any Indian court or extorting an oppressive rate of interest.[45]

Secondly, Palmer sought the licence of the Governor-General in Council in 1816 to lend money to the Nizam for the reorganisation of the Hyderabad army and to ensure that their wages were paid regularly. As Governor-General Lord Hastings was engaged in hostilities with the Marathas and Pindaris the arrangement was seen as beneficial to British interests which counted on the support of Hyderabad. Hastings took the opinion of his Accountant-General on the proposal, and acted on his advice that the 1797 Act appeared restricted to the Company's own territories, and that William Palmer as a Native of India was exempt in any case from its provisions.[46]

Palmer was granted his licence and by 1818 the Nizam's debts to the partnership had risen to an estimated seventeen and a half lakhs. At this point Palmer conceived the audacious concept of a completely new loan which would pay off all the old loans, purporting to allow the Nizam to put his administration on a sound financial footing by saving 25 lakhs of rupees a year. The ostensible interest rate of the new loan was twelve per cent, and a proposal for what came to be called the 'Sixty Lakh Loan' was put to Hastings in Council in 1820. In the face of opposition from Council members who wanted more information, or who suspected that the true rate of interest was more than twelve per cent, the licence was granted, although only with the casting vote of the Governor-General.[47] At this, the zenith of his career, in the confidence of the Nizam's Chief Minister, Chandu Lal, and with the public support of local British Government, Palmer had achieved an unparalleled ascendancy in the internal affairs of Hyderabad. 'Their badged chuprassis', wrote Charles Metcalfe on succeeding Henry Russell as Resident in 1820, 'went everywhere, intoxicated with authority. The firm became an agency to collect anyone's debts on commission, and held villages to siege or stormed them, to wring out payments'.[48]

Palmer's lifestyle matched his power. Metcalfe, who had accepted Palmer hospitality when he first came to Hyderabad, remarked of these days that, 'it seemed as if the wealth which flowed in was too great to be exhausted by any degree of expenditure'.[49] Yet, even Metcalfe who became Palmer's bitter political opponent, paid tribute to Palmer's attractive and charismatic personality. Colonel Meadows Taylor, best known in later life as the author of 'Confessions of a Thug', then an officer in the Hyderabad army who had married William Palmer's daughter, drew a picture of his father-in-law as a man of great personal charm and erudition:

> There was a fascination about him quite irresistible to me, his knowledge was so varied – classical, historical, and political . . . his fund of knowledge and great store of anecdote made him a delightful and improving companion.[50]

But, 1820 the year in which Palmer carried his sixty lakh loan and rode triumphant, closed with disaster when the decision of the Court to overrule Hastings and revoke the original licence of 1816 was received in India. Worse yet was the news in 1821 that the Court also disapproved the sixty lakh loan. Thereafter Palmer was on the defensive as he sought to save his business from ruin. In 1823 the opinion of the law officers of the Crown that the Usury Act *did* apply to the Palmer partnership was received and published. Palmer's network of British support collapsed as Metcalfe, who was resolutely determined to counter the excessive influence of Palmer in Hyderabad, replaced Russell as Resident. Although Governor-General Hastings sought to shield Palmer and his partners as long as he could, the significance of his impending return to Britain was not lost on William's half brother, John. He advised William to look around for a dependant of whoever would succeed Hastings.[51] Once Hastings had left India in 1823, later to defend his involvement in Palmer's dealings, his British political base was destroyed. Placed under pressure to reveal his accounts with the Nizam's government it became clear that the interest on the sixty lakh loan exceeded the permitted twelve per cent. Accusations of bad faith on Palmer's part redoubled, and once he was forbidden to have any dealings with Chandu Lal, save through the Resident, Metcalfe, his credit with the government of Hyderabad was gone. By 1825 the House of Palmer had ceased to trade, involving more than 1200 investors, most of whom were civil and military servants of the Crown and Company.[52] In later years Palmer and his partner, Rumbold, strove to recover their loans, but the sums advanced still had not been fully recovered by the time of Palmer's death in 1867.

At first sight it appears that Palmer's downfall was the direct consequence of a breach of the legislation prohibiting financial dealings by British subjects with Indian rulers. Even Metcalfe agreed that, 'If Mr. William Palmer and his native associates had kept aloof from European partners they would have escaped the interpretation of illegality'.[53] Technically the issue seemed to turn on whether the presence of British subjects as minority partners brought the whole within the provisions of the Act. It was an irony that the technical argument which ruined Palmer was belatedly resolved in his favour. Hastings, back in England, continued to press the issue that since Palmer was a Native of India he was exempt. In 1825 the Chief Justice overturned the original ruling of the law officers and ruled that the 1797 Act was *not* applicable in Hyderabad since, as a penal law, it could not be enforced in the territory of a sovereign Indian ruler.[54] The ruling came too late for Palmer.

Though the provisions of the 1797 Act were the technical instruments of Palmer's downfall, the fundamental question was one of British influence and control in Hyderabad. Palmer used his status as a Native of India to start a business which would not have been sanctioned for a British subject. In applying for a licence when he accepted Rumbold as a partner, Palmer brought his business formally within the British sphere of control. It led Metcalfe to argue with some justice,

> Here is a native subject of the British empire, half British by his birth, British in language and education, and habits, belonging to the British community in Hyderabad, living under the protection of the British flag, and within the precincts of the British Residency, owing all his advantages to British power and influence, and pretends he is not legally bound by order of the British Government.[55]

Palmer boldly sought the ultimately irreconcilable, exemption from the provisions of the 1797 Act whilst seeking the backing of British authority in conducting a business prohibited to British subjects. Whilst the private interests of British officials and the needs of public policy coincided, Palmer flourished. He fell when his House reached a position of such dominance in Hyderabad that it eclipsed the influence of the official Resident. 'They had completely monopolised the money market, they acquired an ascendancy over the Minister that rendered him a creature of their will'.[56] The House of Palmer had achieved just that power against which Parliament had thought it necessary to legislate in 1797. Its political utility had ended with the successful campaign against the Pindaris and Marathas. British or Eurasian, the House of Palmer now stood in the way of the exercise of official British influence. It had to go.

If William Palmer's career was broken by the failure of his British connection, it had depended too on the trust and co-operation of the Nizam's Chief Minister and the Indian banking community in Hyderabad, of whom Banketi Das was a public member of the partnership. One aspect of the study of the lives of prominent Eurasians who lived up country or in the Indian states, men such as Palmer, Skinner, Hearsey and others, is the high degree of social interaction between upper class Eurasian and Indian society. It was in vivid contrast to the more segregated lives of Eurasians in the Presidency towns where their need to assert their position within British society led them to emphasise their European credentials and disavow as far as possible their maternal ancestry.

British officials themselves, once outside the rigid etiquette and social ranking of the Presidency towns, often displayed a more relaxed attitude when up country and in Indian states to the accidents of birth and occupation of fellow Europeans. To some extent the limitations of European society forced this upon them unless they were to lead solitary lives. Frederick Shore, most of whose official career was spent away from Calcutta, observed with some regret that those such as he 'are obliged to associate with shop-keepers, sergeants and clerks, who however respectable their line, have no pretensions to be gentlemen'.[57] Since British civil servants and military officers were notoriously preoccupied with their status as gentlemen, and their wives with the precedence due to their husband's rank, their views of relationships with Indians and Eurasians were voiced the loudest at the time. But they did not speak for all the British community of the early nineteenth century. There was another British world — that of business — where concerns over rank and station mattered less, and trust between people more than national ideology. The Bengal indigo planter, William Huggins, remarked of commerce that it brought all races together, 'to intermix amicably to settle the concerns of their common interest, forgetting distinctions of colour, birth, religion, which only affect the ignorant and useless'.[58] Far to the south at Madras the merchant, Thomas Parry, whose company celebrated its bicentenary in 1988, was content to take Christopher Breithaupt, the Eurasian son of a Danish missionary, as his business partner in 1813. His views on the Indians with whom he worked for nearly forty years are a refreshing contrast to the stereotype characteristic of the official view:

> In the management of my manufacturing establishments and money concerns [sic] in this Presidency I have generally employed native agents. In their zeal and integrity I have always placed the fullest confidence, and that confidence has never been abused.[59]

The more independent the Indian state the more British and Eurasians living there accommodated themselves to an Indian way of life. The army officers of Ranjit Singh, for instance, were expected to settle in the Punjab, marry locally, not to eat beef, smoke in public, not offend against the Sikh faith.[60] The further from Calcutta, as a rule of thumb, the easier the racial interface. Colonel William Gardner, a celebrated British commander of irregular cavalry, described a memorable breakfast with his friend James Skinner at his home near Delhi. Robert Skinner was there – 'a greater dandie than ever, and had more gold and silver chains about him than baron Frank had in Magdeburg dungeon'. Several Englishwomen, Skinner's friends Chand Bukus Khan and Shemskin Bahadur, together with Skinner's children of 'all hues and colours' made up the convivial party.[61] When not on campaign Skinner, and other affluent Britons and Eurasians, lived the lives of rich Indian landowners. James Gardner, for instance, the eldest Eurasian son of Colonel Gardner, was described as 'riding round his estates and a great number of villages of his own of which he is the lord and master'.[62]

In a city such as Lucknow where there were few, if any, eligible British women, Britons and Eurasians lived with or married Indian women long after the practice was frowned upon in Presidency towns. George Beechey, for instance, Court painter to the King of Oudh, married Houssiana in 1837. They had a son – Stephen Richard. George also left an illegitimate daughter.[63] Nor was the marriage of Eurasian women to Muslim men unknown. It is unlikely that Lucknow society looked askance when Mrs. Whearty, the widow of George Walters, went to live with Buksh Ali Khan, although British opinion in India was most disapproving.[64] By the 1830s a high proportion of the British population at Lucknow was indeed Eurasian, many of them shopkeepers and traders, some employed at Court and others in Oudh's military service.[65] For some, their Indian interests in time superseded any commitment to their British origins. The Rotton family provides such an instance. It was descended from Richard Rotton, an officer serving with the Marathas, who was pensioned off in 1803 despite his urgent appeals for British employment rather than a pension. Like many ex-Maratha officers he received no such appointment, whilst his pension of Rs 130 a month just covered the costs of sending his children to school in Calcutta. Rotton found employment in the Oudh army, in which one of his sons, Felix, also served. At the siege of the British residency at Lucknow in 1857, Felix's Indian loyalties prevailed over his British ancestry when he and some of his sons were numbered amongst the insurgents. According to the official report, 'He did nothing to help the British although the descendant of an European himself . . . all his children capable of bearing arms were hostile to us'.[66]

★

On the evidence it was easier for the Eurasian elite living in Indian states to be accepted on their own merits, whether within the resident European community or the upper strata of Indian society. Unlike British India there were no formal restrictions on their employment whether in the civil service of Indian rulers or as military officers. Whereas the place of the Eurasian in British India was after 1791 limited and secondary, no such disadvantages attached to Eurasians in Indian states on account of their part-British ancestry. Indeed, in many Indian states Eurasians were welcomed positively in civil and military capacities. In even a small Indian state a Eurasian might achieve opportunities inconceivable within British territory. Perhaps the most extraordinary of all was the adoption as her son and heir of David Sombre by the Begum Sombre of Sirdhana. He was the son of her Eurasian force commander, George Alexander Dyce, who had married the Begum's step grand-daughter Juliana.[67]

There were a number of factors which may explain the welcome which Eurasians received in Indian states. It seems likely that some Indian rulers, adjacent to a British power with whom political relationships had necessarily to be conducted, found it flattering to their self-esteem to have Europeans in their employ at their courts. Eurasians clearly were an acceptable substitute for the British subjects barred to them by treaty. That seems certainly to have been so at the court of Oudh where the British Resident was told in 1837 by the King's Minister that 'when the King could not employ Europeans: he took Indo-Britons and the nearer they resembled Europeans as to complexion the more his Majesty favoured them'.[68] Even the King's band, which accompanied him in the English country dances which he enjoyed and the Resident deplored so much was Eurasian.

British and Eurasian traders also helped fulfil the acquisitive desires of the rulers of Indian states, whose long purses gave ample opportunity for European enterprise. These needs made possible the immense fortune accumulated by the French adventurer, Claude Martin, combining his role as a Major-General in the Company's Army with that of chief supply agent and banker to the ruler of and the European community in Lucknow. At Hyderabad William Palmer filled a similar role, dealing extensively in European goods for the Court of Hyderabad, and remarking that 'the consumption of jewels in this Government is very great'.[69]

If European employment in general and Eurasian in particular at Indian courts was often prompted by gratifying the needs or flattering the self-esteem of rulers, their employment as military officers had a more practical purpose. They depended entirely on the ruler's goodwill and were independent of his Indian subjects. Their loyalty could therefore generally be counted on in the state's internal politics, although in the case of conflict with the British divided loyalties inevitably arose. Holkar's execution of the Eurasian, Major Vickers, and two other European officers in 1804 seems to have been over this question of loyalty. They had declined to stay in his army when war broke out with the British.[70] James Skinner had felt that loyalty strongly enough, even though dismissed from the Maratha service, to stipulate to General Lake that he should not be called upon to fight against his former employers.[71]

The particular value of European-style units in the Indian armies of the early nineteenth century was their potential for use within the ruler's own state. Overpowerful or refractory subjects could be brought to heel. Revenue demands could be enforced by troops led by officers owing loyalty to the ruler alone. Ranjit Singh used his formidable forces in the Punjab for such purposes, as did Hyderabad. So too in Oudh where the brigade commanded by the Eurasian Roberts was employed at Sultanpore in 1837, 'to assist the Aumil of that district in overcoming or coercing as the case may be some refractory zemindars who have lately refused to pay their revenues to the Government'.[72] Eurasian military officers provided their employers with a non political force on which they could rely.

The reality of Eurasian employment in Indian states calls into question the popular British stereotype of Eurasian as limited in ability, activity, and enterprise. To the extent that truth lay behind the stereotype it owed more to lack of opportunity in British India for Eurasians than to their birth or upbringing. Given the opportunity, as many educated Eurasians were in Indian states, or even in the Company's own irregular forces, the evidence is that they enjoyed the confidence of their employers. The careers of Eurasian commanders – Skinner, Foster and Hearsey for instance – show no lack of the leadership qualities popularly supposed by British opinion in India to be reserved to themselves alone.

7

The Eurasian Struggle for Self Advancement

For some thirty years the Eurasian elite of British India seemed largely to have accepted the discrimination which had been their lot since the late eighteenth century. But in the 1820s a new spirit was abroad amongst them as social, educational, occupational and political initiatives were taken, all designed to enhance their position in the resident British community. This new-found drive was most evident in Calcutta, where most educated Eurasians lived, but was paralleled to a lesser extent in the smaller Presidency towns of Madras and Bombay.

Eurasian undertakings of this period were many and varied. Schemes for settling Eurasians in farming communities were broached, philanthropic committees set up, and apprenticing societies established. Debating groups flourished, the correspondence columns of the English language press in India were used to press the Eurasian case and publicise new initiatives. A new school in Calcutta, the Parental Academy, planned to offer a better education for Eurasians than hitherto available in private and charity schools. Most boldly of all, at the end of the decade Eurasians protested publicly at their uncertain legal position, and at their exclusion from the covenanted service of the Company.

The question arises, why did a Eurasian response to their marginalisation occur later rather than sooner, as might have been expected? In seeking an answer, the natural reluctance of Eurasians to identify themselves as such rather than as British, a lack of leadership until John Ricketts stepped forward, and a tacit acceptance of the status quo, go some way towards an answer. But, the catalyst for action rather than acceptance, for the wide variety of Eurasian initiatives in the 1820s, lay in altered circumstances – the growth in Eurasian numbers and concern at changing Government policy. These together seemed to threaten the very basis of the established and protected, if inferior, Eurasian place in British society in India. Those Eurasians who looked ahead saw an expanding population too large to be accommodated in Government employment, their historic mainstay. Worse yet, they saw their present place threatened by British encouragement of a new cadre of Western educated Indians, eager also for Government employment and willing to work for lower wages.

The threat to the prospects of the Eurasian 'middle class' was real indeed. They were directly affected by successive attempts to reduce the spiralling costs of British Government in India in the early nineteenth century. By 1810 young men in Britain were being advised not to go out to India unless they had definite prospects of employment since, 'there have been so many retrenchments in all the public services'.[1] Eurasian officers who had been employed during the Maratha war of 1803–4 in the Company's irregular military found themselves out of work as their units were disbanded. In the 1820s Eurasian prospects of military employment, either in the Company's irregular units or in the army of Hyderabad were diminished, though not entirely closed, by a new policy of seconding regular officers from the Company's army.[2] It is not surprising that these measures have been subsequently interpreted as part and parcel of a 'period of calculated repression, political, economic and social by the British', aimed specifically at Eurasians.[3] Though such a conclusion is understandable from the later Anglo-Indian point of view, Government policy seems to have had less to do with specific anti-Eurasian discrimination than attempts by the Company's directors to cut the ever rising costs of government and to retain their own patronage. Thus, of the decision to prohibit further employment of local officers in Hyderabad, it was observed that up until then it had been a 'sort of plaything for the Resident and a source of patronage to his friends'.[4] Nevertheless, the effect of the new policy was to reduce an important source of local patronage from which Eurasians had hitherto benefited.

More serious yet to Eurasians was the increase in the 1820s in the numbers of Western educated Indians, willing and eager to work for lower salaries in Government offices. Charles Fenwick expressed the very real sense of Eurasian alarm at the development which threatened the very heartland of their place in British society in India, observing that the speed with which Indians were acquiring English,

... will soon overstock the transcribing market, if such a thing has not already happened. The East Indians, I know, begin to feel themselves pinched for room. Many of the offices of authority begin to teem with Hindu writers, as also the mercantile concerns.[5]

To those who spoke for Eurasians – John Ricketts, Charles Fenwick and James Kyd in particular – the future looked more precarious yet. Ricketts foresaw, unless Eurasians could improve their educational standards, widen their choice of occupation and reverse the ban on their employment in the Company's covenanted service, a 'large redundant Eurasian population out of employ . . . begging and borrowing, pilfering and stealing, starving and perishing'.[6]

There were three separate, but interconnected strands in Eurasian attempts in the 1820s to meet what appeared to the most percipient to be a fundamental threat to their position and prosperity, limited though that was. The first, which might be termed *occupational*, sought to find substantial new areas of Eurasian employment in trade, farming, commerce and seafaring. The second, *social and educational*, aimed to raise the educational standards of Eurasians and to fit them for careers in the upper reaches of government service. The third, *political*, pressed for the removal of legal distinctions between Eurasian and British subjects, and attempted to reopen covenanted service to the best educated and ablest of them. Occupational, social and educational activities are the subject of this chapter. The political aims and achievements of Eurasians are the topic of the next.

Later Anglo-Indians have been tempted to portray the wide variety of Eurasian communal activity in the 1820s as the product of a united community striving to improve its position in the face of British resistance or indifference.[7] The reality was not as clear cut. The dilemma for Eurasians that community action might distance them from, rather than integrate them with the main body of the British in India, was reflected in patchy support for community interests. If some Eurasians were far-sighted and energetic, many others were apathetic. One correspondent to the *Bengal Hurkaru* in 1828, observed of the Eurasian reaction to the efforts of John Ricketts to improve their situation, 'it is a matter of surprise to see the coolness with which he is treated by his fellow countrymen, the Indo-Britons, for whose welfare he endeavours his utmost efforts'.[8]

Eurasian passivity may, in part at least, be explained by an acquiescence in their given place in society. Perhaps many Eurasians held back from active participation in community projects for more positive reasons. Money was scarce for most, with little to spare for the many ambitious and speculative projects which were proposed. Others did not want publicly to be identified as Eurasians, or, particularly in the case of political agitation, feared for their jobs should there be government displeasure. Thus the promotion of Eurasian interests in the 1820s depended on a small though committed group of activists. It was unfortunate for the Eurasian cause that even these were not always united in their views. Dissension amongst them, the bitter conflict which marred the start of the Parental Academic Institution at Calcutta was one instance, weakened the overall impact of their efforts.

*

Although there was a general consensus amongst Eurasian leaders that their community should widen its employment opportunities from its narrow clerical and government base, there were differing opinions on where the best scope lay. Two schools of thought emerged in the 1820s, each with its own protagonist. James Kyd, who had made his fortune as the Company's master ship builder at Calcutta, argued a craft based route. In his *Thoughts, How to Better the Condition of Indo-Britons*, he listed more than forty trade occupations which Eurasians could undertake, and argued that they would have the advantage over Indian competition which he accused of waste of time and lack of application.[9] Charles Fenwick, who had been a Baptist missionary and farmer at Sylhet, argued a contrary view in his *Essay on the Colonization of Hindostan by East Indians*. He believed that the opportunities in trade for Eurasians were far too few to create the number of jobs which were needed. He argued that if Eurasians were to improve themselves colonisation 'appears the only feasible and effectual means of encouraging the grand object of accelerating the march of their prosperity, and of advancing their importance in the world'.[10]

Attempts, led by Kyd and Ricketts, to develop opportunities in trade preceded efforts to put Fenwick's colonisation proposals into effect. In 1825 Ricketts was instrumental in launching the Calcutta Apprenticing Society of which Kyd became the Secretary and Reginald Heber, the Bishop of Calcutta, the Patron. Calcutta's example was followed at Madras. At first the prospects seemed promising, and Kyd used his own shipyards to provide apprenticeships and show what could be achieved:

Kyd was so proud of the manner in which they had been physically built up by carpentry and blacksmithery, that at the second annual meeting of the Society he paraded his young men before the public to exhibit their fine physique.[11]

However, the societies soon ran into problems. Parents at Madras wanted their sons in 'gentlemanly' occupations as clerks rather than in trade. British firms in Calcutta demanded large premiums to take on boys as apprentices and, reflecting the difficult economic situation of the late 1820s, 'felt that there was not enough work to go round for them to share with newcomers'.[12] The lack of opportunity in India, and of funds to send boys to be apprenticed in Britain, brought most of the activities of the apprenticing society to an early end.

One branch of the Calcutta society, the Marine Apprenticing Society, managed to continue operating until 1828. The grant of a surplus and unseaworthy ship by the Bengal Government, which was moored on the Hooghly, enabled 150 boys to be taught the basics of practical seamanship. By 1827 some progress had been made. 190 boys had been accepted for training and some were already serving on pilot vessels, whilst others were considered ready for assignment to country shipping. But, once again lack of funds cut short a promising venture. The Society could only afford to rig the ship and depended on the Government to pay the living expenses of the boys, and on the Marine Assurance Company of Calcutta to pay the wages of the Master and his crew. The failure of the Marine Assurance to meet its obligations in 1828 left the Society with assets of Rs 3187 to meet obligations of Rs 8000. Worse yet, in February 1828 it was reported that the 'School Ship cannot last much longer. She is already in such a crazy condition, that it is not safe to have even her lower mast stepped'. By April the ship had been sold and the children sent back to their orphanages or else to serve in other ships on the river.[13]

By 1828 the hopes of Eurasian activists that trade or marine apprenticeships might prove an important source of new employment for their youth had proved largely illusory. Private funds were clearly quite inadequate to provide the scale of investment needed, and Government financial aid was limited to no more than was already contributed to house the would-be apprentices in their orphanages. Attention now focussed on the alternative option – the settlement of Eurasians in farming communities on the land.

The Eurasian Struggle for Self Advancement

★

Since the middle of the eighteenth century the settlement of people of European descent on the land in India had been one of the issues to which the East India Company in London was most consistently opposed. The reasons ranged from the lofty heights of Philip Francis's argument in 1774 that 'the land belongs as of right to the natives', to a much more pragmatic concern that an influx of Europeans, 'especially those of the lower order', would antagonise the Indian population since, 'they are prone to domineer and oppress the natives from a sense of their own personal and national superiority'.[14] But the danger of a challenge from an indigenous population of European descent, voiced by Charles Grant who feared that if colonisation were allowed, 'a new race might spring up, with larger pretensions, and more intractable than the Hindus', was an important consideration with the Company.[15] These fears were amongst the deepest reasons for excluding Eurasians from the Company's covenanted service in 1791. They may explain too the failure of Sir Alexander Johnston, then Chief Justice of Ceylon, to carry through his ambitious proposal in 1810 to set up a Eurasian settlement there. He had envisaged almost a state within a state in which Eurasians from every British territory in South East Asia would have enjoyed all the freedom of British subjects under the Crown.[16]

There were a number of still born attempts in the early nineteenth century to settle Eurasians on the land. As early as 1786 it was suggested that they might be used to reclaim the Sunderbans in the Bay of Bengal.[17] In 1826 the rising interest in Britain of the advantages of colonising Australia with free settlers was probably reflected in the proposal that if the Company's officers in India were offered the same rights as Royal officers had, to settle in Van Dieman's Land or New South Wales, it 'would be felt as a great benefit by those officers who have families by Asiatic mothers'.[18]

Although none of the early proposals for colonisation were carried through and the Company in London continued to be discouraging, their Governors in India took a more positive line in the 1820s. Governor-General William Bentinck and the influential Sir Charles Metcalfe in Bengal were persuaded of the potential of selective British immigration into India. They were convinced too that the settlement of Eurasians on the land would pose no political threat.[19] Bentinck's Governors, John Malcolm at Bombay, and Stephen Lushington at Madras, shared his views and were prepared to encourage experimental settlements with practical assistance. Once the ban of Eurasian land ownership in the Bengal and Bombay Presidencies had been lifted during the tenure of Governor-General Lord Hastings, the way was legally open for attempts at Eurasian colonisation in the late 1820s.[20]

There was a larger consideration in the minds of the main promoters of Eurasian colonisation, Charles Fenwick and John Ricketts, than just the creation of new employment for Eurasians, important though that was. They shared a vision of a permanent and satisfactory place for Eurasians in India in their own right. Eurasian vulnerability to dependence on Government employment was clear to Ricketts who did not believe that, 'any Government or State on earth can ever furnish a never-failing source of competent livelihood for a whole nation of clerks'. He urged a greater degree of self reliance on the part of Eurasians.[21]

Charles Fenwick was largely in agreement with Ricketts' views. 'A permanency of footing in the country' through land ownership was his recipe for the Eurasian way ahead. He published detailed and carefully costed proposals for Eurasian farming communities which would raise crops and products as diverse as poultry, turtles, sheep and pigs. Eurasians, Britons, and Indians alike would, he thought, all benefit from such communities. Eurasians would have honourable and profitable employment. The British traveller, instead of uncomfortable and unhygienic lodgings, 'would at the end of every given stage, have a comfortable Inn or Farm to go to, and a smart and intelligent Indo-Briton to attend on him'. Indians, wrote Fenwick, would find 'spiritual improvement . . . through the association with intelligent Christians living among them engaged in similar occupations and leading them by example and precept'.[22]

Fenwick's plans raised considerable interest. There were those, however, who whilst applauding his vision, doubted the practicality of his schemes. They wondered whether local Indian inhabitants would buy the produce of their Eurasian neighbours, and even whether they might prove hostile. Others speculated that farming might not be as profitable as Fenwick claimed. Some doubted too whether Eurasians would relish a farming life:

> The present generation of them being mostly brought up as Gentlemen by their fathers and used to all the choice delicacies which a good table could afford, of course aspire to be placed on the same rank with their European brethren as it respects political elevation. With such habits and ideas and

without any training and practice in agriculture, I am at a loss to conceive how they could be prevailed upon to take upon themselves the occupation of downright farmers.[23]

There was scepticism too of the proposals which John Ricketts himself put forward in 1828 that a Commercial and Patriotic Association should be formed in Bengal. More than one hundred attended the first meeting at Calcutta to launch the Association.[24] The plan was to found a joint stock company, financed by individual subscriptions, which would produce sugar, cotton and indigo. Its management would be delegated to members living in up country Bengal. The English language press, which had been heavily lobbied by Ricketts before the meeting, was at best lukewarm to the project. The *India Gazette* wished it well in view of the trouble that had been taken to set it up. The *Bengal Hurkaru* thought there were better ways of accomplishing the objective, but *John Bull* dismissed the whole idea as a 'farrago of nonsense and radicalism'.[25]

The pessimists were vindicated when the Commercial and Patriotic Association was still born. So too was an East Indian Colonization Fund proposed at Futtegurh on the model advocated by Fenwick.[26] However, two experimental colonies were established, one near Bombay and the other near Madras. Both had official backing, some financial help, and made a hopeful start.

In 1829 the colony near Bombay was reported by the Governor, John Malcolm, to be flourishing. The Bombay Government had granted premises at Phoolshair, fifteen miles north-east of Poona, together with forty-two acres of land to the East Indian Colonization Committee of Bombay. The Committee had raised Rs 30,000 by public subscription to support up to 12 apprentices, growing tobacco, cotton and fruit, and learning furniture making and printing. Since the Government had banned the sale of alcohol for several miles around, it was thought that the apprentices and their teachers would be safe from temptation.[27] At Madras, a Eurasian Philanthropic Association set out that year to undertake a scheme very similar to that at Bombay. The Madras Government added Rs 7000 to the Rs 35,000 raised by public subscription to settle a small group of apprentices on the land. Approximately fifty acres of unused land were granted to the Association on a twenty-one year lease at a nominal rental of R 1 an acre. The Shevaroy Hills, near Salem, were chosen as the site at which apprentices, as at Phoolshair, were to grow potatoes, coffee and wheat crops, and be taught furniture-making. The original plans of the Association also envisaged a farm in Madras itself, and an inn on the road to Bangalore.[28]

Before long the early optimism which these two projects had created was dispelled. The Phoolshair colony, which at one time had more than a hundred residents, soon ran out of money in consequence of the higher than expected start up costs, and the need to repair the palace which was in a ruinous condition. Mr. Lundt, who was placed in charge and given a horse to emphasise his importance with the locals, combined his new responsibility with his existing post as superintendent of the nearby Botanical Gardens. He, accused of 'moral turpitude', bore most of the blame for the failure of the colony in 1830, whilst the schoolmaster, Mr. Challen, was described as being almost as ignorant as his pupils, and the doctor – an assistant apothecary – apparently 'could not be parted from Bacchus'.[29]

There were management problems too at the Madras settlement since none of the Management Committee had any agricultural experience. Thus the settlers 'were not accompanied by anyone able to initiate them into the most ordinary elements of agriculture'. There were difficulties in finding suitable recruits, for all were unemployed, willing to try anything, and some at least 'were of unsteady habits, others were lazy and indolent'. As funds drained away there were disagreements within the Management Committee before the experiment was abandoned and the remaining money transferred to the Madras Civil Orphan Asylum.[30] With the failure of both colonies the hopes that the establishment of large numbers of Eurasians on the land would provide an effective answer to their employment problem were effectively ended, though the dream lived on through into the twentieth century.[31]

The efforts of Eurasian leaders to diversify Eurasian employment into trades and agriculture achieved little that was tangible. Many factors contributed to the failure; poor project organisation, inadequate financial resources, and lack of practical knowledge. Two factors in particular appear of special importance. Firstly, though the economic problems of Eurasians were well understood in official circles by the 1820s, Government financial aid was slight although there was some disposition to assist. Governor-General William Bentinck agreed that, 'there has been little opening for their enterprise', and added, 'I should greatly rejoice to see a wider field opened for the industry of the class in question'.[32] But he had his doubts, widely shared, of the community's willingness to help itself. 'East Indians', wrote Charles Fenwick in 1828, 'are doing little or nothing to promote their future prosperity'. Secondly, the deep rooted unwillingness of educated Eurasians to be redeployed from their offices in the cities to lives in trade and agriculture had much to do with the failure of the apprenticing and farming policies of the 1820s. Few Eurasians seem to have shared Charles Fenwick's belief that his countrymen 'would find it easy to live very comfortably by the results of their labours'.[33]

For educated Eurasians the question was not so much one of betterment, but a quest for status and acceptance as 'gentlemen'. Trade and farming were *not* gentlemanly occupations. Farming in particular with its inevitable manual labour, placed Eurasians on the wrong side of the colonial equation, wherein the 'rulers' directed and supervised, and the 'ruled' provided the labour force. One Eurasian, writing to the *Bengal Hurkaru* in 1829, summed up the general attitude:

> It seems as if the mere name of being a Government servant, holds them back like a charm in their servitude – some time back I met with a few East Indians, without employment, who declared themselves a thousand times more willing to become drummers and fifers, than farmers; and more lately I met with a larger number of them, in the same condition, who thought the life of a farmer beneath a gentleman and such they considered themselves! O Mora! O Tempora![34]

This general reluctance of Eurasians to compromise what they saw as their social situation by manual labour was shared by girls and boys alike. James Kyd, noting that many Eurasian girls who did not marry were reduced to financial distress, argued in vain that 'shoe making is a fashionable employment to young Ladies of the highest rank in England'.[35] Eurasian women with any claim to gentility considered shoe making and similar occupations – hat making and millinery – socially demeaning. In 1824 the Managers of the Bengal Orphan Society pleaded – unsuccessfully – with the Court in London that the Eurasian daughters of British officers in their care should be returned to London. They argued that there was no opportunity for the girls to learn any useful livelihood because they had a 'very misplaced and inconvenient disposition to look upon the occupations of honest industry with Contempt and Aversion'.[36]

If the need to widen the scope of Eurasian employment in the 1820s seemed a major priority to their leaders, so too was improvement in the educational opportunities available to their sons. In this they had three strategic objectives. The first was to equip more

Eurasians for the greater responsibilities in Government service, which they hoped their political representations might achieve. The second was to advance Eurasian status within the British community in India. The third was to counter the threat to the Eurasian near monopoly of the better jobs in the uncovenanted service posed by a growing cadre of Western educated Indians.

The problem took on a new urgency in the early 1820s as progressively fewer Eurasians had the resources to send their children to school or university in Britain. Only the wealthiest, men like James Skinner or James Kyd, could afford to do so, and they were exceptions to the rule. Although British civil and military officials continued to send their Eurasian children to England for education or 'finishing', Eurasians of the second or third generation, typically earning Rs 200 a month, had no choice but to educate their children in India. The general standard of teaching was poor, and put Eurasians at a disadvantage in their search for full acceptance by British society. 'Not half of the East Indians are sent to England for their education, and that education which those receive in this country hardly amounts to as much as would be taught in a respectable free school at home', remarked a correspondent of the *Bengal Hurkaru*, adding, 'If an European education were more widely spread among East Indians, they would stand more chance of indiscriminate association with Europeans'.[37]

The problem for Eurasians was that, for the first time in the 1820s, not only did they have to struggle for social acceptance in British society, but they faced a new challenge to their economic base as the work horses of British administration. 'A few years', Eurasians were warned in 1829, 'and Hindoos will be on an equal footing with yourselves; and if you remain stationary while they advance, I leave you to consider that the present state of things will not continue'.[38]

The threat to the Eurasian status quo first emerged at Calcutta in 1817 with the foundation of the Hindu College, which was backed by Government funding in the 1820s. By the end of the decade there were 400 boys at the college, learning the English language and history, literature and natural sciences, as well as Bengali writing and arithmetic.[39] Its students, who spoke only English when at the college, clearly posed a threat to their Eurasian contemporaries, dependent on the very limited standards of the free and private schools of Calcutta.

For all its individual importance Hindu College was just one element in the rapid spread of Western knowledge and education, generated by religious, secular and official bodies in British India of the early nineteenth century. Schools were a central aspect of all missionary work. Every mission station had its school. The Baptists, for instance, had 60 paying students at their school in Serampore by 1811. Seven years later it has been estimated that some 11,000 Indian students attended their 92 schools spread through the Bengal Presidency, often taught by Eurasians from their own Benevolent Institution in Calcutta.[40] The School Book and the School Societies of Calcutta, in which the philanthropist David Hare played a prominent part, had 166 schools under management by 1825.[41] And although the Government's Committee of Public Instruction, set up in 1823 to fulfil the Company's obligations under the Charter Act of 1813, was embroiled at first in a debate over whether public instruction should be in the vernacular or English, by the late 1820s the advocates of the use of English had won the day. Substantial grants were made to secular educational institutions. The Calcutta Madrassa received Rs 30,000, and the Hindu College Rs 25,000 in 1827. Little was granted at Madras, but at Bombay the Native School Book Society received Rs 12,270 and the Poona College Rs 15,000.[42]

Eurasians were simultaneously threatened by and involved in the dynamic educational environment of the 1820s, especially in Calcutta. The threat was the erosion of historic Eurasian exclusivity as the language intermediaries between Briton and Indian. They were involved as their leadership urged Eurasians to improve their educational attainments in order to safeguard and improve their place in British society. The Parental Academy, a school dedicated to Eurasians, whose role and achievements are discussed later, was central to Eurasian aspirations. But there were many other Eurasian educational initiatives. Debating societies flourished, an Oriental Society met from 1825 on. An East Indian Association was set up in 1829 to 'promote the intellectual, moral and political improvement of all classes of society, but specifically of Eurasians'.[43]

Though the extension of Western learning to Indians threatened Eurasian tenure of Government appointments, it opened up another employment opportunity. As early as 1803 it had been suggested that teaching was a suitable employment for them.[44] Headmasters for the new schools of the 1820s were brought from England wherever possible, but many Eurasians were employed as teachers, at salaries ranging from Rs 40 a month to Rs 150. A few became Headmasters themselves. Marcus Rochford, for instance, taught at the Upper Military Academy, Kidderpore before becoming Headmaster of the Parental Academy in 1829–30, and was on the staff of the Madrassa later. James Lorimer, the Headmaster at the Parental Academy from 1831–7, had been educated there.[45] The ranks of Eurasian teachers included the talented Henry Derozio, who, in his brief career as a teacher at the Hindu College, made a singular and controversial contribution to the educational debate of his day.

*

Neither Derozio's background – he was of Portuguese descent – nor his career as a poet, teacher, and journalist were typical of other Eurasian prominents. Where men like Ricketts and Byrn were circumspect and pragmatic, Derozio was flamboyant and controversial. Whilst their contribution was made in committees and the organisation of projects, Derozio's was personal and charismatic. It was brief in time, lying between the publication of his first book of poems in 1828 and his death from cholera at the age of twenty-two in 1831.[46]

If Derozio's poetry first made his name, it was his three year spell as a teacher at the Hindu College which thrust him into contemporary and subsequent controversy. 'Of all teachers', wrote Peary Chaud Mittra, one of his students, 'Mr. H.L.V. Derozio gave the greatest impetus to free discussion on all subjects, social, moral, and religious . . . this led to a free exchange of thought and the reading of books which otherwise would not have been read'. The result was explosive. 'The convulsion caused by Derozio was great. It pervaded almost the whole house of every advanced student. Down with Hinduism! Down with Orthodoxy! was the cry everywhere'.[47] Derozio's enforced resignation from the Hindu College in 1831 was the inevitable consequence of irate protests from the orthodox Hindu managers of the College, and the controversy has survived him. Derozio has been depicted as the progenitor of extreme westernisation in Indian education which 'denied the validity of their entire cultural heritage', and 'led his students into a cultural no-man's land'.[48]

At the time of the requests for his dismissal from the Hindu College Derozio vehemently rejected accusations that he was an atheist, or that he had incited his students to a lack of respect for their parents or religious beliefs. He defended his approach to Western liberal thought on the needs for rational enquiry into given truths, whether political, social or religious. 'How', he asked, 'is any opinion to be strengthened but by completely comprehending the objections that are offered to it and exposing their futility? And what more have I done than this?'[49]

Perhaps the defence was somewhat disingenuous, for whatever he may have intended, he was well aware of the disturbing consequences of his 'rational' approach to teaching on the sons of conservative Hindus, whose parents were more interested in the qualification of their sons for Government employment than a fundamental examination of the basis of their religious beliefs. But it is hard to see in Derozio, a young teacher aflame with his own discovery of Diderot, Rousseau, Lock and Pope, as subsequent critics would have it, the founder of an educational movement which rejected all that was Indian. Derozio's soul is in the poetry which he wrote, romantic, replete with classical allusion, and often drawing for its inspiration on the people, the customs and the stories of India. Many of Derozio's sonnets and shorter poems, 'To India – My Native Land', 'Ode to the Persian of Hafiz', and the 'Song of the Hindustanee Minstrel', took Indian themes. In his most ambitious work, 'The Fakeer of Junghera', Derozio set his Indian love story by the great rock, Junghera, a place of pilgrimage rising from the Ganges.[50]

Derozio took little notice of the social boundaries which separated Britons, Indians and Eurasians. He did not approve of the prevalent Eurasian distaste for the education of their sons alongside Indians believing that, 'It is quite delightful to witness the exertion of Hindu and Christian youths striving together for academic honours'.[51] He founded an Academic Association in 1828 which brought together his Indian pupils and prominent members of the British 'establishment' in literary discussion and debate.[52] When he founded the *East Indian Journal* after his removal from the Hindu College, he emphasised that it would not take any narrowly racial view towards society, but 'that it will advocate the just rights of all sections of the community'.[53] His friends were drawn from a diverse circle, linked by his interests in literature, education and social reform, whatever their race. There were many Britons amongst them for, 'his talents obtained admission for him into the best society of the day'.[54] He had been educated with and was close to many leading Eurasians.[55] Indians also were amongst those who planned to raise a memorial to him after his death.[56]

Derozio had his detractors, both British and Eurasian. The *Oriental Herald* thought his poetry, 'high in the perilous regions of exaggerated passion, and falsetto sentiment', and observed that it was only Derozio's Eurasian birth which made it remarkable, adding cruelly that, 'It is . . . as if a Briton of the time of Severus, had suddenly written a poem in good Latin'.[57] Others found fault with Derozio's vanity, foppishness and extravagance.[58] Despite carping critics Derozio became a source of great pride to Eurasians. That pride though was more apparent after his death – for, as the *Bengal Hurkaru* commented on the publication of his poems, 'It is with great regret we learn that the support his work has achieved has been chiefly confined to the European community, comparatively few Indo-Britons having subscribed to it'.[59] In British eyes indeed the fulsome tributes of the Eurasian community to Derozio after his death seemed only to bear out yet again its general lack of educational and intellectual attainment.[60]

★

The Eurasian activists of the 1820s believed that an improvement in the quality of education available to their children in British India was a vital element in their attempts to improve the social and economic wellbeing of the community. They felt that well educated Eurasians would not only be more socially acceptable in British society, but also better equipped to take advantage of the opening up of Government covenanted employment which they hoped to achieve. In pursuit of this aim the Parental Academic Institution was founded by John Ricketts in 1823, to be modelled on the English public schools. Of all the Eurasian initiatives of the 1820s, the Parental Academy, as the school was called at Calcutta – a similar attempt at Madras did not succeed – was the most successful and longest to endure.[61] Its importance in the history of the painful birth of a Eurasian community in India is all the greater since its founders saw it as a public institution, rather than just a school. Each year the Managers published details of its progress, the numbers of its pupils and teachers, its financial situation as well as of its academic successes. They reported too on their unsuccessful attempts to obtain Government grants, and the level of financial support which they received from the Eurasian and British community. These reports provide a comprehensive record of the school's early years, with all its problems. They illustrate vividly the problems for even the best-off in paying their sons' fees, the difficulty in getting and keeping good teachers, and the lack of official Government support for their project.

The numbers of private schools for boys, with which the PAI was to compete, had begun to grow in the Presidency towns from the 1780s to meet a growing need for 'middle class' education in British

India. Their clientele were the sons of the British or Eurasian parents who were financially unable to send their sons back to Britain to be educated, and the Eurasian sons of civil and military officers considered too dark in colour for an education in England. Most of these schools accepted Indian as well as British and Eurasian children. The rise in the availability of schools for boys was paralleled by a growth in the number of institutions for girls, most with little academic pretension, but strong on the social skills felt necessary to attract a husband. Clearly the quality of education at private schools, which depended almost entirely on the capability of the proprietor, was rudimentary as John Palmer pointed out in 1802:

> The whole range of Education to be had [in Calcutta], comprises reading, writing and arithmetic, but to judge by the slowness and imperfection of acquisition in these humble branches, I fear that there must result a considerable waste of time to all the children of the present day who are retained in Bengal.[62]

By the 1820s there were more schools in Calcutta, with more ambitious aims, and when the Parental Academy was launched in 1823 it entered a relatively crowded private educational sector. As well as numerous 'seminaries' for girls, the Dhurrumtollah Academy, Archer's, the Serampore College, and the Calcutta Academy, amongst others, competed for those boys whose parents could pay their fees. The curricula offered had certainly widened since the start of the century. David Drummond's Dhurrumtollah Academy, which he ran with great public panache – his parents' days when boys showed off their attainments were almost theatrical events – taught the Latin classics and English Literature as well as more practical subjects such as book-keeping. Henry Derozio, one of Drummond's pupils, owed much to him. The Calcutta Academy, owned by the Eurasian Frederick Linstedt had, by 1821, an even more ambitious range of studies – on paper at least. Boys were taught the basics of English grammar, geography, arithmetic through to physics, natural philosophy, hydrostatics and hydraulics. The study of surveying, fortification, navigation and book-keeping prepared boys for their future occupation. French, Persian and Bengali were offered. So too were the 'social' subjects – music and dancing.[63]

The declared aim of the Parental Academic Institution in 1823 was to 'improve the standards of education that then existed', hopefully at a lower cost. Christians of every denomination were invited to become founder members of its new school – the Parental Academy.[64] At first it was hoped that there would be a girls' as well as a boys' school, but attempts to set one up failed for lack of support.[65] Although a mission to improve educational standards for Eurasian boys was the declared aim there was a hidden agenda, never publicly voiced, but no less important for Eurasian parents. Unlike many other private schools of the time, no Indian boys were admitted. The Parental Academy gave Eurasians a school which would be exclusive to them. Indeed, once it was established, many of the Eurasian boys at the Dhurrumtollah Academy were moved over to it.[66] Until 1835, at the very least, there were no Indian pupils at the Parental Academy.[67] The failure to attract sufficient candidates to form a girls' school may well be explained by the fact that, unlike boys' private schools, the ladies' academies of Calcutta did not have Indian girls amongst their pupils.

It has been argued that the foundation of the Parental Academic Institution, which followed a meeting at John Ricketts' house, was a demonstration 'of a widespread community determination to improve educational standards'.[68] The evidence is, however, like so many Eurasian initiatives of the time, that it was the work of a small band of determined activists, operating in a context of general apathy and some criticism. There were those who thought that it was misguided to give a liberal and 'gentlemanly' education to Eurasians and that it would be far wiser to train them in useful trades.[69] Only thirty-six Eurasians contributed to the initial funds for the school. Just Rs 3402 were raised, and of this almost one half came from four donors – James Kyd, Willoughby Da Costa, Charles Reed and Robert Frith.[70]

Short of money from the start, the firm establishment of the Parental Academic Institution was jeopardised further by dissension amongst its founders. Within two months of its launch they were split into Anglican and Dissenting factions. The issue was the appointment of two Congregationalist ministers, the Revv. Hall and Warden, as teachers. The Anglican majority on the Committee dismissed them. Ricketts resigned as Secretary in protest, and a General Meeting was called by the outvoted minority on the Committee. When it met Ricketts was censured for resigning but reinstated on the new Committee which excluded the Anglican majority. They left to establish the rival Calcutta High School, under the patronage of Bishop Heber, which struggled on eventually to become St Paul's High School in 1847.[71] The Parental Academy continued under the leadership of Ricketts and his new

Dissenting majority on the Committee. Thus the slender resources of the Eurasian community were divided as two schools took the place of the one originally planned, to the detriment of both.

Until the Parental Academy received a legacy of 2 lakhs from John Doveton for the school in Calcutta, and the same to restart the school in Madras in 1855, continual financial crisis hindered its development. Donations from the European community in Calcutta averaged only Rs 2000 a year and fell off sharply in the early 1830s after the bank failures of that time. Thus the school was almost entirely dependent on its income from fees. Its rates were set at around the level of the other private schools of the day, Rs 36 a month for boarders and Rs 12 for day boys. A problem which emerged at once, and which illustrates the economic weakness of even the best off sector of the Eurasian community of the day, was the difficulty which most parents had in paying their sons' school fees. In the first decade of the school's existence never less than one quarter and generally around a half of fees were in arrears at the year end. As the Managers pointed out the consequences to the school's development were severe. It was not possible to buy premises to save the rent, nor could well qualified teachers be engaged. The financial problems were reflected in the rapid turnover of both teachers and pupils in the early years of the Parental Academy. There were six headmasters between 1823 and 1837. Assistant teachers came and went with equal rapidity. Between 1824 and 1837 there was not one year in which the school's teaching staff was unchanged from the preceding year, and on occasion senior boys were enlisted as junior teachers. The turnover in students matched the turnover in teachers, averaging 44% a year.[72]

It was natural therefore that the Managers, pressed by financial worry, should look to the Government for help, particularly since other institutions, the Benevolent Institution and the Hindu College, received official grants. A first and unsuccessful attempt was made in 1826, and repeated with no better result the next year. At the time it was taken as clear evidence of discrimination against Eurasians as such, a view accepted by the Anglo-Indian community of the twentieth century.[73] It is, however, debatable whether such a conclusion can be supported. When the Bengal Government turned down the Parental Academy's request it made clear that its policy was to support charitable and public institutions, and that the Parental Academy did not fit into either of these categories. There was concern too that any government contribution would merely subsidise those Eurasian parents who so signally failed to pay their sons' fees. It was pointed out to the Managers that, 'you have failed to realize a large amount of individual subscriptions'.[74] But what government officially withheld, individual officials supplied. Most of the significant sums donated to the funds of the Parental Academy between 1824 and 1835 came, not from Eurasians, but the private pockets of senior Government officials – Governors-General Lord Amherst and Bentinck, and members of the Council – the Hon. W. Bayley, and Sir Edward Grey. In particular, Sir Charles Metcalfe was a regular donor; his gift of Rs 5000 in 1835 allowed the Managers to clear the school's outstanding debts.[75]

For all the recurrent financial difficulties the school survived, and by the 1830s could point to some real achievements. Its student numbers had built up from the 53 with which it started to 172 by 1835, at which time if offered an ambitious curriculum and employed eight full-time teachers. It succeeded in one of its major aims of allocating a high proportion of its income to its teaching staff. In 1828 one third of income was spent on teachers' salaries compared with two fifths at the Calcutta Free School.[76]

Much of the credit for the survival of the Parental Academy must be given to the real dedication of those involved in its management. Two of the early headmasters, William Masters (1824–8) and James Lorimer (1831–7) played conspicuous parts.[77] They were backed by the Management Committee led by Wale Byrn. It was said of him that, 'the Institution is in his heart, he acknowledges no man as his friend who is not a friend of the Parental Academy'.[78] He became Secretary and Visitor in 1824, and served continuously as such until his retirement in 1849, continuing to be Visitor until his death in 1855. From 1830 he lived on the school premises, paying rent for his accommodation and acting, in addition to his other duties, as School Superintendent. It was his persuasion of John Doveton to make the school the main beneficiary of his will which placed the Parental Academy, later to be renamed the Doveton College, on a firm financial footing at last. Byrn was supported by a remarkably cohesive and long serving Management Committee most of whom held senior positions in the Company's uncovenanted service.[79]

After 1835 the Parental Academy faced severe competition from new and financially better-backed schools, such as La Martinière and St. Xavier's in Calcutta. These syphoned off teachers and pupils from the Parental Academy whose numbers declined from a high point of 213 in 1838 to 121 in 1841. The salary of Rs 600 a month which William Masters earned as the first Headmaster of La Martinière was roughly three times what he had earned when at the Parental Academy. Nevertheless the Parental Academy survived into the twentieth century, and numbers of its students achieved respectable positions in administration, the law and education.[80]

For all the determination of its founders and their achievements against all odds, the history of the Parental Academy illustrates again the inherent conflict between the aspirations of educated early nineteenth century Eurasians for a greater integration into British society in India, and a Government policy on education which was beginning the move to provide 'properly trained Indians for its subordinate services'.[81] In Bengal alone, by 1830, there were more than 6,000 Hindus and almost 1,000 Muslims at Government sponsored schools as against 100 or so Eurasians at the Parental Academy.[82] By the 1840s Eurasians were losing out to the competition from Indians whose education was geared to passing the public examinations for entry into uncovenanted Government service, rather than the making of English 'gentlemen'.

The premise of the founders of the Parental Academy had been that a superior education for Eurasians would knit them more closely into the British community of India by providing a well educated cadre for Government service at senior levels. The strategy failed, for neither did it link Eurasians more closely to Britons, not did it bring the hoped for bulwark against increasing competition from Indians for the core employment of the Eurasian community. Eurasians were progressively sidelined in the practical benefits to be had from the spread of Western education in India.

Although credit must be given to the Eurasian leaders of the 1820s for their sustained efforts to develop new possibilities of employment and better educational opportunities for their sons, they failed to achieve the improvement in the social and economic situation of the community which had been their objective. The obstacles which they encountered lay partly within their own community, as well as in factors without. The unwillingness of many Eurasians to consider types of employment which were considered socially unsuitable may be seen as a reflection of the very artificiality of colonial society itself in which government employment was the apex of social standing, and in which other potentially lucrative professions – the law and medicine – were dominated by British non officials. But, if Eurasians failed to grasp the slender chances offered to them, they received little encouragement from Government. If the accusations of the later Anglo-Indian community go too far in suggesting a deliberate policy to disadvantage and depress their community, it must nevertheless be accepted that British authority displayed relative indifference to the various Eurasian initiatives of the 1820s. Some low-level financial support was indeed forthcoming for apprenticing and farming schemes, and as individuals British officials were often privately generous. But British policy in the 1820s was beginning to recognise the need, for reasons of its own interest as much as for more laudable motives, to involve Indians in their own government. This necessarily diminished the hitherto protected and special place of Eurasians.

Eurasian leaders saw the danger clearly. Educational, social and occupational initiatives were an important part of their plans to fend off the coming threat to their status quo. But they had a greater ambition yet, to regain the acceptance which they had lost in the 1790s – to be reinstated *legally* as British subjects. Should they achieve this, careers in the covenanted service would be open to them, the legal privileges of Britons accorded, and at a stroke they would overcome the invidious distinction of being of British descent but not recognised as fully British. It seemed to them that the East India Company would never recognise their claim. Boldly, they resolved to appeal over the Company's Directors to the ultimate authority for India's affairs – Parliament at Westminster. Their Petition, which was received and debated in 1830, was the centrepiece of a newfound Eurasian resolve to take the initiative, to regularise their status, and to be fully accepted as British, *not* Indian.

8

Political Protest
The East Indians' Petition of 1830

On the 27th December 1829 John Ricketts, the representative of Eurasians in Calcutta, arrived in London with the East Indians' Petition, which he was charged to present to Parliament. The timing was appropriate for the date was approaching for the renewal of the East India Company's Charter. Parties were already in the field pressing their special interests; by 1830 no less than 257 petitions had been received protesting against a renewal of the Company's profitable monopoly on trade with China. Select Committees had been set up in 1829 to review the Company's powers, at a time when it was not out of the question that it might be stripped of its governing role in India.[1]

Other petitions from India were received by Parliament at the same time as the petition from the Eurasians of Calcutta. The British inhabitants of Bengal petitioned that the Company's powers to admit or expel British subjects from India be removed. Leading Indians, led by Ram Mohan Roy, requested the right to sit on juries, hitherto the preserve of Christians alone.[2] Although the East Indians' Petition was but one of the many received at the time, it was singular since it was the public protest of the great majority of the educated Eurasians of Calcutta at their racial categorisation. It is believed, though it cannot be proved for certain since the original petition is no longer in the Parliamentary records, that between 600–700 of the 1176 'respectable' Eurasians living in Calcutta and Bengal at the time had signed.[3] They asserted they were British, not Indian, and petitioned to be treated as such.

Their action was largely prompted by a fundamental change in Government policy. From the time of Governors-General Cornwallis and Wellesley, Eurasians, though denied covenanted posts, had benefited from the exclusion of Indians from responsible positions in the Government's uncovenanted service. In the 1820s the rising cost of Government – the Company's Indian debt rose between 1822 and 1828 from £29 million to nearly £40 million – began to make the use of suitably qualified Indians, at salaries well below those paid to Britons or Eurasians, an increasingly attractive proposition.[4] What seemed to be needed, as soon as the educational system could deliver them, was a supply of inexpensive Indian administrative workers. In 1825 the Directors in London urged their Bengal Government to give preference to Indians for law appointments. Next year the policy became quite explicit – 'the first object of improved education should be to prepare a body of individuals for discharging public duties'.[5]

The arrival of Governor-General Lord William Bentinck in 1828, charged with a brief to retrench Government expenditure, and personally in favour of the need to involve Indians in their own government, gave a decisive impetus to a process which had already begun. There was a utilitarian rationale for his policy – the reduction in cost of Government – but it accorded with his liberal views on the natural justice of advancing an Indian role in the British government of India, views which ran ahead of the general thinking of his time. He would have liked the Governor-General to have had the power to appoint any Indian, Eurasian, or European to the covenanted service of the Company, and to send them to Haileybury for training.[6] Had he been allowed he would have included Indians in the new legislative council which he envisaged.[7] 'India', he argued in 1837 after his return, 'must be governed for its own sake, not for the sake of 600 to 1000 individuals who are sent from England to make their fortunes'.[8] Progress towards his laudable objective was in practice limited to an increase in the responsibility and pay of the uncovenanted civil service. Its members were employed more extensively in revenue collection as Deputy Collectors and as Civil Court Judges at salaries of up to Rs 400 a month.[9]

To educated Eurasian opinion of the 1820s the change in Government policy brought, as has been discussed, great fears over their job security. Yet, the opening up of more responsible roles for the uncovenanted civil service and the drive for lower costs of Government, seemed to offer greater opportunities for them as well. The Eurasian argument, which John Ricketts put to Parliament in 1830, emphasised the pool of qualified Eurasians able to take on greater responsibilities, at a much lower cost than by importing civil servants from Britain. As he pointed out, a Eurasian could do the job of a Collector or Judge at a much lower cost than an expatriate Briton, since he unlike his British counterpart, would not be concentrating on amassing a fortune to enable him to return to Britain as soon as he could.[10] Supporters of this argument argued the case in Britain. James Sutherland felt that a Eurasian, 'would think himself very handsomely rewarded' by a third of the salary paid to a British civil servant. But, he had to admit that 'one half of what would content an Anglo-Indian would content a native'.[11] Eurasian interests lay, therefore, in the maintenance of the established principle that British subjects should continue to occupy the senior civil and military posts in British India, provided that Eurasians were also accepted as British and allowed to occupy these posts, even if at a lower salary.

If the feeling which educated Eurasians had in the 1820s that they were being marginalised in the British community was the context for their political protest, their belief was that if they were readmitted to the covenanted ranks of the British civil service their social status would be restored. The preamble to their petition accepted that the 'abolition of those social prejudices' which Eurasians felt so keenly could not be resolved by legislation, but that the existence of civil disabilities for Eurasians tended, 'to place your petitioners in the situation of a proscribed class, to prevent their amalgamation with the European population, and to create and perpetuate against them the most mortifying and injurious prejudices'.[12]

The central issue of the East Indians' Petition of 1830, on which its success or failure has to be judged, was the question of Eurasian legal status. They asked Parliament to rule that they were 'British Subjects', entitled to all their rights and privileges, and *not* 'Natives of India'.

*

The Petition of 1830 at the least brought Eurasian grievances to the attention of a wide political circle for the first time. Ricketts claimed subsequently, 'We have given a shock to the mist of prejudice, by which we were enveloped, and have emerged from obscurity to light'.[13] The debate upon the Petition engaged the Company's Government and British society in India. In Britain it involved Parliament, the Board of Control, and the Company's Directors. The consequences of the debate were to prove decisive to the future status of Eurasians in India. Where there had been a lack of clarity before, there was little doubt after.

Ricketts came ashore on 1st March 1831 at Madras after a long and eventful journey back from London – his ship had run aground off Rio de Janeiro. He had successfully arranged the presentation of the Petition to Parliament and had given evidence to Select Committees of both its Houses. The hero's welcome which he received was evidence of the significance attached to his mission by Eurasians, and of the hopes which they now entertained. Neither the Eurasians of Bombay nor Madras had played any part in the Petition which was on behalf of the Calcutta Eurasians, but the Eurasians of Madras recognised their interest in offering to pay Ricketts' costs whilst he was in Madras and organised a banquet in his honour. More than one hundred of them, a high proportion of the relatively small educated Eurasian population there, sat down with Ricketts as the guest of honour at a dinner, 'to which all the elegances of the season contributed'. Speeches and musical toasts followed. Ricketts' health was drunk to the specially composed 'Ricketts March', whilst 'Money in their Pockets' was the derisive accompaniment to the toast to the East India Company.

The occasion was so convivial that many of the guests stayed on carousing until the early hours, well after the grave and serious Ricketts had gone to bed. By the end of March Ricketts was back in Calcutta. His welcome there was just as warm. On the 28th March he addressed a meeting of Eurasians at the Town Hall to report on his mission. He was greeted with acclaim, voted a silver vase (which he left in his will to his eldest son), and a portrait, later painted by Charles Pote. A public dinner was held, enlivened with speeches and no less than fourteen toasts. Once again Eurasians made clear their lack of faith in the Company's concern on their behalf. To the toast of 'The Court of Directors; and may the happiness of the Subjects under their sway be the end and aim of their Government', the musical accompaniment was to the refrain of 'There's nae such Luck about the House'.[14]

The reception which Ricketts received from Eurasians in India was certainly a personal tribute to the considerable efforts which he had made on their behalf, even though at this high point of congratulation he still found it necessary to rebut suggestions that he had profited personally from his visit to England. His reception was a clear public expression of a feeling of achievement amongst Eurasians. At last they had aired their grievances, received a hearing from Parliament, and had found influential friends in Britain prepared to argue their case. Ricketts had spoken for the beliefs of many Eurasians when, with characteristic bluntness, he told the Select Committee of the House of Lords that, 'To the East India Company as a body they owe nothing. They have received from it no sympathy or redress . . . nothing but studied insult, contemptuous indifference, or at best empty profession'.[15] He believed on his return that for once all Eurasians were united. Though – not surprisingly – there had been little positive response from the Company to the Petition whilst he was in London, Ricketts nevertheless was sure that there were Government ministers and members of Parliament who supported the Eurasian case.

*

The East Indians' Petition embraced all Eurasian grievances in the fields of education, employment and legal status.[16] Firstly, the educational policy of the Company was attacked for denying to the Parental Academy in Calcutta the financial support which had been made available to the Benevolent Institution and the Hindu College. Secondly, Eurasians complained at their exclusion from covenanted service, and that they were also excluded from uncovenanted posts in the judicial, revenue and police services. They alleged too that they were being hindered in taking up employment with independent Indian states. Thirdly, they protested at their position before the law which they argued was ambiguous. Outside Calcutta Eurasians, unlike British subjects, were subject to the Muslim civil and criminal law of the Company's courts along with all other Indian subjects. In consequence, as Christians, they maintained that they lay outside the rule of civil law by which their marriages could be confirmed, their wills validated and succession to property determined. There were other legal grievances too. Bengal Government regulations which gave the Company the right to bring its native subjects to justice even when outside Company territory, and which allowed the Company to detain those who were not British subjects without trial, were held to apply to Eurasians as well.[17]

In fact Eurasians were very short of specific examples to support their case that they were practically disadvantaged by their status at law. Eurasians who lived in up country Bengal had their marriages and wills registered in Calcutta without any difficulty. Ricketts himself, when giving evidence to the Select Committee on the matter, could not produce a single instance of injustice to Eurasians in Company courts, or any example where the legitimacy of Eurasian marriages or wills had been contested. Nor could he supply a case of a Eurasian being detained without trial, commenting weakly that, since he lived in Calcutta his experience of what went on in up country Bengal was very limited.[18] Why then did Eurasians argue so strongly that their legal status was so critically important when it seemed to have so little practical significance?

*

The real issue for Eurasians was not that few, if any, of their numbers suffered any practical injustice from being answerable to the Company's courts when outside Calcutta. The question was one of principle. British subjects were largely exempt from the Company's judicial system which applied to 'Natives of India' alone. Eurasians sought to be recognised as 'British Subjects', who alone were exempt, and who alone were legally eligible for covenanted service.

The vital legal distinction between 'British Subjects' and 'Natives of India' originated in the provisions of the Regulating Act of 1773 which had established Supreme Courts in the Presidency towns which were quite independent of the Company's own judicial system. The Supreme Courts had jurisdiction over *all* residents, of whatever race, in Madras, Bombay, and Calcutta. The Act, however, conferred on the Calcutta Supreme Court an additional *personal* jurisdiction over all British subjects resident in Bengal, Bihar, and Orissa. They were exempt from the Company's country courts in all criminal and most civil matters.[19]

The 1773 Act also laid down new rules for jury service. Juries, on which Eurasians had in the past customarily served, were henceforth to be composed exclusively of 'British Subjects'. The Act, however, failed to define who were or were not British subjects. In the years immediately after 1773 it seems that educated Eurasians of British stock were considered 'British Subjects'. They still were appointed from time to time to covenanted civil and military posts up until 1791. Eurasians continued to sit on juries. Charles Weston was one of at least two 'country borns' amongst the jury which convicted the Maharajah Nuncomar in 1775.[20] But by the end of the century, although Parliament had provided no guidance on whether Eurasians were British subjects or not, the Company had decided the matter through its own Regulations which had the force of law in British India. In 1787 it determined that all Europeans in Bengal who were *not* British subjects were subject to its courts.[21] In 1791 Eurasians were excluded from covenanted service on the grounds that they *were* 'Natives of India', a ruling confirmed by regulations in 1809 and 1813 which applied to Eurasians who had been born out of Christian wedlock. A decision of the Calcutta Supreme Court in 1822 that a Eurasian child born to a Briton married to an Indian was 'to all intents and purposes a British subject', was simply ignored by the Company.[22]

The Eurasian ambition to be declared 'British Subjects' and thus become eligible for covenanted employment was undoubtedly the primary aim of their Petition. There was, however, a secondary but important consideration which added urgency to their quest for British legal privileges. It related directly to the Eurasian plans of the time to gain new employment for their community as farmers. The Eurasians in the projected farming colonies, as matters stood, would be subject to the Company's courts once out of the Presidency towns. Eurasian leaders of a community little disposed to leave its urban life, recognised that if its members were to be persuaded to move up country in any considerable numbers, then the question of their legal status there needed to be addressed. The issue was illustrated in an editorial of the *Bengal Hurkaru* which cited the alleged case of a Eurasian woman who was, 'compelled by brutal chowkeydars to walk in the sun, in the hot season, a distance of three miles to the Magistrate's Kutcheree'. In regretting that Eurasians stayed wedded to their city life the editor observed,

> But who can wonder at it when they look at the cause, the state of the law. In Calcutta, an East Indian enjoys the protection of British law; but, in the Mofussil, with all the intellectual superiority of a European, and animated, perhaps, by truly British sentiments, to what indignities is he not liable?[23]

The question of their status before the law was far from being the minor technical matter of little consequence to Eurasians, which to observers it seemed to be. Charles Wynn, the Member of Parliament who commended the Petition to the House of Commons on 4th May 1830, saw their legal status as fundamental to the problem of Eurasians. It was,

> . . . not merely a grievance in itself, but it gave rise to a feeling among the half-castes that they stood in a different situation from their European relations, with whom they would otherwise mix on a basis of equality, and to whom they were in point of fact, equal in this country [England].[24]

*

There was a considerable political risk in the decision of Eurasian leaders to appeal over the Company's head to Parliament. Their gamble depended on the willingness of Government either to legislate in their favour, or through the Board of Control, established in 1784 to supervise the Company, to overrule the Court of Directors. But, since the Petition of 1818 to the Company had achieved nothing, the risk seemed worth the taking; indeed to be the only alternative open to them.

It was inevitable that a petition from Eurasians asking to be recognised as fully British in a colonial society which, for political, social and racial reasons had already decided that they were not, should arouse controversy. Many in British official and non official society in India thought they were well enough off as they were, and that their claim was an impertinence and absurdity. At the time Emma Roberts described the 'great stir [which] has been made by this portion of the community', their meetings in the Town Hall and frequent letters to the press observing that they,

> descant with more eloquence than judgment upon the wrongs of their country, sometimes arrogating to themselves the glories of their maternal ancestors, and at other times claiming the rights of Englishmen, and demanding to be placed in official situations under a government which they represent to be little better than an usurpation.[25]

The very act of Eurasian public political protest, an explicit challenge to their designated place in colonial society, provoked hostile comment. John Ricketts became the butt of sardonic satire, described as a 'queer little man with a sharp nose', who would make a good Guy Fawkes.[26] In *Confessions of an Eurasian*, Ricketts was cast as 'Middlerace', the representative for a Eurasian petition, tongue-tied, gauche, and who mistook the liveried doorman at the Company's offices in London for the Chairman of the Company.[27] Even a decade after the Petition, Eurasian temerity in petitioning Parliament was described as a search by them for 'livelihoods which incur no speculative risk, and render necessary no greater average of daily labour than they had always performed'.[28]

Not all in India were hostile to the Eurasian cause. The editorials of several English language newspapers suggest that local non official British opinion had some sympathy for Eurasian aspirations, and were prepared to argue that there were real grievances to be rectified. The *Asiatic Journal* asked in 1825, what other example there was 'in ancient or modern times' where a community, 'from the circumstances of its birth, and from no inherent defect of body or mind, became outcastes in the eyes of their superstitious fellow nationals'.[29] The refusal of the Court of Directors to accept the Supreme Court's ruling in 1822 that Eurasians, if born of Christian parents, were entitled to the same privileges as British born subjects, was attacked by the *Calcutta Gazette*. The *Bengal Hurkaru*, of all newspapers the most consistently supportive of Eurasian hopes, gave extensive coverage in its correspondence columns and support in its editorials to the progress of the Petition. 'They [Eurasians] have a right', wrote the editor in March 1830, 'to believe that His Majesty's Ministers would pay attention to their just claim, as subjects of an important colony of the Crown, than [to] a body of merchants who have reason to consider India merely as a great farm'.[30]

Though favourable press comment was welcome to Eurasian leaders, the views of senior Company officials were of greater significance. Some were more favourable than others. Stephen Lushington, the Governor at Madras, showed his sympathy by inviting Ricketts, on his return to India in 1831, to a reception and dinner at Government House. The next year he gave Rs 500 to the Eurasians of Madras who intended to follow up the Calcutta Petition with their own, and agreed to ensure that Eurasians would no longer be excluded from revenue, judicial and police appointments.[31] Sir Charles Metcalfe, now a member of Council for Bengal, who had been in his youth at the head of those hostile to Eurasian interests, had become a firm advocate for the removal of Eurasian civil disabilities. His advice to the Governor-General William Bentinck was that, 'the East Indians of mixed breed ought to be placed on the same footing as British subjects'.[32]

The supportive views of Lushington and Metcalfe were not, however, shared by John Malcolm, the Governor at Bombay. He was undoubtedly very much in favour of practical schemes to develop useful employment for Eurasians – colonisation, training as engineers and surveyors. But he emphatically did not agree that Eurasians, as a group, should be treated as British subjects. He accepted they were linked by language, habits, and religion, but separated by colour, social class and ability. Malcolm was glad that Eurasian 'proceedings in Bombay have hitherto been marked by moderation and good sense', a probable reference to the failure of the Bombay Eurasians to associate themselves with the Calcutta Petition. Eurasians were, as far as Malcolm was concerned, useful allies to, though not equal with, the British. He did not feel that their advancement would be attained, 'by meetings, speeches, or memorials, or by the grant of privileges, or any equality of right which can be conferred on this class'. They were to earn their place 'through persevering industry, frugality and honesty'.[33]

No opinion was more critical to Eurasian hopes amongst British officials in India than that of the Governor-General, William Bentinck. It has been written of him that, 'against the tide of British opinion, he particularly favoured Eurasians'. His wish to appoint a Eurasian officer, James Achmuty, as an aide-de-camp when he arrived in India in 1828, and his courteous treatment of Lieutenant-Colonel James Skinner, suggest that Bentinck, with his inherent lack of racial prejudice, was not antagonistic to Eurasians as individuals. But that was as far as it went, for Bentinck thought that Eurasians as a group were politically unimportant. In 1829 he minuted:

> Their number is inconsiderable. The evident disposition of all who raise themselves to opulence and consideration is to take their place with Englishmen according to their rank. The lower classes are not politically to be distinguished from natives, excepting that, as Christians, they are, of course nearly allied to us.[34]

Since Bentinck believed profoundly that an Indian contribution to the administration of their own country should be encouraged, it ran counter to that policy to support an extension of British privileges to Eurasians. He dissented from Metcalfe's minute which urged acceptance of Eurasians as British subjects, noting in its margin that he could not see, 'the justice or policy in giving to East Indians any advantage over natives. They possess no superiority in education, and are much inferior in wealth and importance socially'.[35] Bentinck, who was personally committed to equality of opportunity in Government service without regard to colour, race or creed felt a strong antipathy to the nature of British rule, which he described in 1837 as, 'cold, selfish and unfeeling; the iron hand of power on the one side, monopoly on the other'.[36] As far as he was able he was prepared to use his influence to advance Indians in Government service rather than Britons or Eurasians. Thus the Eurasian ambition to be treated as British was essentially in conflict with the fundamental direction of Bentinck's policy.

*

There was a natural concern amongst the Calcutta Eurasians over taking such a controversial step as to appeal over the heads of their chief employers, the East India Company, to Parliament itself. There were some, who recognising their vulnerability as employees, hesitated at first to associate themselves with what would undoubtedly seem a political, if not disloyal, act.[37] Indeed, what became the East Indians' Petition of 1830 did not start as a considered protest by the Eurasian community at large. It was at first a reactive response to the Supreme Court's decision in 1822 that Eurasians who were illegitimate could *not* be considered British subjects. Charles Reed, who had lost the case, decided to appeal to the King in Council against the ruling. He, and three prominent Eurasians, Willoughby Da Costa, Jacob Heatly, and George Imlach, set out to raise funds for the appeal.

Until 1825 when John Ricketts, who had been one of the original subscribers was appointed Secretary, little seems to have been accomplished. Ricketts brought his habitual zeal to bear. By the following February a first draft of the Petition had been prepared, only for it to meet several years of delay as legal firms in Calcutta and London scrutinised it. But, in February 1829 the Petition had been finally drafted, adopted by the Committee, and was placed in the Town Hall for signature. Unhappily it was to the accompaniment of an unedifying public dispute led by Charles Reed and Jacob Heatly, who had originated the petition. They accused Ricketts of commandeering the Petition, and of acting as 'sole and universal Functionary, President, Secretary, Ambassador, and Financier'.[38] Ricketts defended himself and insisted that he had no prior intention of acting as the community's delegate in London until he had been pressed to accept the task.[39] Since Ricketts had to take unpaid leave and claimed no more than his costs on the journey to London and back, he made a considerable financial sacrifice in the cause of what he considered his public duty. From the unedifying welter of charge and countercharge, one fact stands out. Had it not been for Ricketts' drive and resolution the Petition, seven years in consideration, would probably never have reached Parliament.

As Ricketts set sail for London with the Petition, late in 1829, there were some reasons to hope for its success. There had been signs in recent years that Parliament was taking a more liberal attitude towards Eurasian aspirations. The Jury Act of 1826 readmitted Eurasians to jury service, and by 1828 they once again took their place alongside British subjects.[40] The Company too had reinterpreted and modified its ban on Eurasians in its covenanted service. From 1827 on only first generation Eurasians were to be excluded.[41] Liberal legislation in the late 1820s gave some hope that there might be a favourable context in which the Petition would be received. The repeal of the Test and Corporation Acts in 1828 and the debate over the Catholic Relief Bill seemed to Ricketts to be 'hopeful auguries that their case might not pass unheeded'.[42] Whether or not Eurasians had received any encouragement from sympathisers in London cannot be told, but it is conceivable that Charles Wynn, who was President of the Board of Control from 1822 to 1828, may have given some favourable indication, for he had been instrumental in restoring the right of Eurasian widows to benefit from Lord Clive's Fund and had introduced the Jury Bill of 1826 to Parliament.[43]

Once Ricketts had arrived in London he found some in positions of political importance who were sympathetic to the Eurasian case. But they were outnumbered by those who were either uninterested or hostile. Attempts to put the case privately to the Duke of Wellington and Robert Peel were politely rebuffed. Meetings with the Chairmen of the Company, and more significantly with the Board of Control, brought nothing more than an undertaking to look at the detail of Eurasian legal grievances. Lord Ashley, a Commissioner of the Board of Control, who had initially showed strong support and agreed to introduce the Petition to Parliament, withdrew, perhaps under pressure from Lord Ellenborough, then the President of the Board. By February 1830 Ricketts had concluded that 'nothing in satisfactory or tangible shape was to be looked for at India House . . . that great imperial mart for lucrative patronage for India' – in which educated Eurasians wanted so much to share.[44] Success now depended on an introduction of the Petition to Parliament, and a positive reaction there.

By March 1830 the Earl of Carlisle had agreed to introduce the Petition to the House of Lords. Charles Wynn agreed to take Lord Ashley's place and warmly commended the Petition to the House of Commons. In the debate which ensued, Stuart Wortley, Secretary to the Board of Control, maintained the official line that there was no discrimination against Eurasians as such. Most speakers, however, supported the Petition. Charles Wynn argued to the House, which had relieved the civil disabilities of Roman Catholics and was about to do the same for Jews, 'that men should not be shut out from all offices of trust, simply because they derived their being from its [India's] original inhabitants'. He attacked those who argued that, since Eurasians were looked on with 'contempt' by the population of India, they must be excluded from office as having, 'first placed these individuals in a state of degradation and then to use that

Political Protest

degradation as a reason for continuing it'. Other members spoke in his support. Sir James Mackintosh termed theories of natural racial superiority, 'one race born to command and another to obey', as 'the cornerplace argument of the advocates of repression'. Cutlar Fergusson 'bore testimony to the honour of the half-caste', and maintained that before the law 'they should be equal to the European of the full blood'.[45]

When Ricketts left London on his way back to India he had achieved his object of hearings by both Houses of Parliament and had given evidence to the Select Committees of both. He also had assurances that Eurasian complaints concerning their problem as Christians liable to be judged by Muslim law in the Company's courts would be examined. On the central question, however, whether they would be accepted as 'British Subjects', the outlook was less than hopeful. During the debate on the Petition in the House of Lords, Lord Ellenborough, whose position as President of the Board of Control was crucial to Eurasian hopes, had come out strongly against Eurasian aspiration.

> It should, however, be borne in mind [he said] that the petitioners did not require an equality of civil rights, but an admission to privileges to which the native population at large were not entitled, and this they demanded notwithstanding they were the offspring of Europeans by native women.[46]

Perhaps it was unfortunate for Eurasians that their Petition coincided with Lord Ellenborough's tenure at the Board of Control, rather than that of his more sympathetic predecessor, Charles Wynn. It was just as unfortunate that Parliament was dissolved shortly after the Select Committee hearings, and that all proceedings lapsed in consequence, leaving the Company and the Board of Control free of such political pressure as there was on behalf of Eurasians.

It was whilst Ricketts was preparing to return to India in June 1830 that the Company, with unusual speed, wrote to the Bengal Government with its official response to the Petition. It made clear that first generation Eurasians, especially those who were illegitimate, were not to be treated as British subjects but as Christian Natives of India, that 'they should be on exactly the same footing, both in respect of rights and obligations as other natives of India'. As to the Eurasian claim to be admitted to covenanted service, the Company reiterated its view that whilst Indians were excluded so too would Eurasians be. It was just as adamant that Eurasians would not be exempted from the jurisdiction of their courts for if 'they were subject to a different law from the other natives of India, they would be erected into a separate and privileged order'.[47]

A few technical legal crumbs were offered to Eurasians, but only insofar as they were Christians. Special provision was made for Eurasians who died intestate in up country Bengal, although even here the Company was not prepared to depart from the custom in India of an equal division of assets amongst surviving children. It *was* conceded by the Company to be unfair that Christian defendants should be subject to the fatwas (adjudications) of Muslim law officers. In 1832 judges of the Company's courts were given the power to appoint 'respectable natives' as assessors or jurors in cases where the defendants were Christian.[48]

But, beyond this nothing was conceded by the Company. Their view had prevailed. Eurasians were 'Natives of India', not 'British Subjects'. The euphoria raised amongst the Eurasian community at Ricketts' homecoming was quickly dispelled.

*

For all that it had failed in its primary object, the Petition had found supporters both in India and London, and the renewal of the Company's charter in 1832 provided a second chance for Eurasians to urge their case. There was talk in 1831 of a further Petition. In August Ricketts chaired a meeting at Calcutta to discuss another attempt, but since there were no funds available to pay the costs of sending a representative to London, the resolve of Eurasians seemed to ebb swiftly away.[49] Suggestions that Eurasians should retain a Member of Parliament to lobby for their interests were not followed up. Nor was Ricketts' proposal that the Company should be pressed to set up training colleges in India, from which Eurasians might graduate as covenanted servants.[50]

There are several possibilities which may explain the failure of Eurasians to build on their political initiative of 1830. Eurasian society was financially weak and suffering, in common with the European community as a whole, from the consequences of the Calcutta bank failures of the time. There was little money to spare for new petitions without some hope of success. A loss of leadership seems to be another important factor. The first petition had depended on the drive and enthusiasm of John Ricketts. He was loath to return to England a second time, since it had been made clear to him that leave of absence from his job would not be granted again.[51] In 1832 he was one of the few Eurasians appointed as a civil court judge. Perhaps his appointment was convenient for the Government, for he was stationed far from Calcutta. His death in 1835 removed the one Eurasian leader with the determination necessary to push the political issue onwards. There was no-one to replace him, nor did anyone try.

Looking back twenty years later it was suggested by one contributor to the *Calcutta Review* that the chief reason for the abandonment by Eurasians of their efforts to be accepted as British was their own inertia. Government appointments were still available for Eurasians, which 'made it an easy matter to enjoy such clerkships . . . no sooner did things arrive at this state, than the East Indians became apathetic in the great work in which they had been engaged'.[52] The conclusion fitted in well with the stereotype of Eurasians as unambitious. An alternative interpretation is that there was a realistic recognition amongst Eurasians, who were dependant on the Company for their employment, of the weakness of their political position after the failure of the first petition, particularly after the Company's Charter was renewed in 1833. The terms of its renewal did indeed give them some illusory hopes of the advancement of their interests.

These hopes were sustained by the debate on the renewal of the Company's Charter which continued through 1832. Ricketts' evidence to the Select Committees of 1830 was placed before the Select Committees of 1832. Sir Alexander Johnston and others added favourable evidence on behalf of Eurasians.[53] When the Charter was eventually renewed two provisions of the Act seemed to promise some improvement in both their legal position and of higher grade employment in the Government of India.

Firstly, the establishment of a Law Commission for India, with powers to review the existing judicial system and the problems posed by the diverse ethnic and religious populations under British jurisdiction, allowed the position of Eurasians before the law to be examined afresh. As the Commission began its work in 1836, the complaints of the Eurasian community were brought to its attention.[54] Secondly, Eurasian leaders were encouraged by the declaration of clause 87 of the Charter Act that neither birth, nor religion, nor colour – the aspiration of Lord William Bentinck – would in future be counted as a bar to employment by the Company. Naturally this raised expectations amongst Eurasians that there would be greater opportunities of more responsible roles in government for them. This expectation was, however, tempered with the apprehension that since the Charter Act also finally removed the Company's control over the inflow of Britons into India, Eurasians would in future be in competition with British immigrants as well as Western educated Indians.[55]

But, whilst Parliament promised a review of the legal system in India and equality of opportunity for all whether British, Eurasian, or Indian in Government service, it left the practical interpretation and implementation to the East India Company. Secure now in the renewal of its Charter the Directors of the Company wrote swiftly in 1834 to their Government in India and gave comprehensive instructions on how the provisions of the Act were to be carried out. They announced a fundamental shift of policy towards a common judicial system for all, 'whether of Western or Eastern extraction', to be operated by the Company's courts, and urged their Government in India to start moving in that direction. As the Legal Commission started its work they recommended that it should listen to views from all sections of the British and Indian communities. In a pointed reference, however, to the East Indians' Petition of 1830 they made it clear that no-one had a prescriptive right to be heard – 'No such right belongs to those who petition the Houses of Parliament in this country'.[56]

Although the Company was determined that their courts would provide the basic judicial system in British India, and that in due course the Supreme Courts in Presidency towns would be brought within their system, they intended that 'Englishmen' – British subjects – would be tried on criminal charges broadly in accordance with the practice in Britain. No guidance was given concerning the circumstances under which a Eurasian would be judged 'English' for the purpose of criminal trial. In practice it seems that they were not if they were born to Indian mothers unmarried to their British fathers. 'If a person of mixed blood', it was explained to a Parliamentary Select Committee in 1852, 'had been educated at Eton, and afterwards at Cambridge', he would be 'treated as a native under the criminal law' in India.[57]

The Company's rejection of the Eurasian claim to be treated as British before the law may easily be interpreted as one of racial prejudice, but such a conclusion oversimplifies. British immunity from Company courts in up country Bengal was a matter of concern from early in the nineteenth century, for British indigo planters had used this exemption in many instances to coerce the Indian cultivators of their crops. The Company faced a dilemma in reconciling the essential need by the economy of Bengal for a successful indigo industry with protecting its Indian cultivators from oppression by powerful British planting interests. In the early 1830s the Company sought to redress the balance and to bring British planters within the scope of the Company's civil jurisdiction – to immense protests from the British indigo planters.[58] Their failure in the long-term to provide that protection led directly to the Bengal indigo disturbances of 1859–62.[59] Had the Company accepted Eurasian claims, the numbers of those claiming exemption from the Company's jurisdiction in up country Bengal would have risen significantly at a time when policy was clearly directed at *reducing* the exceptional privileges of British subjects before the law. Eurasian aspirations were affected by a policy consideration wider than that of their particular interest.

The Company's interpretation of clause 87 which purported to remove race, creed, and religion as a bar to Company's employment – 'it does not break down or derange the scheme of our government as conducted principally through the instrumentality of our regular servants' – brought no comfort either to Eurasians. The Directors made it clear that there was to be no special treatment for Eurasians. 'Fitness is henceforth to be the criterion of eligibility', in a new world in which British settlers were expected to compete with Eurasians and Indians for the uncovenanted appointments of which Eurasians had hitherto enjoyed a near monopoly.[60]

Any hope that Eurasians may have entertained that the Charter Act of 1833 would bring a new prospect of greater employment and acceptance were to prove misplaced. 1833, as far as educated Eurasians were concerned, marked the end of an era of special protection and the start of a new in which they were to be in direct competition for Government employment with an increasing number of Western educated Indians and a rising inflow of Britons. Between 1830 and 1859 the non official British population of British India increased fivefold from just over 2,000 to around 10,000. The value of an educated Eurasian work force to Government was effectively marginalised. Little, if anything, was achieved by their Petition of 1830, nor was to flow from the liberal sentiments of the Charter Act of 1833.

Aftermath

It took time for the visible effects of new British policy to show through. During the 1830s and 1840s the occupational profile of educated Eurasians looked much as it always had done. Most of those living in Calcutta still worked as clerks in Government or in legal and business offices. Schoolteaching was now a larger source of employment. A few Eurasian men obtained commissions in the Company's regular Army.[1] Wale Byrn's sons were accepted, and so too was James, the illegitimate son of Sir Charles Metcalfe. Although officially not eligible as a first generation Eurasian, he was nevertheless commissioned into the Bengal Regiment.[2] But cases such as these were exceptions to the general rule and depended on fathers able to exert considerable influence. No Eurasians, nor Indians, were appointed to the covenanted civil service, a wholly British preserve until competitive examinations were introduced in 1855 – and only a very few for many years thereafter.

After 1830 Indians continued to make headway in the senior ranks of the Bengal uncovenanted civil service, in which the appointments of Deputy Collector and Sadr Amin (civil court judge) carried important responsibilities and higher salaries. In February 1832 twenty-three Sadr Amins were appointed, of whom only four can be identified as Eurasians.[3] The case of the Eurasian, George Meyer, who was turned down for such an appointment in that year suggests that positive discrimination against Eurasians for such posts already existed. It was reported that 'it is no secret that members of government here were directed in their rejection of East Indian candidates, by instructions from Lord William [Bentinck].[4] Bentinck's policy of involving Indians in the government of their own country was supported by the emphasis given in the Company's despatch of 1834 to the need to provide education for 'natives of full-blood' to enable them to compete more successfully.

Aftermath

By the 1840s many more appointments as Deputy Collectors and Sadr Amins were available in Bengal, and most were occupied by Indians. Two in three of the Deputy Collectors and virtually all the Sadr Amins were Indians, although the posts were theoretically open to Britons and Eurasians.[5] It was possible nevertheless for Eurasians of talent to rise through the ranks of the uncovenanted civil service to very responsible positions. George Kellner became Military Accountant General before his knighthood and appointment as Financial Commissioner for Cyprus. At Bombay, Charles Forjett, the son of an Army officer who served at Seringapatam, rose from assistant surveyor to Sadr Amin, and distinguished himself as Commissioner for Police in 1857.[6] Nevertheless, educated Eurasians were convinced that they were discriminated against, claiming in a Memorial to Parliament of 1853 that, 'the door to preferment is literally closed against your memorialists' countrymen, while many of them are perfectly qualified to fill them'.[7]

Just as in the 1820s 'lack of respect' for Eurasians by Indians had been pressed into service as a convenient post hoc rationalisation for their exclusion from covenanted service in 1791, so from the 1830s it served to justify their under representation in the new higher levels of uncovenanted Government service. By the 1850s such a belief was ingrained in the British view of Eurasians. William Bird, who had acted as Governor-General in 1844, told the Select Committee of 1852 that few Eurasians had been appointed civil court judges, not for reasons of 'incompetency', but because in general they were 'not respected either by the natives or Europeans'.[8]

Practical considerations, as well as a flattering reaffirmation of British self-belief that *they* were respected by Indians, doubtless influenced the policy which discriminated against Eurasians. Indians preferred to be tried by and have their civil suits determined by men of their own race, and the ambition of Western educated Indians to exclude Eurasians from competition for desirable Government appointments may have provided British ears with an acceptable message of lack of respect for Eurasians. The economic argument counted too, for Eurasians, though less expensive than imported Britons, were more expensive to employ than Indians. At an even deeper level, though by the 1830s British rule in India seemed more secure than at any previous time, there was still concern at its shallow roots amongst the Indian population. To Charles Metcalfe's observation in 1829 that, 'We are to all appearance more powerful in India now than ever we were. Nevertheless our downfall may be short work', Governor-General William Bentinck noted, 'This is very possible'.[9] He saw the advantage in building an Indian cadre strongly linked to British rule through its education and government employment, withdrew financial support from any 'College or School of Native learning' and gave wholehearted backing to the allocation of educational funds to English language schools for Indians.[10] When Thomas Macaulay described in his Minute on Education the intent of his educational policy to create, 'a class who may be interpreters between us and the millions we govern – a class of persons Indian in blood and colour, but English in taste, in opinions, in morals and intellect', he had Bentinck's entire concurrence.[11] Though the educated Eurasians of British India and the role which they had fulfilled for the last fifty years fitted precisely with Macaulay's description of the class which he sought to create, it was not to them whom he referred. 'Natives of the full-blood', as they were termed, would provide the administrative arm of British Government in the future. For the last fifty years Eurasians had not been British enough. After 1835 they were not Indian enough.

By the later years of the nineteenth century the hold of Eurasians on even mid level Government employment was weakening fast. Between 1870 and 1890 the numbers of Eurasians in Calcutta with Government posts paying between Rs 100 and Rs 300 a month fell from 101 to 65, whilst those posts held by Indians rose from 120 to 191.[12] Eurasians, nevertheless, continued to depend substantially on occupation in the public sector for their livelihoods. Fortunately for them the new technology of the mid nineteenth century brought a source of employment for many of the better educated. Steam power on India's rivers [one of John Ricketts' sons, John Andrew, was for many years the Secretary of the Steam Navigation Company]; the post and telegraphic services [Brendish and Pilkington were the Eurasian telegraphists who signalled the arrival of the rebellious sepoys at Delhi in 1857]; and above all the railways which employed many as inspectors, drivers, firemen, guards and station masters, took the place of the government clerkships which had sustained the Eurasians of the late eighteenth and early nineteenth centuries. Thus there were many Eurasians who held on to their 'middle class' status through to the twentieth century. The Stark and Madge families, established in Calcutta since the late eighteenth century, were representative of those employed in the postal service, as headmasters, in mechanical engineering, library work, the missions, and who might even serve as magistrates.[13]

Yet, for the majority of the Eurasian population the problems of education and employment, already so evident in the early nineteenth century, persisted throughout its course despite the efforts of Bishop Cotton and Sir Henry Lawrence in particular to bring greater educational opportunity to a higher proportion of the poorer sector.[14] Reports into the community's social and economic situation in Calcutta first in 1891 and again in 1919 revealed the vast scale of the problem for poor Eurasians and the failure of previous attempts to alleviate it.[15] Their findings noted the relatively small but respectable and comparatively well off sector at the head of what was now officially termed the Anglo-Indian community, but vividly described the plight of the majority with little or no education, largely unemployed and unwanted by employers, making a living as best they could whilst living in deplorable conditions. John Ricketts' vision one hundred years earlier of 'a large and redundant Eurasian population out of employ . . .' sadly had been prophetic.

★

The Eurasians of British India were only one, albeit one of the most numerous, of the populations of mixed race which were the inevitable and enduring legacy of European colonial intervention in several continents around the world. Whether in the Americas, Africa, India, Asia or the Pacific these populations, though geographically far distant, shared common characteristics.[16] They were in general highly dependant on the colonial power, and often used as an intermediate group to serve colonial government. Typically colonial regimes, whether in Asia or the Americas, tended to exclude their domiciled descendants, 'white' or 'mixed', from the levers of power, wealth and control which were jealously retained by authorities of the parent country. Governors came out from Europe and returned there at the conclusion of their term of office.[17]

A general observation which may be made of colonial societies is that mixed race populations sprang from and were often the victims of a system which, for a variety of reasons, made little provision to their men of wives from their own race. Children of mixed race were the inevitable consequence of local relationships which, though generally tolerated, were nevertheless officially irregular, and which compromised a public code of male behaviour which could never be sustained. Once travel to India became easier in the later nineteenth century and greater numbers of British women were prepared to come to India to marry, so toleration of deviation from the approved code of public behaviour there diminished. British civil servants who married local women in the later nineteenth century were liable to transfer or to be passed over for promotion.[18]

Eurasian populations were the living evidence to colonial whites of the distressing frailty of their men. They undermined, in the most public manner possible, concepts of colonial rule which depended ultimately on maintaining the illusion of the racial superiority of white European males. The consequent dilemma for Eurasian populations was how they might identify fully with their parent colonial societies, on which they were economically dependant and to which they were culturally bound. They shared in what has been termed the 'imagined community of nationalism' as fully as their European fathers and forefathers, but were denied participation on equal terms.[19] In turn the predicament of colonial authority was how far should it go in acknowledging its children of mixed race. In practice it seems that there was an uneasy compromise in colonial societies between disavowal and acceptance. Parental responsibility and considerations of Eurasian utility to the regime were in tension with concepts of Eurasian political unreliability and the damage which full acceptance might be thought to do to perceptions of white prestige. The racial rhetoric and the stereotyping of Eurasians as morally and behaviourally inferior to Europeans which was so common in colonial societies was no doubt an overt expression of the supposed superiority of character and quality of Europeans. It may well be thought also to have been prompted by a European wish to distance themselves as far as possible from the public consequences of their private behaviour.

The years between 1773 and 1833 were a period of social as well as political transition for the British in India. The easygoing attitudes towards the cohabitation of British men with Indian women, so prevalent in the eighteenth century, gave way to public condemnation of anything other than marriage to British women. Though the British of the early nineteenth century in India conformed to a greater degree to the new morality, the fundamental problem of the imbalance in numbers between British men and women remained unresolved. By the 1830s the better off in British society were more likely to marry British women. But for the majority of British colonials no such option was open. Few British soldiers had British wives. The moral casuistry of the condemnatory rhetoric of their consequent behaviour is in itself remarkable; so too was the propensity by officialdom to shift the blame on to 'the women of the country who communicate "this bitter scourge of unlawful embraces"', for the prevalence of venereal disease amongst the army rank and file.[20]

The practical consequences of the moral guilt implicit in British failure to live up to their public ideals was commonly transferred to their Eurasian children. As early as 1789 Captain Innes Munro recommended, 'a swingeing tax upon all who come under the denomination of mulattoes, or, as they are called in the East Indies, "half-casts"'.[21] By 1823 the *East India Military Calendar* solemnly averred that:

> Experience has proved that every father of illegitimate offspring is subject to great expences [sic] on their account . . . It will occur to the experience of such unfortunate parents, that no race possesses more ambition, or greater turn for personal indulgence than these Indo-Britons.[22]

★

Whilst the racial ambiguity of the Eurasians in British India, neither fully British nor fully Indian, was at the heart of their problems in British society, economic factors contributed to the deterioration of their social position in the early nineteenth century. The society, of which they were recognised, albeit grudgingly, as members was itself a small, artificial and relatively self sufficient implant in India. Not many Britons, whatever their aspirations, achieved great wealth. Only upper civil servants, senior military officers, professionals, and commercials with access to capital and lines of credit could hope to return to Britain with more than a modest competency at the end of their years in India. The exclusion of Eurasians from covenanted civil service denied their elite one major potential source of wealth. The competition from British commercials and professionals who entered India in ever increasing numbers after 1813 cut Eurasians off from the other.

Educated Eurasians of the day, and Anglo-Indian historians since, have held the East India Company's policies primarily responsible for the limits which were placed on Eurasian opportunity, and for the extent of poverty amongst their community. Eurasians of the calibre of Ricketts, Byrn, Kyd, Skinner and others clearly had the ability to fulfil roles well beyond those allowed them. The gap between their aspirations and the possibilities within the system was immense, and the Company had little mind to close it. But the premise on which the Company's policy was based, that whether they liked it or not, Eurasians *were* 'Natives of India', made the grant to them of British privileges inexpedient, the more so once Indians had begun to be readmitted to responsible roles in Government service from the 1820s. Special Eurasian interests were not allowed to stand in the way of a new policy designed to build an Indian cadre supportive of British rule. That resolve was in no way shaken, perhaps even reinforced, by the Eurasian political agitation which led to their Petition of 1830, and which failed even to preserve their hitherto protected position in Government service.

The Eurasian problem in British India was one of class as much as race. That problem was present from the moment British soldiers were stationed in India. Most Eurasians were the children of fathers who, in Britain, would have left the fields to work in factories and for a life in the dreadful slums of her industrial towns and cities. In assessing official policy towards Eurasians in India the class attitudes of the time need to be borne in mind. The early nineteenth century has rightly been described as a time in Britain for the working classes in which, "The people were subject simultaneously to two intolerable forms of relationship: those of economic and of political repression'.[23] In India the acceptance of some degree of parental and racial obligation, spurred on by the more mundane considerations of social order and British prestige, promoted the development of free schools, orphanages, and attempts to find employment in later life suitable to the class of Eurasian children. Although the Company hoped at first that the local British community would bear the costs, its financial involvement grew as the need expanded and once it was clear that private charity could not cope with the rising numbers of destitute children of British fathers and Indian mothers. For this credit must be granted, perhaps not so much to the Directors in London, as to their servants in India to whom the social problem was so evident and who pressed for additional funds to alleviate it.

The greatest problem of all arose from the inability of British society in India to provide jobs in adult life for all Eurasians. A Government machine which expanded in line with the growth of British power in India fortuitously provided for many educated Eurasians, but the narrow confines of a self-contained British society offered inadequate scope for the many who had few skills and no advantages of birth. Though the Company's Army looked after its own, either as non combatants or as soldiers' wives, many were forced to subsist as best they could. The role of Government as primary employer of course reinforced the economic dependency of Eurasians of all classes. In that role Government served its own ends and needs, yet provided at what seemed to it an appropriate level for the Eurasian children of its employees. The unsuccessful attempts of the 1820s to diversify Eurasian employment out of Government dependency illustrate, in the general unwillingness and inability of Eurasians to venture into new fields, an established culture of dependence on British official employment. This in turn reinforced amongst educated Eurasians an attitudinal identification with the colonial regime. They were thus vulnerable to and unprepared for the greater competition which they had to face in Government service after 1833.

External circumstances rather than an internal desire forced the pace in the development of what may be described as the reluctant Eurasian, and later the Anglo-Indian, community. The poverty of many and the racial inheritance of all marked it in British eyes as a distinctive class, which at all times required some form of economic protection, even if this was felt by the community itself always to be inadequate.[24] Indeed it always *was* inadequate. Nineteenth century technology, and employment on the railways in particular later supplanted the reliance of early days on clerical employment in India. Railway cantonments largely replaced Government offices as focal points of a still protected community, but a community which was the victim of all the social, economic, and structural disadvantages common to all the mixed race descendants of the European colonial adventure, wherever it took place.

Biographical Appendix

Achmuty family

John (1772–1836), Richard (1774–1816), and James (1775–1864) were the Eurasian sons of Colonel Arthur Achmuty and his Portuguese wife, Ursula. Their father boasted that he had paid for their appointments to the Company's covenanted service. All three remained in the Company's service despite the exclusion of Eurasians after 1791. Richard retired from the civil service in 1808, John served until 1827. James rose to General Officer rank.

Barretto Family

Descended from Captain Manuel Barretto who came to India in 1505. Two of his descendants were Governors of Goa in the sixteenth century. Leaders, in the eighteenth and early nineteenth centuries, of the Calcutta Portuguese community. Owners of Barretto's, a successful agency house. Joseph and Luis endowed the new Roman Catholic Cathedral at Calcutta in 1796. Barretto funds built churches at Serampore, Dum-Dum, and contributed generously to charity relief work in Calcutta.

Brightman, Edward (1780–1833)

Son of Edward Brightman Snr. and his wife Mary. Owner of Brightman's House of Agency. Married Mary Jones in December 1803. His son, John, followed Edward into the family business. One of the original founders of the Parental Academic Institution in 1822.

Biographical Appendix

Buckingham, William (1799–1831)

Eurasian son of a British soldier, educated at the Lower Orphan School, Calcutta. Posted when 13 as a drummer to a Bengal Native Regiment. Served for several years, married, experienced physical and mental breakdown. Intended to become a mystic in the jungles of Saugor Island. Given shelter when destitute by the Baptists at Serampore. Helped there with odd jobs until started to accompany the brethren on missionary journeys. Accepted as a missionary, posted to Jessore, where served until his death in 1831.

Byrn(e), Wale (1803–1855)

Convention has it that he was 'the son of an Irishman who came out to the country and married an East Indian lady'. 'Wally' was born 7 March 1803, and was the step-brother of Colonel Byrne of HM Army. (Stark and Madge, *Worthies*, pp.36, 38). There are difficulties in the accepted account. His 'father', also Wale Byrn, a sergeant in the Artillery at Fort William married Mary Christian in 1792. The baptism of an elder sister to Wale was registered in 1793, and of younger brothers, William and Charles Frederick in 1805 and 1807 respectively. Both brothers were mentioned in Wale's will in 1842, but there appears no record of Wale's baptism in 1803. There must be speculation over Wale's relationship to Colonel John Byrne, whose widow was appointed one of the guardians of Wale's children at his death. It seems improbable that Colonel Byrne, born in 1786, was Wale's step-brother, as has been claimed. Perhaps a cousin, perhaps even his father. Educated at Farrell's School, Calcutta. Joined uncovenanted service as a draughtsman to the Chief Engineer, Bengal. Transferred to the Military Board office, rose to Head Accountant and ultimately Senior Uncovenanted Assistant to the Secretary to the Government of Bengal. Acted as Deputy Collector for Calcutta.

Active in social work. Secretary to the Calcutta CMS Association, Governor of the Free School, Secretary and Visitor to the PAI. A close colleague of John Ricketts in Eurasian communal activity. Vestry member at the Old Mission Church, Calcutta.

Well connected socially. Married twice. His relative, Colonel John Byrne, ADC to several Governors-General, assisted in the appointment of Wale's three sons to military commissions. His two daughters married covenanted civil servants.

Carey, Maria (1741–1801)

Married Peter Carey, a mariner, 1754. Described as a 'country woman'. Survived imprisonment in the Black Hole, Calcutta in 1756. A Roman Catholic of Portuguese descent. Burial entry in Calcutta Roman Catholic Cathedral Records for 28 March 1801. Plaque placed by West Bengal Government in her memory close to the sanctuary.

Carstairs, Peter (1803–1861)

Born Madras. Educated by the LMS. First employed in the Accountant General's office, Madras. Obtained contract for clothing the Madras Army. Secretary to the Madras Widows' and Orphans' Fund for twenty years. Retired to England and stood unsuccessfully for Parliament. Died at Richmond.

Da Costa, Willoughby (1785/6–1841)

No record of birth. One sister, Jane, two brothers: George and Philip, both heavily in debt to Willoughby at his death. Married Lucy Harrison, a Eurasian, May 1805 and settled Rs 30,000 on her. Supervisor, Calcutta Mint. Close friend of John Ricketts and executor of his will. Active Baptist and involved in many community affairs. Member East Indians' Petition Committee; one of the founders and a committee member of the PAI, 1824–35. Joint treasurer with Ram Mohan Ray of the Commercial and Patriotic Association, 1828.

A man of some affluence. At his death, his brother George who owed him more than Rs 22,000, was one of many debtors to his estate.

Derozio Family

A Portuguese Protestant family. Michael Derozio (1742–1809), merchant, was one of the early benefactors of the Serampore Baptists, donating Rs 1000 to the foundation of the Lal Bazaar Chapel. His son, Francis (1779–1830) was an accountant with the firm of James Scott. The family were well enough off to send one of their children to Scotland for his education, and lived comfortably in the Lower Circular Road. A family of strong musical interests.

Henry Louis Vivian Derozio (1809–1831) poet, teacher, journalist, second of the five children of Francis and his wife Sophia, was educated at Drummond's, Calcutta. Left at 16, spent a short period at his uncle's indigo factory before employment as a sub editor and contributor to the *India Gazette*. His first collection of poems was published in 1827. From 1828 until his forced resignation in 1831 taught at the Hindu College. Shortly before his death in 1831 of cholera, launched the *East Indian*, a periodical which did not survive his death. Unmarried. Buried South Park Street, Calcutta.

Dick, George Stewart and Paris

Although their births have not been traced, both brothers were Eurasian, perhaps born to one of the several members of the Dick family serving as civilians and senior army officers in Bengal at the end of the eighteenth and start of the nineteenth centuries.

George Stewart (c.1800-post 1852)

Was active in Eurasian community affairs. Married Mary Cassidy, Calcutta, September 1816. Several children. Son George Thomas, baptised December 1821, subsequently served in the Madras Army, reaching rank of Lieutenant-Colonel.

George Stewart was in business as a wine merchant and later as a general merchant in Calcutta. No mention after 1852. His grandson, George Paris Dick (1866–1941) returned to India as an advocate in 1893. Member Legislative Council; President, Anglo-Indian and Domiciled Community Association, Nagpur branch.

Paris (c.1800–?)

Even less is known. Educated in England, where he qualified as a doctor. Was in India in 1825, but returned to England soon after.

Doveton, John (1801– 1853)

Circumstances of birth obscure. Perhaps the illegitimate son of Gabriel Doveton, baptised at Vepery in June 1801. Age recorded in death certificate indicates, however, birth in 1790/91. But certainly son of one of the several Dovetons serving in the Madras Presidency at the time. Probably related to General Sir John Doveton, who commanded Hyderabad Subsidiary force in 1809–16. Educated at MMOAM. Appointed to Hyderabad Army in 1817. Rose to Captain Commandant before resignation and departure to England. Unmarried. A Baptist. Donated 4 lakhs of rupees in his will to the Parental Academic Institutions of Calcutta and Madras. A friend of Wale Byrn and Peter Carstairs.

Fenwick, Charles Augustus (1792–1852)

Illegitimate son of Captain Fenwick. Baptised July 1792 at Berhampore. Married A. Mawbey at Sylhet, July 1831. Perhaps his second marriage. Baptist missionary 1825–30 at Sylhet. In 1831 Superintendent of Buildings and Commissariat Agent at Charaponjee. Later lived at Dhurrumtollah Road, Calcutta. In 1840 Editor, *Commercial Advertiser*. At death, Moulmein 1852, described as a Pleader.

Fink, John Christopher (1796–1856)

Born Ternate 1796. At first an apothecary. Joined Lal Bazaar Baptist Church, Calcutta in 1816. Volunteered for Chittagong mission to Arakanese in 1820 with his wife Mary. Brought up 15 children there. Second son, Robert, after career as Headmaster of local school, rose to be Assistant Accountant-General of Bengal. John returned to and died in Calcutta.

Forjett, Charles (c.1805/10–90)

Son of an officer in the Madras Army. First appointed an assistant surveyor with the Bombay Government. Subsequently official translator in Marathi and Hindustani. Later head of Poona police, Principal Sadr Amin, finally Commissioner of Police, Bombay. Retired to Britain. Unrecognised for his part in forestalling spread of 1857 uprising to Bombay.

His son, F.H. Forjett, who joined the Bombay 59th Foot in 1865 was one of the few Eurasians to be commissioned.

Biographical Appendix

Forster (Foster), Lieutenant-Colonel Henry (1793–1862)

Illegitimate son of Sir Henry Pitts Forster, Master of Calcutta Mint. Served first with Marathas; joined James Skinner as adjutant and second-in-command. Raised a brigade in 1834 to suppress revolt in Rajputana. Active in first Punjab campaign 1845. Like Skinner received a Royal colonelcy. First wife, a Kellner, killed in the Delhi mutiny. Second wife an Indian. All his daughters married military officers. His sons had military careers – William married a Hearsey, Thomas reached Major-General's rank and married his cousin Anne Kellner. His son married a Skinner.

Hearsey, Hyder Yung (1782–1841)

Illegitimate son of Lieutenant-Colonel Andrew Hearsey. Educated at Woolwich after his father's death. Commissioned in Oudh army at age 16, then served with the Marathas. Joined George Thomas and after his defeat branched out on his own with a force of 5000 men. Granted a pension of Rs 800 a month on outbreak of Maratha hostilities in 1803 and served under General Lake. Subsequent employment included a survey of the Ganges through to its source, an expedition to Tibet with George Moorcroft, campaigns against the Gurkhas in 1809 and 1815.

Married Zuhur-ul-Nissa of Cambay, sister of Lieutenant-Colonel William Gardner's wife. His sons served in the army of Oudh. His daughter, Harriet, married her step-uncle, the future General Sir John Hearsey.

Imlach Family

Henry, Alexander and George were the three Eurasian sons of Colonel Henry Imlach, Military Auditor-General, Bengal. All three were baptised at Dinapore in 1794. Henry and Alexander became indigo planters at Kishnagore, where Henry was murdered in 1825. George became a surgeon and apothecary at Calcutta. He and Alexander were active in the development of the East Indians' Petition of 1830.

Jones, Lieutenant-General Sir Richard (c. 1754–1835)

Born at Bombay, parents unknown. Cadet 1771, Lieutenant-General by 1808. Commanded Bombay Army during the Maratha campaigns of 1803–5. Took important part in storming of Bhurtpore. Retired to England and died at Worthing.

Kellner, Sir George Walsh (1825–86)

Son of Francis Daniel and descendant of Lieutenant Paul Kellner of the Wurtemburg Regiment. Educated at the PAI, Calcutta. Entered Government service as a clerk in 1841. Inspector-General of Accounts 1866–70; Military Accountant General 1871–7; Financial Commissioner and Member of Council, Cyprus 1878–83; Assistant Paymaster-General 1884.

Kirkpatrick, William Benjamin (1807–65)

Son of James, a marine pensioner and Sarah, born Calcutta Educated at BBI. Became Baptist minister 1824, Headmaster PAI 1829. In 1834 temporary teacher at BBI. Editor *Orient Pearl* magazine 1835. By 1845 Deputy Register, Sadr Diwani Adalat at Rs 600 a month. Returned to teaching in 1852 at St. Paul's School. Four years later Lecturer in Law and Political Economy at the Hindu College.

Active in Baptist affairs in Calcutta and a supporter of the East Indians' Petition of 1830. Married twice.

Kyd(d) (Kidd), James (1786–1836)

Wealthiest Eurasian of his time. One of three known illegitimate sons of Lieutenant-General Alexander Kyd. Educated England. From 1807 master ship builder to the Company at Calcutta. Inherited considerable wealth from his father. Between 1808 and 1835 built over twenty-five vessels for the Company, including the only line of battle ship built at Calcutta.

An active citizen of Calcutta. Member of Asiatic Society. Highly regarded for his philanthropic and charitable activities. Secretary to Calcutta Apprenticing Society. Did not marry and Kidderpore dockyard was sold on his death. Left personal property of Rs 92,000 and three houses in fashionable areas of Calcutta. The first instalment of the sale price for the dockyard added a further Rs 94,000 to his estate. Left a major legacy to Mary Kyd, whom he recognised as his daughter in 1836.

Linstedt Family

Frederick (1791–1833) and Charles (1788–1844) were the sons of Lieutenant William Linstedt and his wife, Rosalie. Frederick owned and ran the Calcutta Academy, and was a Trustee of the Old Mission Church Evangelical Fund. Charles became Deputy Register of the Military Department, Calcutta and was a committee member of the PAI 1825–1835.

Lorimer, James Augustus (1809–1837)

Baptised Calcutta. Son of Alexander Lorimer, an indigo planter at Jessore, and his wife Eliza. Educated with his brother at the PAI. Joined teaching staff as Head Monitor. Rose to joint Headmaster 1831. Sole Headmaster at death in 1837. Believed unmarried.

Madge Family

Descended from Major Thomas and Captain E.H. Madge who served in Madras in the late 1770s. Until 1912 the family owned property in Madge Lane, Calcutta, off Chowringhee. Elliott Walter Madge (1866–1913) was educated at Mussoorie and the Doveton College, successor to the PAI. After employment at the Government Treasury appointed Superintendent of Reading Rooms at the Imperial Library (now the National Library), Calcutta. The son of W.C. Madge, who had been educated at Edinburgh and was a magistrate. The grandson of D.W. Madge, also a magistrate, Superintendent of the Board of Revenue, and a Governor of the Calcutta Free School.

Members of the Madge family were living in Calcutta up until 1952, perhaps later.

Martindell, Henry Gabriel (1811–1844)

Son of Henry and Eliza Martindell, grandson of Lieutenant-General Sir Gabriel Martindell. Attorney. Married Louisa Richards who died at age 20 in 1840. Lived at Elysium Row (nr. Park Street) Calcutta. Employed as Secretary, Military Widows'

Fund and as an accountant and auditor in the Military Auditor General's Office.

Masters, William (1804–68)

Son of William, a soldier with HM Royal Irish Light Dragoons, and wife Charity. A British subject. Educated after mother's death at Farrell's Academy. First Headmaster PAI 1824–28. Headmaster Verulam Academy subsequently. First Headmaster La Martinière, Calcutta, 1836–44, at a salary of Rs 600 a month. Married Caroline Louisa Crow, a second generation Eurasian, 1836. Teacher at Hindu College, 1853. From 1860 Headmaster Government College, Kishnagur. At time of death Professor of Mathematics. Ancestor of William Masters, the twentieth century novelist.

Sir Charles Metcalfe's Sons

Charles Metcalfe had three sons by a Sikh lady from Ranjit Singh's court, with whom he lived for at least 8 years. All three sons were sent to England into the care of Metcalfe's younger sister. Henry Studholme, the eldest, returned to Calcutta, was in business there, but shot himself in 1840. The second, Frank, disappeared somewhere in India at about this time. The third, James, was born in 1817, educated in London and admitted as a military cadet to Addiscombe. His father endorsed his application as a 'ward'. (*Cadet Papers*, L/MIL/9/180, pp. 524–34, IOR). James was commissioned into the Bengal regiment in 1836 and retired as a Lieutenant-Colonel. Metcalfe acknowledged James as his son in his will, and left him £50,000.

Montague, Charles Jeffs Stephen (1815–57)

Son of Charles Montague, a Matross of Artillery at Fort William, Calcutta, and his wife Rosa. Joined PAI as Third Assistant Teacher in 1832. Headmaster PAI 1838–45. Died en route to England 1857.

Nairne, Major Robert (1763/4–1803)

Born Bencoolen. Reputed natural son of Robert Nairne, sometime Second in Council there. Cadet in 1780, rose to Major with Bengal 6th Native Cavalry. Much admired by General Lake who saved his life when he attacked a tiger armed only with a spear. Lake shot the tiger. Nairne's recklessness led to his death as he led an attack near Kachaura, pressing on when he had been ordered to stand fast. Married to Ann Mercer, natural daughter of Laurence Mercer of the Bengal Civil Service. She remarried in 1817.

Palmer, William (1780–1867)

First son of Lieutenant-General William Palmer and Faissan Nissa Begum. Educated England. Entered the military service of Hyderabad in 1799. Served until 1810. His subsequent banking career at Hyderabad achieved spectacular success until the withdrawal of British support in 1820. Ceased trading as insolvent in 1825. Died in 1867 still trying to recover his debts.

Seven children, all born of Muslims. Last wife was the English widow of Captain Desormieux. His daughters all married British army officers. Two of his sons served in the Hyderabad army, two in the Madras Native Infantry.

Pote, Charles (1794–1859)

One of the Eurasian children of Edward Pote, Resident at Patna, whose collection of oriental manuscripts is housed at Kings College Library, Cambridge. Educated at Drummond's, Calcutta. Worked in London as an engraver. On return to Calcutta employed as a drawing master and practised as a miniaturist and portrait painter. Commissioned for portraits of Sir Charles Metcalfe, David Hare, and John Ricketts. Later employed as Superintendent of the Howrah Custom House. Finally headmaster of the Dacca Pogose School, where he painted the altar piece for the Armenian Church. Believed not to have married. An active member of the East Indians' Petition committee.

Ricketts, John William (1791–1835)

Son of Lieutenant John Henry Ricketts and Bibi Zenut Ricketts. Nephew of Vice-Admiral Sir Robert Ricketts. Placed in the Upper Military Orphanage, Calcutta after his father's death at Seringapatam in 1792. Sent to Amboyna as a clerk where he fathered an illegitimate daughter, Amelia. Decided to become a Baptist missionary. Closely involved with the

Serampore cause all his life. Ill health caused his return to Calcutta and a career in the Board of Customs. The prime mover of Eurasian social and educational and political activity in the 1820s, and the representative for the Parliamentary Petition of 1830. Appointed a civil court judge on his return to India and was Principal Sadr Amin at Gaya at his death.

Survived by his wife Sarah, believed to be the Eurasian daughter of a British surgeon, six of his seven sons and two daughters.

Rochford (Rochfort), Marcus (c.1800-post 1846)

Birth untraced. Perhaps a son of Captain Gustavus Rochfort of HM 67th Regiment, serving in Calcutta c.1806. Teacher at Upper Military Academy, Calcutta. Headmaster PAI, Calcutta, 1829–30. Married Mary Ann Hedges, Calcutta, 1830. In 1835 listed as a teacher at the Madrassa, Calcutta. Between 1842 and 1847 first Headmaster and later Professor of Literature at Mahommed Mohsen School, Hooghly. No longer listed as a Calcutta resident by 1847.

Skinner, Lieutenant-Colonel James (Sikander) (1778–1841)

Of Scottish descent. Son of Captain Hercules Skinner and 'Jenny', believed to have been a Rajput. Educated at the Military Orphanage, Calcutta. Entered Maratha service in the early 1790s. Dismissed with other officers of British descent, despite able service, in 1803 and recruited by General Lake to form an irregular cavalry corps. Continued in British service until his death. Last active appointment was as Brigadier in 1838. Appointed in 1827 to a Royal commission and Commander of the Bath.

Sombre, David Ochterlony Dyce (1808–1851)

Great grandson of the mercenary, Walter Rheinhardt. Adopted by the Begum Sumru, from whom he inherited £500,000 in 1836. Went to England, married Mary Anne Jarvis, daughter of 2nd Viscount St.Vincent on whom he settled £133,000. Elected to Parliament 1841 but unseated for bribery. Committed by his wife for insanity but fled to Continent. His heirs, wife and two sisters, successfully had his will, donating his fortune to the Company to finance a college at Sirdhana, set aside.

Stark Family

Settled in Calcutta from the end of the eighteenth century. Herbert Alick Stark (1864–1938), the first historian of the Eurasian community in India, made his career in the Bengal educational service, rising to Inspector of European Schools, Bengal. A fellow of the University of Calcutta, member of the Bengal Legislative Council, and active in community affairs.

His father was Registrar of the Railway Board, Simla, and grandfather a Headmaster with the CMS. The third of fourteen children.

Stevenson (Stephenson), Major-General Sir Robert (c.1768–1839)

Parents unknown. Appointed Bengal cadet 1783. At one time Quarter Master General, reached rank of Major-General. Commanding at Cawnpore in 1833. Served with Bengal Native Infantry. Believed not to have married but had at least one illegitimate daughter, born of a Malay.

Thompson, John (c.1790–1840)

Clerk in Military Auditor-General's office before baptism in 1811. Appointed to Baptist mission, Delhi in 1812 and served there until his death. Survived by widow, Sarah, and two daughters killed at Delhi in the sepoy revolt of 1857.

Turing Family

Established in the Madras Presidency by Dr. Robert Turing who became Presidency surgeon at Fort St. George. Numbers of his descendants were employed in the eighteenth and early nineteenth centuries in the Company's civil and military service. The John Turing who was rejected in 1791 as a writer was born at Chingleput in 1778 of an unnamed Indian mother. His father, William, who left him 2000 pagodas in 1780, was a Company civil servant. John's namesake and relation (perhaps a cousin), John Turing, appointed a writer in 1795 and who served until 1808, was the legitimate son of John Turing and his wife Mary, also a descendant of Dr. Robert Turing.

Walters, George Hopkins (c. 1777–c. 1827)

One of the two Eurasian sons of Dr. Hopkins Walters, one time physician to Asuf-ud-Daula at Lucknow. Both brothers were educated in England by relatives as their father died on the journey back. George was commissioned in the Dragoons before returning to India on half pay in 1808. After losing all his goods in a fire he came via Cawnpore to Lucknow. His involvement in a public fracas led the Resident initially to oppose his right to reside.

Married a Mrs. Whearty and ran a 'Europe shop' at Lucknow. Their daughter converted to Islam to become a consort of the King of Oudh. After Walters' death, Mrs. Whearty went to live with one of the King's Indian servants. When her daughter fell out of favour at Court she went to live with her mother.

Weston, Charles (1731–1810)

Illegitimate son of the Recorder of Calcutta. Surgeon's apprentice and friend of John Holwell, zemindar of Calcutta, who gave him capital to start his business. Won the 1791 Calcutta Lottery's main prize of Tiretta's Bazaar which gave him a monthly income of Rs 3500. Invested shrewdly in property around Lal Bazaar. Lived in style, leaving over 5 lakhs of rupees, four houses, many paintings, much furniture and silver. A man of musical and literary tastes.

A committed Christian. As Parish clerk of St. John's active in poor relief. Known for his personal generosity. Left Rs 100,000 as a charitable fund to be administered by St. John's. Twice married, to Amelia and then Constantia, both probably Eurasians. Six known children. His largesse in life was matched by generosity in death with a long list of bequests to friends and dependents. His debtors were a wide cross section of Calcutta society, British as well as Eurasian. Buried in South Park Street, Calcutta.

Notes

Preface

1 Since many light-skinned Anglo-Indians classified themselves as British rather than Anglo-Indian the Census authorities concluded that actual numbers seriously understated the Anglo-Indian population. They estimated that Anglo-Indians numbered 168,400 and British subjects 125,500. *Census of India, 1931*, (Delhi, 1933), I:1, pp.425–429.
2 A. Mukhtar, *Non Gazetted Railway Services*, (Government of India Press, 1946), pp.6–7, 23–25, 35–42.
3 *Report of the Calcutta Domiciled Community Enquiry Committee, 1918–19*, (Calcutta, 1920).
4 Although K. Ballhatchet's *Race, Sex and Class under the Raj*, (London, 1980) does not deal extensively with Eurasians as such, it is relevant to the social context and attitudes of the wider British community within which the Eurasian community developed. So too is S.C. Ghosh, *The Social Condition of the British Community in Bengal*, (Leiden, 1970). Chapter Four treats specifically with Eurasians up until 1800.
5 H.A. Stark, *John Ricketts and his Times*, (Calcutta, 1934); *Hostages to India*, (Calcutta, 1936).
6 F.R. Anthony, *Britain's Betrayal in India*, (New Delhi, 1962); A.A. D'Souza, *Anglo-Indian Education*, (Delhi, 1976).
7 E. Abel, *The Anglo-Indian Community*, (Delhi, 1988).
8 *Census of India, 1931*, I:1, p.297.
9 Until the 1750s British soldiers in India were counted in hundreds. By 1790 their numbers in the Company and Royal Armies had risen to just over 18,000. In 1826 there were over 30,000 British soldiers in India. 'General Abstract of the Last Return of His Majesty's and the Company's European Forces in India', Feb. 1790, Home Misc/85,

p.123, IOR; W. Badenach. *Inquiry into the State of the Bengal Army*, (London, 1826), Table 1 facing p.4.

1 – British Men, Indian Women, Eurasian Children

1. Cited in O.C. Kail, *The Dutch in India*, (India, 1981), p.145.
2. M.N. Pearson, *The Portuguese in India*, (Cambridge, 1987), p.101.
3. Kail, *Dutch in India*, p.147.
4. J.J.A. Campos, *History of the Portuguese in Bengal*, (Calcutta, 1919), p.170.
5. C.R. Boxer, *Race Relations in the Portuguese Colonial Empire, 1415–1825*, (Oxford, 1963), p.64.
6. Pearson, *Portuguese in India*, p.102.
7. D. Kincaid, *British Social Life in India, 1608–1937*, (London, 1973), p.18.
8. R. Barlow and H. Yule (eds.), *The Diary of William Hedges, 1681–87*, (London, 1887), pp.78–80.
9. *Ibid.*, p.52.
10. Cited in H.D. Love, *Vestiges of Old Madras*, (London, 1913), II, p.299.
11. *Ibid.*, I, p.533.
12. Abel, *The Anglo-Indian Community*, p.13.
13. F.E. Penny, *The Church in Madras*, (London, 1904), I, p.72.
14. J.T. Wheeler, *Early Records of British India*, (Calcutta, 1878), pp.69, 75–76.
15. Ghosh, *Social Condition*, pp.58–61; 'Statement of Expence (sic) etc.' 1829, Frederick Papers, MSS EUR D 765 920, p.129; 'Annual Statement for the Bengal Army 1828/9, Military Statements, L/MIL/8/37, IOR.
16. Bengal Wills, 1780–5, L/AG/34/29/4–5, IOR.
17. E.W. Madge, 'Baptisms in Calcutta, 1767–77; 1778–82, *Bengal Past and Present*, 1923, XXV, pp.131–55; XXVI, pp.142–68.
18. W. Tennant, *Indian Recreations*, (London, 1803), I, p.79.
19. Letter to a family friend, 1 Sept. 1770, James Rennell Papers, Home Misc./765, p.206, IOR.
20. T. Williamson, *The East India Vade-Mecum*, (London, 1810), pp.414–15.
21. Letter from Surgeon John Stewart, Cawnpore, Feb. 1785, cited in Z.Yalland, *Traders and Nabobs*, (Salisbury, 1987), p.53.
22. L. Stone, *Road to Divorce, England, 1530–1857*, (Oxford, 1990), Table 10:1, p.432.
23. The baptisms of John and Mary in 1774 and 1777 respectively are

Notes

noted in Madge, 'Baptisms in Calcutta, 1767–77'. Bristow married Emma Wrangham in 1782.

24 Z. Yalland, *A Guide to the Kacheri Cemetery etc.*, (Putney, 1983), p.6.
25 Will of Major Thomas Naylor, 1782, Bengal Wills 1780–3, L/AG/34/29/4, IOR.
26 T.O. Dunn, 'An Anglo-Indian Romance', *Calcutta Review*, 295, Jan. 1919, pp.56–71.
27 Williamson, *Vade-Mecum*, I, p.413.
28 N. Saroop, *A Squire of Hindoostan*, (New Delhi, 1983), pp.24–5.
29 Will of Major Samuel Kilpatrick, 1781, Bengal Wills 1780–3, L/AG/34/29/4, IOR.
30 Will of Major-General Claude Martin, Wellesley Papers, ADD MSS 13863, BL.
31 Will of Lieutenant Robert Grant, 1780, Bengal Wills, 1780–3, L/AG/34/29/4, IOR. Grant's will recounts in detail the poignant story of Zeenut, his girl from Patna. He bought her whilst he was ADC to the Nawab of Oudh. Falling ill Grant set off for the sea air of the coast. Zeenut insisted on travelling with him though she was recovering from a miscarriage and was with difficulty persuaded to wait for his return at Patna. He died at Chittagong, leaving her the interest on Rs 7000 for life.
32 Cited in A.F. Stuart, 'Some Notes on the Position of Early Eurasians', *The Asiatic Quarterly Review*, July 1913, p.94.
33 Cited in P. Penner and R. Dale (eds.), *The Rebel Bureaucrat – Frederick John Shore*, (Delhi, 1983), p.206.
34 Yalland, *Traders and Nabobs*, p.89.
35 There were *no* officers above the rank of Lieutenant-Colonel in the Bombay Army of 1784. 'Numbers of Officers in the Bengal and Bombay Armies, 1784', Home Misc./H 363, p.213, IOR; Badenach, *State of the Bengal Army*, Note to Table 1, facing p.4, p.32.
36 *Alexander's East India Magazine*, 1831, I:2, p.55.
37 R. Callahan, 'Cornwallis and the Indian Army, 1786–97', *Military Affairs*, XXXIV, 1970, pp.93–7.
38 W.H. Massey, 'Eastern Sketches or Original Letters from India, 1826–27', MSS EUR B 74, p.85, IOR.
39 I. Munro, *A Narrative of Military Operations on the Coromandel Coast* (London, 1789), pp.49, 186.
40 J. Lunt (ed.), *From Sepoy to Subedar*, (Lahore, 1873), p.24.
41 C. D'Oyly, *Tom Raw, the Griffin*, (London, 1828), p.261.
42 Will of Captain Alexander Paterson, 1785, Madras Wills, 1785–7, L/AG/34/29/187, IOR.
43 Will of Lieutenant-Colonel Humphrey Harper, 1785, *ibid.*.

Poor Relations

44 Will of Lieutenant-General Sir John Pater, 1817, Madras Wills, L/AG/34/29/217, IOR. Pater built a church at Masulipatam in memory of Sapphira's mother, Arabella, but not as suggested by A.Mudie, ['Arabella's Church', EUR MSS B 249, FL/E/2, IOR] because Arabella had been refused Christian burial. She was buried by Church of England rites in 1809, [Madras Burials, N/2/4, f.233, IOR]. When Pater died in 1817 he left two sons born after Arabella's death.
45 S. Goldbourne, (J. Macfarlane, ed.), *Hartley House, Calcutta*, (Calcutta, 1789), p.200.
46 J. Long (ed.), *Selections from the Unpublished Records of the Government of India*, (Calcutta, 1869), I, p.476.
47 Cited in Penny, *Church in Madras*, I, p.507.
48 E. Hobsbawm, *Industry and Empire*, (London, 1968), p.104.
49 'List of Military on board the ship 'The Earl of Mansfield' for Bengal, 25 Jan. 1784'; 'Francis', 8 Jan. 1785', Military Department Records, L/MIL/9/91, IOR.
50 'Return of the Ages and Sizes of the HEIC Recruits on board the "Britannia" and the "Prince William Henry"', 12 Mar.1793, Home Misc./85, p.469, IOR.
51 C. Ross (ed.), *Correspondence of Charles, Lord Cornwallis*, (London, 1859), I, p.228.
52 Massey, *'Eastern Sketches'*, p.198.
53 Fort St. George Military Consultations, 1 June 1814, Board's Collections (hereafter BC), F/4/528, No. 12769, IOR.
54 'New Arrangements for the Medical Department', Jan. 1802, BC, F/4/154, No. 2673, IOR.
55 G. Toynbee, *A Sketch of the Administration of the Hooghly District from 1795 to 1845*, (Calcutta, 1888), pp.134–5.
56 Letter from the Commander-in-Chief's Office, Calcutta, 31 Dec. 1818, Military Department Comps and Misc., L/MIL/5/376, No. 279, IOR.
57 Letter from G. Young to Lord Cornwallis, 20 Apr. 1791, War Office Out-Letters, 1789–92, WO/4/297, PRO.
58 R.K. Renford, *The Non-Official British in India to 1920*, (Delhi, 1987), p.10.
59 Letter from the Commander-in-Chief's Office, Calcutta, 31 Dec. 1818.
60 *Standing Orders of the Tenth Regiment*, (Palermo, 1815), pp.35–40.
61 Register of Marriages at Trichinopoly, 1805–42, USPG Archives, C/IND/GEN, Box 1(2), RHL.
62 Proceedings, Madras Military Proceedings, 11 May 1810, P/256/67, No. 4341, IOR.

Notes

63 'Regarding the Provision made for Women and Orphan Children left destitute on the departure of King's Regiments etc.', Military Department Comps and Misc., L/MIL/5/376, IOR.

64 'Establishment of Lock Hospitals', BC, F/4/200, No. 4502, IOR: Ballhatchett, *Race, Sex and Class*, pp.10 f..

65 C.A. Bayly, *Imperial Meridian*, (London, 1989), p.115.

66 C.H. Philips, *The East India Company, 1784–1834*, (Manchester, 1940), pp.188–91.

67 M.M. Sherwood, *The History of Little Henry and his Bearer*, (Wellington, 1815). An edifying story of a little English boy and his Indian man-servant who becomes a Christian.

68 R.G. Wallace, *Fifteen Years in India*, (London, 1822), p.34.

69 Cited in S. Kelly (ed.), *The Life of Mrs. Sherwood*, (London, 1854), p.426.

70 Bombay Public Consultations, 15 Feb. 1815, BC, F/4/503, No. 12032, IOR.

71 It was common practice in British wills for a proviso that executors were to determine whether a child born to an Indian companion within nine months of their protector's death was to be accepted as his. See: Will of James Dumoulin, 1781, Bengal Wills 1780–3, L/AG/34/29/4, IOR.

72 M.M. Sherwood, *The History of George Desmond*, (Wellington, 1821), p.189.

73 Letter from Rev. G. Walton, Salem, 25 July 1834, South India Tamil Correspondence, Box 6, Folder 4, Jacket B, LMS Records, CWM Archives, SOAS.

74 E. Roberts, *Scenes and Characteristics of Hindostan*, (London, 1835), I, p.42.

75 Wallace, *Fifteen Years*, p.138.

76 S.S. Browne, *Home Letters from India, 1828–41*, (London, 1878), p.17.

77 E.J. Thompson, *The Life of Charles, Lord Metcalfe*, (London, 1937), p.101.

78 Extracts from Bengal Wills, 1780–5, L/AG/34/29/4–5 and 1830–2, L/AG/34/29/ 46–52, IOR. By 1830–2 the proportion of civilians keeping Indian companions was much less – 12% – than of military officers –28%. The same overall pattern is apparent in Madras wills of the time.

79 Return of Baptisms for the Archdeaconry of Calcutta, 1830, Bengal Baptisms, N/1/26, IOR.

80 L. Stone, *The Family, Sex and Marriage in England 1500–1800*, (London, 1988), p.381; B.Joarder, *Prostitution in Nineteenth and Early*

Twentieth Century Calcutta, (New Delhi, 1985), p.8; 'Diary of David Sombre', M.A. Forester (ed.), *Dyce Sombre against Toup etc.*, (London, 1855), I, pp.359–368.
81. Williamson, *Vade-Mecum*, I, p.452; Return of the Number of Cadets and Writers appointed etc. 1813 to 1833, Accounts and Papers, 1833, XXVI, Paper 536, IOR; Wallace, *Fifteen Years*; p.339.
82. J. Statham, *Indian Recollections*, (London, 1832), p.39.
83. Roberts, *Scenes and Characteristics*, III, p.97.
84. J. Malcolm (K.N. Pannikar, ed.), *The Political History of India*, (London, 1826), II, pp.141–2.
85. I. Burton, *The Life of Captain Richard F. Burton*, (London, 1893), p.108.
86. *The East India Military Calendar*, (London, 1823), II, p.417.
87. R. Heber, *Narrative of a Journey through the Upper Provinces of India*, (London, 1827), I, p.42.

2 – Charity and Children in Care

1. R. Cobbe, *Bombay Church*, (London, 1766), p.105.
2. *Annual Report, 1835*, BFS, NLC.
3. Monthly Meeting of Governors, CFS, 14 May 1817, Records of St. Thomas's School, Kidderpore.
4. 'List of Gentlemen appointed to the Civil Service etc.', 1762–84, Home Misc./H 79, Part 1, IOR.
5. The fund received several valuable individual legacies. See Biographical Appendix: – Charles Weston and the Barretto family. C.Lushington, *The History, Design and Present State of the Religious, Benevolent, and Charitable Institutions founded by the British in Calcutta etc.*, (Calcutta, 1824), p.339.
6. Public Letter from Bengal, 23 June 1814, BC, F/4/458, No. 11168, IOR.
7. 'Fund for the Maintenance of the Orphans of the Company's Military Officers etc.', Home Misc./H 85, pp.49–53; Military Letter from Bengal, 25 July 1805, BC, F/4/192, No. 4311, IOR.
8. 'Memorial of the Management of the Military Orphan Society, Bengal, 1824', BC, F/4/712, No. 19454, IOR.
9. Lushington, *Calcutta Institutions*, p.259.
10. 'Return of European Officers in India', 31 Oct. 1784, Home Misc./H 363, p.213, IOR.
11. 'Destitute Orphans of King's Regiments', Military Dept. Comps and Misc., L/MIL/5/376, IOR.

Notes

12 'Sketch of the Orphan School Establishment at Alipore in 1828', BC, F/4/1240, No. 40737, IOR.
13 Cited in Kelly (ed.), *Mrs. Sherwood*, pp.433, 503.
14 'An Account of the Free School, Calcutta, Midsummer 1818', St. Thomas's School.
15 Public Letters from Bombay, 19 July 1815; 20 Dec. 1817, BC, F/4/503, No. 12032; F/4/561, No. 13788, IOR.
16 'An Account of the Free School, Calcutta, and of its Proceedings, Midsummer 1818', St. Thomas's.
17 Love, *Vestiges of Old Madras*, III, p.351; 'Rules and Regulations of the BFS', 13 May 1815, BC, F/4/503, No. 12032, IOR.
18 Penny, *Church in Madras*, I, pp.286, 349.
19 Correspondence of Rev. J. Marshman, India Missionary Papers and Correspondence, BMS Archives, IN/19A, RPC.
20 Malcolm, *Political History of India*, II, p.138.
21 R. Porter, *English Society in the Eighteenth Century*, (London, 1982), pp.165–7.
22 'Rules and Regulations of the BFS', IOR.
23 Public Letter to Bombay, 27 June 1810, BC, F/4/561, No. 13788, IOR.
24 Marshman Correspondence, RPC.
25 *Proposals for the Institution of a Free School Society in Bengal, 1789*, (Calcutta, 1796), pp.3–6.
26 Military Letter from Fort St. George, 11 Aug. 1817, BC, F/4/557, No. 13669, IOR.
27 A. Bell, *Report of the Military Male Orphan Asylum at Madras*, (London, 1812), p.22.
28 Porter, *English Society*, p.165.
29 *Annual Report, 1817*, BBI, RPC.
30 'Minute of Sir John Malcolm', 10 Oct. 1829, *Select Committee on Affairs of the East India Company, 1832*, I Public, IX, Appx.I, pp.531–41.
31 'Minutes of the Vestry at Tanjore', 20 July 1787, BC, F/4/222, No. 4871, IOR.
32 *Annual Report, 1834*, CFS, St. Thomas's.
33 'Minute of Sir John Malcolm', *Select Committee, 1832*, pp.531–41.
34 *Annual Report, 1835*, CFS, St. Thomas's.
35 Extracts from Returns of Annual Expenditure; 1810, BMOS; 1830, BFS; 1820–1, 1832–4, CFS.
36 'Rules and Regulations of the BFS', 13 May 1815, IOR.
37 'Minute of Sir John Malcolm', *Select Committee, 1832*, footnote to p.533.

38 Letter from Rev. C.W. Gericke, 31 Jan. 1792, Jodrell Papers, Photo Eur 136, IOR.
39 'Minute of Sir John Malcolm', *Select Committee, 1832*, footnote to p.533.
40 J. Cordiner, *A Voyage to India*, (Aberdeen, 1820), p.91.
41 Lushington, *Calcutta Institutions*, pp.252–54.
42 *Annual Report, 1835*, BFS, NLC.
43 A.C. Das Gupta (ed.), *Selections from the Calcutta Gazette*, (Calcutta, 1959), VI, p.5.
44 Bell, *MMOAM Report, 1812*, pp.23, 34, 106–9.
45 B.B. Misra, *The Indian Middle Classes*, (London, 1961), pp.192–3.
46 *Annual Reports, 1831, 1835*, BFS, NLC.
47 Bengal Public Consultations, 3 Sept. 1819, BC, F/4/564, No. 13862, IOR.
48 Bell, *MMOAM Report, 1812*. pp.106–9.
49 *Annual Report, 1827*, BBI, RPC.
50 Public Letter to Fort St. George, 4 Mar. 1789, BC, F/4/98, No. 2006, IOR.
51 Letter to Bombay, 31 Mar. 1756, BC, F/4/182, No. 3494, IOR.
52 *Annual Reports, 1834, 1835*, CFS, St. Thomas's.
53 'Cost of Children etc.', Frederick Papers, II, pp.129–31, IOR.
54 'Minute of Sir Thomas Munro', 15 Nov. 1824, BC, F/4/787 R, No. 21363, IOR.
55 G.D.H. Cole and R. Postgate, *The Common People, 1746–1946*, (London, 1987), p.278.

3 – Eurasian Employment: A Limited Opportunity

1 Tennant, *Recreations*, I, p.57.
2 Burton, *Life of Captain Richard Burton*, I, p.507.
3 H.R. Panckridge, *A Short History of the Bengal Club*, (Calcutta, 1927), p.9.
4 F.J. Shore, *Notes on Indian Affairs*, (London, 1837), I, p.110.
5 Military Letter from Fort St. George, 2 Jan. 1799, BC, F/4/59, No. 1312, IOR.
6 G. Valentia, *Voyages and Travels to India, Ceylon etc.*, (London, 1809), I, p.468.
7 Yalland, *Traders and Nabobs*, p.111.
8 Shore, *Notes on Indian Affairs*, I, p.119.
9 Adam Maxwell claimed he had been appointed by the Peshwa Baji Rao as his mukhtar to represent his interests to the Governor-General. The case against Maxwell was that he had fraudulently pretended he had

Notes

influence. Baji Rao paid Maxwell his fee of Rs 11,500 but later alleged he had neither appointed him nor agreed a fee. 'Asiatic Intelligence', *Asiatic Journal*, XXIV, Sept. 1837, pp.8, 46, 70.

10 Renford, *Non-Official British in India*, p.9.

11 See Biographical Appendix: James Kyd, Peter Carstairs, James Skinner and William Palmer.

12 Colonel J. Young to William Bentinck, 4 July 1830, Bentinck Correspondence, MSS EUR E 424/4, IOR. In 1835 it was decided to appoint Kyd, Radhakant Deb and Dwarkanath Tagore as additional justices of the peace for Calcutta. General Letter from Judicial Department, Fort William, 16 Nov. 1835, BC, F/4/1720, No. 69358.

13 Almost three quarters of the girls who were married out of the LOA Calcutta, between 1800 and 1818, became the wives of Company soldiers or bandsmen. Two in five were married off to Royal soldiers. All received a trousseau valued at Rs 25. Appendix to undated Memorandum, c.1819/20, Military Dept. Comps. and Misc., L/MIL/5/376, IOR.

14 Letter from Commander-in-Chief to Secretary to Government, Bengal, 31 Dec. 1818, *ibid.*.

15 Four out of five of the boys leaving the LOA between 1782 and 1820 were posted to Company regiments as bandsmen. Lushington, *Calcutta Institutions*, Appendix II, p.xlvii.

16 *Alexander's*, I, Dec. 1830–June 1831, p.204; Military Letter from Bombay, 17 Sept. 1823, BC, F/4/803, No. 21506, IOR.

17 Code of Military Regulations, 1806, V, Clothing and Dress, No. 66, Army Dress Regulations, Archives Photo No. 8204–731, NAM; W.Y. Carman, *Indian Army Uniforms under the British*, (London, 1969), pp.99–102.

18 The careers of many of the 64 boys who left the LOA in 1818 can be traced through the Bengal Baptismal, Marriage and Burial records. Most became drummers, married Indian Christians, and served with the Company's army until their death often in up country Bengal. Bengal Public Consultations, 27 Aug. 1819 – 3 Sept. 1819, IOR.

19 Military Letter from Bengal, 27 Nov. 1829, BC, F/4/1240, No. 40737, IOR.

20 H. Sharp (ed.), *Selections from Educational Records*, (Calcutta, 1920), II, pp.345–8.

21 W. Huggins, *Sketches in India*, (London, 1842), p.84. It was not until the Sepoy uprising of 1857 that Eurasian military units served in the British Army. They included the Lahore Light Horse, Peshawar Eurasian Regiment and the East Indian Regiment. Though it was

agreed that they had served well all had been disbanded by the mid-1860s.
22 'The Humble Petition of Jonathon Seville', 25 Mar. 1835, Correspondence and Notes of the Hon. F.J. Shore, Home Misc./790, IOR.
23 B.B. Misra, *The Central Administration of the East India Company, 1773–1834*, (Manchester, 1959), p.277.
24 Will of Patrick Sutherland, 1856, Bengal Wills, L/AG/34/29/94, IOR.
25 Inventory of Wale Byrn, 1855, Bengal Inventories, L/AG/34/27/156, IOR.
26 Petition of Herbert Pyefinch, 17 Nov. 1779, Petitions, Haileybury Records, J/1/9, p.277, IOR.
27 'Return of Assistants etc.', 1783, Home Misc./238, p.344, IOR.
28 *Ibid.*, p.339.
29 *Ibid.*, p.326.
30 W. Thacker and Co., *The Bengal Obituary*, (London, 1851), p.301.
31 'Grants of Several Small Pensions etc.', 1813, BC, F/4/423, No. 10383; Military Dept. Comps and Misc., 1806–19, L/MIL/3/378, IOR.
32 'Humble Memorial to Rt. Hon. Lord William Bentinck etc.', 25 Feb. 1835, BC, F/4/1593, No. 64578, IOR.
33 'Statement of the Military Board Establishment, Calcutta', 5 Apr. 1829, Frederick Papers, II, p.1, IOR.
34 'Assistants in Public Offices', *The Calcutta Annual Register and Directory, 1831*, (Calcutta, 1831), pp.339–45.
35 Public Letter from Fort St. George, 19 Nov. 1833, BC, F/4/1454, No. 57134, IOR.
36 Proceedings, Board of Revenue, Fort St. George, 10 July 1800, BC, F/4/165, No. 2829; Bengal Consultations, 29 Dec. 1820, BC, F/4/681, No. 18863, IOR.
37 Attachment, Minute of J.F. Thomas, 25 Jan. 1836, Correspondence, C Series, 1705–1860, C/IND/MADRAS 2.f.i., USPG Archives, RHL.
38 *Ibid..*
39 Military Letter from Fort St. George, 21 Oct. 1831, BC, F/4/1338, No. 531155, IOR.
40 J. Murray, *On the Topography of Meerut*, (Calcutta, 1839), p.11; TS transcript of an unknown set of Indian dress regulations, Marquess of Cambridge Papers, 8204–731, NAM.
41 D.G. Crawford, *A History of the Indian Medical Service, 1600–1913*, (London, 1914), I, p.510; II, p.118.
42 Letter from Military Department, 8 July 1823, Bombay Letters

Notes

Received, 31 Oct.–29 Dec. 1824, Correspondence with India 1803–57, L/MIL/3/1724, pp.162–3, IOR.
43 Das Gupta (ed.), *Calcutta Gazette*, VI, p.351.
44 The Engineer Institution had problems with its Eurasian boys many of whom were insubordinate and left before finishing their courses. Public Letter from Bombay, 31 May 1826, BC, F/4/959, No. 27217, IOR; 'Minute of Sir John Malcolm', 10 Oct. 1829, *Select Committee, 1832*, I Public, Appendix I, pp.513–4.
45 'Settlement of Europeans in India', *Select Committee, 1832*, General Appendix V, p.268.
46 *Calcutta Annual Register and Directory, 1831*, pp.347–77.
47 'Statutes of the Bishop's College, Calcutta', BC, F/4/767, No. 20799, IOR.
48 *Report of Proceedings connected with the East Indians' Petition to Parliament*, (Calcutta, 1831), p.48. See: Biographical Appendix – Dick Family.
49 See: Biographical Appendix – Charles Pote.
50 *Ibid*. – Linstedt Family.
51 'Annotated Register of LMS Missionaries', LMS Records, CWM Archives, SOAS.
52 Report from the Revv.Tyerman and Bennet, Mauritius, 7 Dec. 1827, Home Odds Personal, Box 12, Folder 1, p.38, LMS Records, CWM Archives, SOAS.
53 *Annual Reports of the WMS, 1814–37*, I-VI, SOAS.
54 E.D. Potts, *British Baptist Missionaries in India, 1793–1837*, (Cambridge, 1967), p.246.
55 'Missionary Buckingham', Correspondence up to March 1832, *Periodical Accounts of the Serampore Mission*, IX, pp.586, 615, RPC; See: Biographical Appendix – William Buckingham.
56 *Periodical Accounts of the Serampore Mission*, Jan-Dec 1829, IV, p.75, RPC.
57 Roberts, *Scenes and Characteristics*, III, pp.53–4.
58 See: Biographical Appendix – Imlach Family; E.Palmer, 'The Palmers of Hyderabad', MSS EUR D 443/1, IOR.
59 Huggins, *Sketches in India*, p.84.
60 Letter from 'A Mechanic who has had Apprentices', 17 Mar. 1825, *Bengal Hurkaru*.
61 Shore, *Notes on Indian Affairs*, I, p.105.
62 *Annual Report, 1813*, BBI, RPC.
63 Only fourteen of the 79 Eurasian uncovenanted civil servants employed at Madras in 1836 earned more than Rs 250 a month. 37 earned less than Rs 150. Memorandum, 1836, C/IND/MADRAS 2.f.1., USPG Archives, RHL.
64 *Alexander's*, IV, July-Dec. 1832.

65 Statham, *Indian Recollections*, p.44.
66 Inventory of Sarah Ricketts, Bengal Inventories, 1848, L/AG/34/27/142, IOR.
67 Stark, *Hostages to India*, p.130.
68 'List of East Indians', *Calcutta Annual Register and Directory, 1831*, pp.372–7.

4 – Eurasians in the Official Eye

1 Anthony, *Britain's Betrayal*, p.v.
2 D'Souza, *Anglo-Indian Education*, pp.1–14.
3 Court Book, 19 Apr. 1791, B/113, p.17, IOR.
4 H.E. Busteed, *Echoes of Old Calcutta*, (Calcutta, 2nd ed. 1888), p.73.
5 Petition of Henry Powney, 1776, Petitions, Haileybury Records, J/1/9, p.255, IOR.
6 V.C.P. Hodson, *List of Officers of the Bengal Army, 1758–1834*, (London, 1927), IV, Appendix C, p.597.
7 'Fund for the Maintenance of the Company's Military Officers etc.', Home Misc./85, pp.49–53; 'Memorial of the Military Orphan Society, Bengal', BC, F/4/712, No. 19454, IOR.
8 Bayly, *Imperial Meridian*, pp.147–55.
9 Public Letter to Fort St. George, 25 May 1798, BC, F/4/512, No. 12299, IOR.
10 E. Thompson, *Sailor's Letters etc.*, (London, 1767), I, p.10; Statham, *Indian Recollections*, p.33.
11 H. Pearson, *Memoirs of the Life and Writings of the Rev. Claudius Buchanan D.D.*, (Oxford, 1817), I, p.187.
12 D. Arnold, 'White Colonization (sic) and Labour in Nineteenth Century India', *Journal of Imperial and Commonwealth History*, XI:2, 1983, pp.133–58.
13 Ray died on his way out to India in 1766, G.F. Grand (W.K. Firminger ed.), *The Narrative of the Life of a Gentleman Long Resident in India*, (Cape of Good Hope, 1814), p.3.
14 Valentia, *Voyages and Travels*, I, p.24.
15 Military Letter from Madras, 11 Aug. 1817, and Advocate General's Opinion, BC, F/4/557, No. 13666, IOR.
16 Munro, *Narrative of Military Operations*, p.50.
17 C. Grant, *Observations on the State of Society among Asiatic Subjects of Great Britain*, (London, 1813), Note to p.181.
18 Letter from John Jebb and James Pattinson, 27 Feb. 1818, 'Settlement of Europeans in India', *Select Committee, 1832*, Gen. Appendix, V/38, pp.257 f..

Notes

19 'Arguments for transferring the Company's Military Establishment etc.', Warren Hastings Papers, ADD MSS No. 39382, p.33, BL.
20 Letter from Governor-General Cornwallis, 6 Mar. 1789, Bengal Letters Received, 1 Nov. 1788–12 Mar. 1789, E/4/47, IOR.
21 Public Letter to Bombay, 27 June 1819, 12 Nov. 1813, BC, F/4/503, No. 12035; Political Letter from Bengal, 11 June 1812, BC, F/4/401, No. 10087, IOR.
22 'Settlement of Europeans in India', *Select Committee, 1832*, Gen. Appendix, V/38, pp.257 f..
23 Roberts, *Scenes and Characteristics*, III, note to p.98.
24 *Alexander's*, V, Jan.–June 1833, pp.369–74.
25 Penner and Dale (eds.), *Frederick John Shore*, p.86.
26 S. Ghosh, *Social Condition*, pp.85–8.
27 C.C. Prinsep, *Record of the Services of the Honourable Company's Civil Servants in the Madras Presidency, 1741–1858*, (London, 1885), p.146.
28 'Return of the Numbers of Writers and Cadets appointed, 1813–1833', Parliamentary Papers, 1833, XXVI, No. 536, IOR.
29 Stark, *Hostages to India*, pp.68–75.
30 J.H. Parry and P.M. Sherlock, *A Short History of the West Indies*, (London, 1965), pp.161–8.
31 Letters from George Younge to Major-General Medows and Lord Cornwallis, 6 May 1790, War Office Out-Letters, 1789–92, WO 4/297, pp.113, 138, PRO.
32 Court Book, 25 Jan. 1792, B/114, pp.836–7, IOR.
33 Letter from Fort William, 24 Dec. 1794, A.C. Banerjee (ed.), *Fort William-India House Correspondence*, (Delhi, 1969), XX, p.493.
34 Application of Henry Haldane, 1793, Records relating to Entry into the Service, 1753–1940, L/MIL/9/108, No. 875, IOR.
35 Letter to H. Inglis, 14 July 1797, 'Correspondence of David Scott', Home Misc./730, p.82, IOR.
36 Resolution, 1 Mar. 1792, Minutes and Memoranda of General Committees etc., D/35, p.82, IOR.
37 Hodson, *Bengal Army Officers*, III, p.351, Cadet Papers, L/MIL/9/134, pp.383–5, IOR.
38 See: Biographical Appendix – Sir Charles Metcalfe's sons.
39 Ghosh, *Social Condition*, p.84.
40 Court Book, 23 and 28 Jan. 1795, B/120, pp.1004, 1008–9, IOR.
41 See: Biographical Appendix – Achmuty family; Richard Jones; Robert Nairne; Robert Stevenson.
42 C. Lushington, *Calcutta Institutions*, Appendix, p.lxvii; Letter to Major Sandys, Aug. 1804, cited in Pearson, *Memoirs of Buchanan*, I, p.300.

43 Lushington, *Calcutta Institutions*, Appendix, p.1xvii.
44 Military Letter from Bombay, 11 Mar. 1816, BC, F/4/538, No. 12948. Bombay, Bengal and Madras all insisted on the same qualifications for benefit.
45 Lushington, *Calcutta Institutions*, p.268; Letter to Fort William, 25 Feb. 1793, Reply, 27 Oct. 1793, Banerjee (ed.), *Fort William-India House Correspondence*, 1792–6, XX, p.391; Military Consultations, Fort St. George, 22 Apr. 1795, BC, F/4/211, No. 4716, IOR.
46 Military Consultations, Fort St. George, 22 Apr. 1805, *ibid.*.
47 Military Letter to Fort St. George, 7 Sept. 1808, BC, F/4/360, No. 8774, IOR.
48 Letter from Commander-in-Chief to Secretary to Government, Bengal, 31 Dec. 1818, Military Department Comps. and Misc., L/MIL/5/376, IOR.
49 Military Consultations, Fort St. George, 2 Apr. 1805, BC, F/4/211, No. 4716, IOR.
50 Secret Department, Fort St. George, 28 Oct 1824, BC, F/4/787 R, No. 21363, IOR.
51 Minute of Sir Thomas Munro, 15 Nov. 1824, *ibid.*.
52 Memorandum, undated c.1820, Military Dept. Comps. and Misc., L/MIL/5/376, IOR. The argument that Eurasians had lesser needs than Europeans which justified a lower allowance than paid to British wives of soldiers, was used to justify lower allowances for Eurasian missionaries than British, and even for a reduction to two fanams a day in 1824 for Eurasian prisoners in Madras gaol from the five fanams paid to British prisoners. Public Letter to Fort St. George, 26 May 1824, Despatches to Madras, E/4/929, pp.1007–9.
53 Military Letter from Bengal, 1 Oct. 1825, BC, F/4/1115, No. 29907, IOR.
54 Statement of Expence (sic) etc., Frederick Papers, II, pp.129–35, IOR.
55 Military Letter to Bombay, 8 Feb. 1832, Petition of East Indians, Bombay, 13 Nov. 1833, BC, F/4/1454, No. 57236, IOR.
56 Minute, 30 Oct. 1827, Minutes and Memoranda of General Committees etc., D/77, p.75, IOR. Editorial, 3 June 1828, *Bengal Hurkaru*.

5 – Towards a Reluctant Community

1 N.P. Gist and R.D. Wright, *Marginality and Identity*, (Leiden, 1970), p.15.
2 Report of a Meeting, 23 Mar. 1825, *Bengal Hurkaru*.
3 Report, 1825, *Oriental Herald*, VII, p.373.

Notes

4 Letter from 'An European', 23 Mar. 1825, *Bengal Hurkaru*.
5 Minute on Colonial Settlement, 30 May 1829, C.H. Philips, (ed.), *The Correspondence of Lord William Bentinck, 1828 – 1835*, (Manchester, 1940), I, p.209.
6 Eighth Annual Report, 1830, PAI, *Doveton College Reports*, NLC.
7 Editorial, 21 Dec. 1830, *Bengal Hurkaru*.
8 M. Banton, *Race Relations*, (London, 1967), p.314.
9 N.C. Chaudhuri, *The continent of Circe*, (London, 1965), p.123.
10 F. Bernier, A. Constable (ed.), *Travels in the Moghul Empire, 1656– 1668*, (Westminster, 1891), pp.209, 404.
11 Boxer, *Race Relations in the Portuguese Empire*, p.64.
12 L. Grandpré, *Voyage dans l'Inde et au Bengal*, (Paris, 1801), p.136.
13 J. Kindersley, *Letters from the Island of Teneriffe etc.*, (London, 1777), p.272.
14 Goldbourne, J. Macfarlane (ed.), *Hartly House*, p.204.
15 Cited in Stuart, 'Notes on Early Eurasians', *Asiatic Journal*, July 1913, p.95.
16 J.Z. Holwell, *A Genuine Narrative of the Deplorable Deaths of the English Gentlemen and others etc.*, (London, 1758), pp.29, 56; See: Biographical Appendix – Maria Carey.
17 There was concern when Colonel Gardner's Eurasian granddaughter married Mirza Unjun Sheka, a descendant of the Mughal emperor in 1835 lest some might think, 'that European ladies are willing to enter the zenana of native princes'. Roberts, *Scenes and Characteristics*, III, p.140. Mukadeera Ouleea, the daughter of George Walters, was the 'English Begam' in the zenana of the King of Oudh, much to the disgust of the traveller, Mrs F. Parkes, *Wanderings of a Pilgrim in Search of the Picturesque*, (London, 1850), I, p.83.
18 T.H. Maddock to Lord William Bentinck, Bentinck Correspondence, IOR.
19 Bengal Military Consultations, 6 Nov. 1789, BC, F/4/127, No. 2343; 'Monthly Returns of Public Patients in the Lunatic Asylum etc.', 6 Jan. 1834, Bengal Public Consultations, P/13/6, IOR; W.Ernst, *Mad Tales from the Raj*, (London, 1991), p.81.
20 Cited in Stuart, 'Notes on Early Eurasians', *Asiatic Journal*, July 1913, p.94.
21 Julius Imhoff, who died in 1788, was the step-son of Governor-General Warren Hastings. He left his sons in the care of the Calcutta banker, John Palmer. Palmer to Hastings, 21 Aug. 1802, General Correspondence, XLVII, 1801–2, Warren Hastings Papers, ADD MSS 29178, pp.254–6, BL; S.Grier, *Letters of Warren Hastings to his Wife*, (Edinburgh, 1905), p.450.

22 Heber, *Narrative of a Journey*, I, p.69.
23 Letter from Ensign A. Le Gallais to David Le Neven, 15 Nov. 1844, 8410–166–1, NAM.
24 M.W. Bellew, *Memoirs of a Griffin*, (London, 1843), I, p.165.
25 Roberts, *Scenes and Characteristics*, III, p.20.
26 Cited in Stuart, 'Notes on Early Eurasians', *Asiatic Journal*, p.96.
27 Wallace, *Fifteen Years*, p.75.
28 Bellew, *Memoirs*, I, p.130.
29 It was reported of Eurasian drummers and their wives in the 1840s that 'We have seen many a couple come to be married, who could not even make the responses to the service in English'. 'Englishwomen in Hindustan', *Calcutta Review*, IV, July–Dec. 1845, p.124.
30 Letter from 'An European', 23 Mar. 1825, *Bengal Hurkaru*.
31 Williamson, *Vade-Mecum*, I, p.457.
32 Roberts, *Scenes and Characteristics*, III, p.95.
33 Marchioness of Bute (ed.), *The Private Journal of the Marquess Hastings K.G.*, (London, 1858), I, p.295.
34 Ship launchings from Kyd's dockyard were occasions attended by fashionable society. The Governor-General, his wife, 'and almost all the beauty, rank and fashion of Calcutta' – 400 guests in all – attended the launch of the 'General Kyd' in 1813. Occasionally all did not go well. When the 'Agnes' was launched in 1829 she capsized as guns fired and 'Rule Britannia' struck up. She floated on her beam down to Coolie Bazaar, fortunately without loss of life. Thacker and Co., *Bengal Obituary*, p.242; H.D.Sandeman (ed.), *Selections from the Calcutta Gazettes* etc., (Calcutta, 1869), IV, p.337; Report, 23 Feb. 1829, *Bengal Hurkaru*.
35 P.L. Van den Berghe, *The Ethnic Phenomenon*, (New York, 1981), p.108.
36 M. Martin (ed.), *The Despatches, Minutes and Correspondence of the Marquis Wellesley K.G.*, (London, 1836), II, p.135.
37 Statham, *Indian Recollections*, p.42.
38 *Anglo-India; Social, Moral and Political etc.*, (London, 1838), II, p.135.
39 Board Minutes, 26 Dec. 1831, Box 22, p.95, LMS Records, CWM Archives, SOAS. The Society decided after the consultation to take a pragmatic approach and relate salaries to the 'need of the individual rather than the office', 5 Dec 1837, Box 25, p.266, *ibid.*.
40 Letter from Rev. J. Reid, Bellary, 15 Oct. 1831, South India Tamil Correspondence, 1817–57, Box 3, Folder 3, *ibid.*.
41 Letter from Revv. Tyerman and Bennet, Mauritius, 7 Dec. 1827, Home Odds Personal, Box 12, Folder 1, *ibid.*.
42 Letter from Rev. J.C. Thompson, Quilon, 24 Sept. 1832, *ibid.*.

Notes

43 Letter from Rev. W. Campbell, Bangalore, 24 June 1831, South India Tamil Correspondence, 1817–57, Box 3, Folder 2, *ibid..*
44 Bell, *MMOAM Report*, p.20.
45 Letter from Rev. W. Miller, Nagercoil, 15 Oct. 1832, Travancore Correspondence, 1832–8, Box 2, Folder 1, LMS Records, CWM Archives, SOAS.
46 Statham, *Indian Recollections*, p.40.
47 Huggins, *Sketches in India*, pp.82, 96.
48 Evidence of J. Sutherland, 16 Mar. 1832, *Select Committee 1832*, I Public, IX, p.120.
49 'Confessions of an Eurasian', *Anglo-India: Social, Moral and Political*, I, pp.362–414.
50 J.H. Stocqueler, *Handbook of India*, (London, 1844), pp.46–50. Stocqueler, who was a past editor of *John Bull*, a Calcutta newspaper as dismissive of Eurasian aspiration as the *Bengal Hurkaru* was sympathetic, thought Eurasians 'devoid of energy' and quite unfitted for higher Government employment.
51 Military Letter from Bengal, 31 May 1828, BC, F/4/1029, No. 28172, IOR; 'Notes from Skinner's Draft Autobiography', 1827, Papers of Colonel James Skinner, 5205–19, NAM.
52 Report, 1825, *Oriental Herald*, VII, p.351.
53 See: Biographical Appendix – Willoughby Da Costa and the Derozio family.
54 Heber, *Narrative of a Journey*, III, p.282.
55 E.A. Chatterton, *A History of the Church of England in India*, (London, 1924), p.127; 'Statutes of Bishop's College, Calcutta', BC, F/4/767, No. 20799, IOR.
56 Letter from Bishop of Calcutta, 10 Apr. 1834, *USPG Annual Report for 1834*, p.181, RHL.
57 *USPG Annual Report for 1833*, p.155; Minutes, 25 Jan. 1836, General Quarterly Meeting, Madras Diocesan Committee, C/IND/1.f.6, USPG Archives, RHL.
58 E.T. Sandys, *One Hundred and Fourty Five Years at the Old Mission Church, Calcutta*, (Calcutta, 1916), II, pp.259–60.
59 E.S. Wenger, *The Story of the Lall-Bazar (sic) Baptist Church*, (Calcutta, 1908), p.27.
60 Penny, *Church in Madras*, II, pp.259–60.
61 Of the 854 members of the Church, 1800–35, 300 were Indians, 50 Portuguese, 503 either British or Eurasian, and one an Armenian; Wenger, *Lall-Bazar Church*, Appendix I, pp.i-xliv.
62 Sandys, *Old Mission Church*, Appendix II.
63 Statham,*Indian Recollections*, pp.49, 377–8.

64 *Reports of the Calcutta Baptist Missionary Society, 1819–29*, RPC.
65 C.A. Fenwick, *Essay on the Colonization (sic) of Hindoostan by East Indians*, (Calcutta, 1828), p.79. See also Biographical Appendix – Charles Fenwick.
66 Letter from 'A Lover of Right and a Hater of Wrong', 9 Jan. 1828, *Bengal Hurkaru*.
67 H.A. Stark and E.W. Madge, *East Indian Worthies*, (Calcutta, 1892), p.6.
68 'Alphabetical Lists of European and East Indian Inhabitants', *Calcutta Annual Directory and Register, 1835*, pp.1–55. Lists the addresses of most 'respectable' Eurasians and Britons living in Calcutta and Bengal.
69 J. Pemble (ed.), *Miss Fane in India*, (Gloucester, 1985), p.19.
70 Sandeman, *Calcutta Gazettes*, V, p.473.
71 Roberts, *Scenes and Characteristics*, I, p.11.
72 J.R. Martin, 'Notes on the Medical Topography of Calcutta', V/27/62/619, p.28, IOR. Many Eurasians lived well into the Indian town of Calcutta and across the river Hooghly at Howrah; Extracts from the Topography and Vital Statistics of Calcutta, 1828–43, V/27/62/220, p.42, IOR.
73 Letter from Rev. J. Hill, Calcutta, 24 Nov. 1827, North India Bengal Correspondence, 1824–8, Box 2, Folder 3, LMS Records, CWM Archives, SOAS.
74 Military Consultations, Fort St. George, 28 Dec. 1827, BC, F/4/1115, No. 29907, IOR.
75 Letter from 'Filius Britannicus', 19 Mar. 1825, *Bengal Hurkaru*.
76 W. Arthur, *A Mission to Mysore* (London, 1847), note to p.48.
77 Report, 18 Mar. 1825, *Bengal Hurkaru*.
78 W.K. Firminger, 'Some Fresh Light on the Old Bengal Lodges', *Transactions of the Quatuor Coronati Lodge*, 2076, XVIII, 1905, pp.157–60, United Grand Lodge of England Library.
79 See: Biographical Appendix – Wale Byrn, Linstedt family, Willoughby Da Costa, John Ricketts, Edward Brightman, George Stuart Dick, Alexander Imlach, William Kirkpatrick, Imlach family, Henry Martindell, Charles Pote.
80 Hodson, *Officers of the Bengal Army*, III, p.352; Will of Bibi Zenut Ricketts, 11 June 1824, Bengal Wills, L/AG/34/29/36, IOR; Records of the Ricketts family, Mrs S.Dyson, London.
81 Letter from Jabez to William Carey, Amboyna, 21 Mar. 1814, India Missionary Correspondence, IN/27, RPC. Ricketts' daughter Amelia was living with Zenut Ricketts, her grandmother, in 1824. Her later life is not known.

Notes

82 Stark, *John Ricketts*, p.115.
83 Cited in Stark and Madge, *Worthies*, p.8.
84 Letter from Jabez to William Carey, Amboyna, 21 Mar. 1816, India Missionary Papers and Correspondence, IN/27, RPC.
85 Wenger, *Lall-Bazar Church*, pp.146–51.
86 Inventory of J.W.Ricketts, Bengal Inventories, 1826, L/AG/27/110, IOR.
87 J.W. Ricketts, *A Series of Letters*, p.vi.

6 – Eurasians Up Country and in the Indian States

1 *Census of India, 1941*, (Simla, 1943), 1:1, Table XIII, p.99.
2 See Biographical Appendix – J.T. Thompson; J.C. Fink.
3 F. Bernier, (A. Constable, ed.), *Travels in the Moghul (sic) Empire 1656–1668*, (Westminster, 1891), p.217. See also C. Grey (H.L.O. Garrett, ed.), *European Adventurers of Northern India, 1745–1849*, (Lahore, 1929), pp.2–4, for a brief account of European military in the service of the Mughals.
4 J. Grose, *A Voyage to the East Indies*, (London, 1766), I, p.79.
5 J. Pemble, *The Invasion of Nepal*, (Oxford, 1971), pp.26–7.
6 Grey, *European Adventurers*, p.212.
7 *Ibid.*, p.36; See: Biographical Appendix – Hyder Hearsey.
8 L.F. Smith, *A Sketch of the Rise, Progress, and Termination of the Regular Corps Formed and Commanded by Europeans in the Service of the Native Princes of India*, (London, 1805), p.60.
9 R.G. Burton, *A History of the Hyderabad Contingent*, (Calcutta, 1905), p.21.
10 Political Consultations, Fort William, 27 Apr. 1831, BC, F/4/1386, No. 55205, IOR.
11 India Political Consultations, 13 Mar. 1837, P/194/31, IOR.
12 'Return of Europeans and East Indians employed in the service of the Nawab of Banda etc.', Political Consultations, Fort William, 4 Feb. 1833, BC, F/4/1498, No. 58831.
13 Grey, *European Adventurers*, pp.72, 169, 224, 303, 319, 360.
14 *Ibid.*, p.303.
15 Martin, (ed.), *Wellesley Despatches*, I, pp.1–9.
16 'Extracts from Treaties with the Native Powers of India etc.', Papers Relating to Indian Affairs, W 2438, pp.1–3, IOR.
17 Smith, *Sketch of the Rise of a Regular Corps*, p.98.
18 Bengal Political Consultations, 29 Feb. 1796, Papers and Letters Relative to the affairs of Oude (sic), 1795–1797, ADD MSS 13522, pp.96–104, BL.

19 Martin, (ed.), *Wellesley Despatches*, I, p.388.
20 Bengal Political Consultations, 9 May 1823, BC, F/4/923, No. 25904, IOR.
21 Political Consultations, Fort William, 12 Nov. 1832 and 4 Feb. 1833, BC, F/4/1511, No. 59583 and F/4/1498, No. 58831, IOR.
22 R. Llewellyn-Jones, *A Fatal Friendship*, (Delhi, 1985), p.97.
23 Bengal Political Consultations, 8 Apr. 1831, P/126/27, IOR.
24 Lindsay was Head Writer of the Residency at Gwalior in 1831. He fled, when discrepancies in his accounts were discovered, to Jaipur where his brother-in-law was an army captain. When he returned reluctantly to Gwalior Lindsay was sentenced to six years imprisonment without labour or irons; Political Letter, Fort William, 4 Mar. 1831, BC, F/4/1284, No. 51541; Criminal Consultations, Fort William, 5 June 1832, BC, F/4/1402, No. 55493, IOR.
25 Bengal Political Consultations, 30 Jan. 1819, P/121/38, IOR.
26 Letter, 20 Sept. 1816, R. Strachey, 'Letters from Lucknow, 1815, 1816, 1817', MSS EUR D 514/3, pp.356-7; Political Letter from Bengal, 3 Jan. 1817, BC, F/4/601, No. 14454, IOR.
27 Proceedings, 21 Nov. 1836, India Political Proceedings, P/194/23, IOR.
28 R. Llewellyn-Jones, *Claude Martin in Early Colonial India*, (Delhi, 1992).
29 H.E. Fane, *Five Years in India*, (London 1841), I, p.232.
30 Letter, 26 Sept. 1838, Browne, *Letters from India*, p.193.
31 Letter No. 5, 5 Oct. 1806, Skinner Papers, 5205-19, NAM.
32 Political Letter to Bengal, 6 Apr. 1825, BC, F/4/916, No. 25807, IOR.
33 Bute, (ed.), *Hastings Journal*, I, pp.292-5.
34 Report, 16 Feb. 1828, *Bengal Hurkaru*.
35 Notes for draft autobiography 1828, Skinner Papers, 5205-19, NAM.
36 Letter No. 7, 12 Mar. 1811, *ibid.*.
37 Letter, 18 Aug. 1820, Papers Relating to William Gardner, 6305-56-5, pp.55-7, NAM. Skinner's fortune was hit hard by losses incurred in the Calcutta bank failures of 1831.
38 Palmer, 'The Palmers of Hyderabad', IOR; Letter to Warren Hastings, 6 July 1802, General Correspondence, Warren Hastings Papers, XX, p.240, BL.
39 W. Prinsep, 'Memoirs of William Prinsep', MSS EUR D 1160/1, pp.251-3, IOR.
40 Thacker and Co., *Bengal Obituary*, p.266.
41 'Affairs of William Palmer and Co.', Bengal Political Consultations, 7 Oct. 1825, Home Misc./743, II, p.45, IOR.

Notes

42 Letter, 13 Sept. 1822, 'Papers Relative to Certain Pecuniary Transactions of Messrs William Palmer and Co. with the Government of His Highness the Nizam', Marquess of Hastings Papers, W 2290, IV, p.182; 'Affairs of William Palmer and Co.', II, p.43, IOR.
43 R. Bingle, *The Marquess of Hastings, 1813–23*, MSS EUR C 256/2, pp.433–40, IOR. Bingle's unpublished thesis examines William Palmer's dealings in extensive detail.
44 13 Geo. III.
45 Political Letter to Bengal, 24 May 1820, Marquess of Hastings Papers, IV, p.6, IOR.
46 Thompson, *Life of Lord Metcalfe*, p.194.
47 Bingle, *Marquess of Hastings*, pp.455, 468–71, IOR.
48 Cited in Thompson, *Life of Lord Metcalfe*, p.195.
49 Affairs of William Palmer and Co., II, p.255, IOR.
50 P.M. Taylor, *The Story of My Life*, (London, 1878), p.62.
51 Bingle, *Marquess of Hastings*, p.475, IOR.
52 Affairs of William Palmer and Co., II, p.257, IOR.
53 *Ibid.*, II, p.80.
54 Z. Yazdani, *Hyderabad during the Residency of Henry Russell, 1811–1820*, (Oxford, 1976), p.123.
55 Cited in Bingle, *Marquess of Hastings*, p.452, IOR.
56 Political Letter from Bengal, 26 Feb. 1823, Marquess of Hastings Papers, IV, p.566, IOR.
57 Shore, *Notes on Indian Affairs*, I, p.108.
58 Huggins, *Sketches in India*, p.90.
59 Cited in G.H. Hodgson, *Thomas Parry, Free Merchant, 1768–1824*, (Madras, 1938), pp.183, 242–3.
60 Grey, *European Adventurers*, p.13.
61 Letter, 22 June 1820, Gardner Papers, 6305–56–5, pp.39–40, NAM.
62 Parkes, *Wanderings of a Pilgrim*, I, pp.379–85.
63 G. Beechey, 'George Duncan Beechey', Photo EUR 106, IOR.
64 Cited in Stuart, 'Notes on Early Eurasians', *Asiatic Quarterly Review*, July 1913, p.100.
65 Roberts, *Scenes and Characteristics*, II, p.145.
66 Cited in Llewellyn-Jones, *Fatal Friendship*, pp.32–3.
67 Forester (ed.), *Sombre against Toup etc.*, David Sombre (see Biographical Appendix) found that his unstable character, poor command of English, and unappealing personal habits offset the advantages that his large personal fortune would have given him in London's fashionable society.
68 India Political Proceedings, 6 Mar. 1837, P/194/31, IOR.
69 Marquess of Hastings Papers, IV, p.275, IOR.

70 H.E. Compton, *European Military Adventurers of Hindustan, 1784–1803*, (London, 1892), p.419.
71 J.B. Fraser, *Military Memoir of Lieut.-Col. James Skinner C.B. etc.*, (London, 1851), I, p.257.
72 India Political Consultations, 13 Mar. 1837, P/194/31, IOR.

7 – The Eurasian Struggle for Self-Advancement

1 Williamson, *Vade-Mecum*, II, p.175.
2 Hodson, *Bengal Army Officers*, IV, p.557.
3 Anthony, *Britain's Betrayal*, p.iv.
4 'Hyderabad, The Nizam's Contingent', *Calcutta Review*, Jan.-June 1849, XI, p.197.
5 Fenwick, *Colonization*, p.29.
6 J.W. Ricketts, *A Series of Letters*, p.44.
7 Stark, *Hostages to India*, pp.93–4.
8 Cited in Ricketts, *A Series of Letters*, p.44.
9 J. Kyd (attrib.), *Thoughts, How to Better the Conditions of Indo-Britons*, (Calcutta, 1828), p.15.
10 Fenwick, *Colonization*, p.23. See: Biographical Appendix – Charles Fenwick.
11 Stark, *John Ricketts*, p.53.
12 *Ibid.*, p.54.
13 Public Letter from Bengal, 23 Feb. 1826, BC, F/4/951, No. 26980, IOR; Das Gupta (ed.), *Calcutta Gazette*, VI, p.324; Stark, *John Ricketts*, pp.54–7; Editorial, 11 Feb. 1828, *Bengal Hurkaru*.
14 Minute of Philip Francis, 12 May 1775; Letter from John Jebb and James Pattinson, 27 Feb. 1818, *Select Committee, 1832*, VIII, pp.181, 259.
15 Grant, *Observations on the State of Society*, p.181.
16 Evidence of Sir Alexander Johnston, 6 July 1832, *Select Committee, 1832*, IV, Judicial, XII, p.182.
17 D.G. Crawford, *A History of the Indian Medical Service, 1600–1913*, (London, 1914), II, p.468. The plan, which envisaged that the sons of officers would be allocated 100 acres each and other ranks 50 acres, was not accepted.
18 Badenach, *State of the Bengal Army*, note to p.28.
19 Minutes by W. Bentinck on European Settlement, 30 May 1829, and by C. Metcalfe on the Future Government of India, 11 Oct. 1829, cited in Philips (ed.), *Bentinck Correspondence*, pp.211, 316.
20 General Letter to Bengal Government, 30 June 1830, *Select Committee, 1832*, I Public, IX, Appendix F, p.243. Whilst the ban on

Notes

Eurasian landholding was raised in the 1820s for Bengal and Bombay, Madras did not come into line until 1830.
21 Ricketts, *A Series of Letters*, Preface.
22 Fenwick, *Colonization*, p.vi; Editorial, 4 Sept. 1828, *Bengal Hurkaru*.
23 Letter from 'East Indian', 12 Nov. 1828, ibid..
24 Das Gupta (ed.), *Calcutta Gazette*, VI, p.388.
25 Cited in Ricketts, *A Series of Letters*, pp.18, 35, 86.
26 Das Gupta (ed.), *Calcutta Gazette*, VI, p.445.
27 'Minute of Sir J. Malcolm', 10 Oct. 1829, *Select Committee, 1832*, Appendix E 1, Public, IX, pp.342–3.
28 Proceedings, Board of Revenue, Fort St. George, 20 June 1831, BC, F/4/1474, No. 57971, IOR; T.G. Clarke, *The Fortunes of the Anglo-Indian Race*, (Madras, 1876), p.19; *References to Madras in the Asiatic Journal*, (Madras, 1889), p.32.
29 'Relative to the formation of an Association etc.', BC, F/4/1259, No. 50964, IOR; Stark, *John Ricketts*, p.64.
30 Clarke, *Fortunes*, p.19.
31 *Guide to the Eurasian and Anglo-Indian Villages*, (Madras, 1882); R.Symonds, 'Eurasians under British Rule', N. Allen (ed.), *Oxford University Papers on India*, (Delhi, 1987), I:2, p.35.
32 Minute by W.Bentinck on European Settlement, 30 May 1829, Philips (ed.), *Bentinck Correspondence*, I, p.211.
33 Fenwick, *Colonization*, p.8; Letter from C. A.Fenwick, 8 Jan. 1829, *Bengal Hurkaru*.
34 Letter from 'R . . . S . . .', 18 Dec. 1829, *Bengal Hurkaru*.
35 Kyd, *Thoughts*. p.28.
36 Memorial of the Management of the BMOS, 29 July 1832, BC, F/4/712, No. 19454, IOR.
37 Letter from 'K', 19 Mar. 1825, *Bengal Hurkaru*.
38 Letter from 'Brasidas', 22 Mar. 1828, ibid.. 'Brasidas' is believed to have been the nom-de-plume of Wale Byrn.
39 P.C. Mittra, *Biographical Sketch of David Hare*, (Calcutta, 1877), p.xii; Rules of Hindoo College, Bengal Public Consultations, 6 Jan. 1834, No. 25, P/13/6, IOR.
40 Potts, *Baptist Missionaries in India*, p.119.
41 D. Kopf, *British Orientalism and the Bengal Renaissance*, (Berkeley, 1963), p.64.
42 T. Fraser, 'Memoir on the Education of Indians', 7 Feb. 1827, *Bengal Past and Present*, Jan–June 1919, XVIII, pp.154–5.
43 Das Gupta (ed.), *Calcutta Gazette*, VI, p.383.
44 Tennant, *Recreations*, I, p.216.
45 See: Biographical Appendix – Marcus Rochford and James Lorimer.

46 T. Edwards, 'Henry Louis Vivian Derozio', *Calcutta Review*, CXLIII, 1881, pp.283–310.
47 Mittra, *David Hare*, pp.16–17.
48 Kopf, *Bengal Renaissance*, p.258; C.A. Bayly, *Indian Society and the Making of the British Empire*, (Cambridge, 1988), p.163.
49 H.L.V. Derozio, (F. Bradley-Birt and R. Das Gupta eds.), *Poems of Henry Louis Vivian Derozio*, (Calcutta, 1923), pp.xlv–liii.
50 *Ibid.*, pp.2, 24, 43, 72, 127.
51 Cited in Stark, *John Ricketts*, p.73.
52 Mittra, *David Hare*, p.17.
53 Das Gupta (ed.), *Calcutta Gazette*, VI, p.706.
54 E.W. Madge, (S.R. Choudhuri ed.), *Henry Derozio, the Eurasian Poet and Reformer*, (Calcutta, 1967), p.17.
55 Charles Pote, Wale Byrn and William Kirkpatrick were Derozio's contemporaries at the Dhurrumtollah Academy.
56 Das Gupta (ed.), *Calcutta Gazette*, VI, p.714. John Ricketts chaired the committee set up to provide a suitable memorial. Rs 900 was raised but misappropriated by a member of the committee. A memorial was raised to Derozio at the South Park Street cemetery by the municipality of Calcutta on the 150th anniversary of his death.
57 Extract from the *Oriental Herald*, 23 Nov. 1829, cited in Das Gupta (ed.), *Calcutta Gazette*, VI, p.420.
58 C.J. Montague (attrib.), *Henry Louis Vivian Derozio*, (Calcutta, 1843), p.51. Montague, a fellow-Eurasian, was unsparing in his criticism of Derozio's talents, dress, public affectations, '. . . it was laughable to see him in the morning, spurred and booted to the knee, on a powerful Arab, coursing the plain'. Whilst allowing that Derozio was 'brilliant' in conversation Montague thought him 'superficial and arrogant'. See Biographical Appendix – Charles Montague.
59 Editorial, 27 Oct. 1828, *Bengal Hurkaru*.
60 Das Gupta (ed.), *Calcutta Gazette*, VI, p.721.
61 *A Brief History of the Parental Academic Institution*, (Madras, 1854), pp.1–19.
62 Letter from John Palmer to Warren Hastings, 21 Aug. 1802, General Correspondence 1801–2, Warren Hastings Papers, XLVII, pp.254–6, BL.
63 'The Educational Establishments of Calcutta Past and Present', *Calcutta Review*, XIII, Jan.-June 1850, p.450; Sandeman (ed.), *Calcutta Gazettes*, V, p.633.
64 *Brief History of the PAI*, p.1.
65 Ninth Annual Report relative to the PAI, 1831, *Doveton College Reports*, NLC.

66 'Educational Establishments', *Calcutta Review*, p.457.
67 Second to Thirteenth Annual Reports, 1824–35, PAI, *Doveton*, NLC.
68 Stark, *Hostages to India*, pp.93–4.
69 Letter from 'Impartial Observer', 21 Jan. 1828, *Bengal Hurkaru*.
70 'Original Donations to the PAI', *Asiatic Journal*, Mar. 1823.
71 General Meeting PAI, 12 June 1823, *Asiatic Journal*, 1823; Anthony, *Britain's Betrayal*, p.406.
72 Second to Thirteenth Annual Reports, 1824–35, PAI, *Doveton*, NLC.
73 D'Souza, *Anglo-Indian Education*, p.88.
74 Fourth Annual Report, 1826, PAI, *Doveton*, NLC.
75 Thirteenth Annual Report, 1835, PAI, *ibid.*.
76 Eleventh Annual Report, 1833, *ibid.*; *Annual Report of the Free School, Calcutta*, 1832–3. One third of the PAI income (32.7%) was spent on teachers' salaries in 1833, compared with just under one fifth (18.8%) at the Free School in the same year.
77 See: Biographical Appendix – William Masters.
78 Twenty-Sixth Annual Report, 1845, PAI, *ibid.*.
79 Second to Thirteenth Annual Reports, 1824–35, *ibid.*. Eight committee members served in each of the eleven years of the period, and a further six for seven or more years.
80 Stark, *John Ricketts*, p.72.
81 J.F. Hilliker, *British Educational Policy in Bengal, 1833–54*, (London University Ph.D. thesis, 1968), p.22.
82 'A Return of the Numbers of Scholars etc.', Bengal Presidency, 30 Apr. 1830, Parliamentary Papers, XXXVI, 17 May 1852, IOR.

8 – Political Protest: The East Indians' Petition

1 C.H. Philips, *The East India Company, 1784–1834*, (Manchester, 1940), pp.287–90.
2 Report, 15 Dec. 1829, *Bengal Hurkaru*; S. C.Crawford, *Ram Mohan Roy*, (New York, 1987), pp.147–56.
3 *Calcutta Annual Register and Directory*, pp.370–7.
4 Philips, *East India Company*, p.262.
5 A. Tripathi, *Trade and Finance in the Bengal Presidency, 1793–1833*, (Calcutta, 1936), p.197.
6 J. Rosselli, *Lord William Bentinck*, (Sussex, 1974), p.200.
7 *Ibid.*.
8 Evidence from Lord William Bentinck, 14 July 1837, *Report from the Select Committee on Steam Communication with India*, Parliamentary Papers, VI, 1837, IOR.
9 Rosselli, *Bentinck*, p.204.

10 *Report of Proceedings, East Indians' Petition*, p.60.
11 Evidence of James Sutherland, 16 Mar. 1832, *Select Committee, 1832*, I Public, IX, pp.120 f..
12 *Alexander's*, I, Mar. 1831, p.338.
13 *Report of Proceedings, East Indians' Petition*, p.xix.
14 *Ibid.*, pp.103–5.
15 *Ibid.*, p.85.
16 Stark and Madge, *Worthies*, Appendix A, pp.49–50.
17 Regulations V of 1809 and VIII of 1813, Bengal Regulations, 1804–18, V/8/18; Regulation III of 1818, Bengal Regulations, 1815–19, V/8/19, IOR.
18 *Report of Proceedings, East Indians' Petition*, p.40.
19 B.N. Pandey, *The Introduction of English Law into India*, (Bombay, 1929), pp.35–6.
20 Busteed, *Old Calcutta*, p.73.
21 Regulations XXII of 1787, Bengal Judicial Regulations, 1780–92, V/8/15, IOR.
22 L.B. Varma, *Anglo-Indians*, (New Delhi, 1979), p.145.
23 Editorial, 18 Jan. 1829, *Bengal Hurkaru*.
24 'Introduction of the Petition of Indo-Britons', 4 May 1830, *Hansard*, 8 Apr. – 4 June 1830, XXIV, col. 378.
25 Roberts, *Scenes and Characteristics*, III, p.95.
26 Cited in Ricketts, *A Series of Letters*, p.87.
27 'Confessions of an Eurasian', *Anglo-India; Social, Moral and Political*, I, pp.395–402.
28 Stocqueler, *Handbook of India*, p.51.
29 'On the Policy of the British Government towards the Indo-Britons', *Asiatic Journal*, XX, 1825, p.107.
30 Editorial, 30 Mar. 1830, *Bengal Hurkaru*.
31 *References to Madras in the Asiatic Journal*, p.35.
32 Minute by Sir Charles Metcalfe, 11 Oct. 1829, Philips, (ed.), *Bentinck Correspondence*, I, p.309.
33 'The General Views of Sir John Malcolm on the East Indian Community', 10 Oct 1829, *Select Committee, 1832*, Appendix I, I Public, IX, pp.531–4.
34 Philips (ed.), *Bentinck Correspondence*, I, p.211.
35 *Ibid.*, I, p.309.
36 Bentinck Evidence, 14 July 1837, *Select Committee on Steam Navigation, 1837*, VI, Parliamentary Papers, IOR.
37 Editorial, 7 Apr. 1829, *Bengal Hurkaru*.
38 Letter from 'Two Indo-Britons, Managers', 29 May 1829, *ibid.*.
39 Letter from John Ricketts, 1 June 1829, *ibid.*.

Notes

40 7 Geo IV.3. widened the juror qualification from 'British Subjects' to 'Christians', thus allowing Eurasians to sit as jurors. They were, however, listed separately as 'non-British Subjects' although they served alongside British subjects on Petty and Grand Juries; List of Jurors, 16 Apr. 1828, *ibid.*.
41 Minutes of the Committee of Correspondence, 30 Oct. 1827, D/77, p.75, IOR.
42 *Report of Proceedings, East Indians' Petition*, p.22.
43 Charles Watkin Williams Wynn, (1775–1850). Member of Parliament, 1797–1850; President, Board of Control, 1822–8; First President Royal Asiatic Society.
44 *Report of Proceedings, East Indians' Petition*, p.5.
45 *Hansard*, 4 May 1830, XXIV, cols. 378–85. Fergusson and Mackintosh were Directors of the Company as well as Members of Parliament.
46 *Ibid.*, 29 Mar. 1830, XXIII, col.962.
47 General Letter to the Bengal Government, 30 June 1830, *Select Committee, 1832*, I Public, IX, Appendix F, p.343.
48 Regulation VI of 1832, Bengal Regulations, 1824–36, V/8/21, IOR.
49 *Alexander's*, III, Mar. 1832, pp.288–91.
50 *Report of Proceedings, East Indians' Petition*, p.xxx.
51 *Alexander's*, III, Mar. 1832, pp.288–91.
52 'The East Indian Community', *Calcutta Review*, XI, Jan.–June 1849, pp.73–90.
53 Evidence of Sir Alexander Johnston, 6 July 1832, *Select Committee, 1832*, IV, Judicial, XII, p.182.
54 W. Stokes, *The Anglo-Indian Codes*, (Oxford, 1887), p.xi.
55 Twelfth Annual Report for 1834, *Doveton College Reports*, NLC.
56 Court of Directors to the Government of India, 10 Dec. 1834, cited in C.Ilbert, *The Government of India*, (Oxford, 1898), p.500.
57 Evidence of F. Millett, 24 May 1852, *Report from the Select Committee of the House of Lords, 1852*, V/4/5, pp.129–30, IOR.
58 'Memorials presented to the Court of Directors against the Act No. XI of 1835 etc.', V/4/41, IOR.
59 B.B. King, *The Blue Mutiny*, (Philadelphia, 1966).
60 Ilbert, *Government of India*, p.529.

Aftermath

1 'The East Indian Community', *Calcutta Review*, Jan.–June 1849, XI, pp.73–90.

2 Thompson, *Life of Lord Metcalfe*, p.340; See: Biographical Appendix – Sir Charles Metcalfe's Sons.
3 Das Gupta (ed.) *Calcutta Gazette*, VI, p.711.
4 *Alexander's*, IV, July 1832, pp.19–21.
5 'Names and Appointments of Sadr Amins and Deputy Collectors', *The Bengal and Agra Directory and General Register*, (Calcutta, 1845), pp.59–65.
6 See: Biographical Appendix – George Kellner and Charles Forjett.
7 'The Memorial of East Indians etc.', *Second Report from the Commons Select Committee on Indian Territories*, 12 May 1853, Parliamentary Papers, XXVIII, Appendix III, pp.113–15, IOR.
8 Evidence of William Bird, 18 May 1852, *Report from the Select Committee of the House of Lords, 1852*, V/4/5, p.113, IOR.
9 Minute by Sir Charles Metcalfe, 11 Oct. 1829, Philips (ed.), *Bentinck Correspondence*, I, p.309.
10 Cited in G. Seed, 'Lord William Bentinck and the Reform of Education', *Journal of the Royal Asiatic Society*, Apr. 1952, pp.70–71.
11 Cited in Sharp (ed.), *Educational Records*, I, p.116.
12 Cited in Wenger, *Lall-Bazar Church*, pp.57–5.
13 See: Biographical Appendix – Stark and Madge families.
14 Abel, *Anglo-Indians*, pp.62–70.
15 *Report of the Calcutta Domiciled Community Enquiry Committee, 1918–9*, (Calcutta, 1920).
16 C.Dover, *Half-Caste*, (London, 1937), pp.164–243.
17 Boxer, *Race Relations in the Portuguese Empire*, pp.67–73; Pearson, *Portuguese in India*, pp.95–9; Anderson, *Communities*, p.46.
18 Ballhatchet, *Race, Sex and Class*, pp.146–54.
19 Anderson, *Communities*, pp.5–7.
20 Letter from J.W. Price, Trichinopoly, 10 Feb. 1805, BC, F/4/200, No. 4502, IOR.
21 Munro, *Narrative of Military Operations*, p.51.
22 *East India Military Calendar*, II, p.417.
23 E.P. Thompson, *The Making of the English Working Class*, (London, 1963), p.217.
24 As late as 1946 eight per cent of the 176,000 subordinate staff appointments on India's railways were reserved for Anglo-Indians and Europeans who started on a higher salary in the grade than did Indians. Salaries rose to Rs 400 a month. Expenditure per head on railway schools, hospitals, running rooms, housing and social institutes, far exceeded the sums allocated to Indian railway staff. Mukhtar, *Non Gazetted Railway Services*, pp.23, 35–44, 58–62, 107–8.

Bibliography

I. PRIMARY SOURCES

A. Records

India Office Library and Records, London

Acts and Codes, 1780–1955.
Bengal, Madras and Bombay Baptisms, Marriages and Burials.
Bengal Public Consultations, 1819, 1834.
Bengal Political Consultations, 1796, 1807, 1819, 1831.
Bengal Regulations, 1780–92, 1804–18, 1815–19, 1824–36.
Board's Collections, 1796–1858.
Correspondence with India 1703–1858.
Home Miscellaneous Series, c.1600–c.1900.
India Political Proceedings 1836, 1837.
Marquis of Hastings Administration Papers, 1824.
Military Correspondence with India, 1803–57.
Military Department; Compilations and Miscellaneous Records, 1754–1944.
Military Statements, 1785–1859.
Military Department Records relating to Entry into the Service, 1753–1940.
Minutes of the East India Company's Directors and Proprietors, 1599–1858.
Minutes and Memoranda of General Committees etc., 1700–1858.
Papers Relating to Indian Affairs.
Parliamentary Papers, 1802–1955.
Petitions, Certificates etc., 1749–1857, Haileybury Records.
Wills, Probates, Inventories and Administrations, 1774–1943.

National Army Museum, London

Army Dress Regulations, Marquess of Cambridge Papers.

National Library, Calcutta

Annual Reports of the Society for Promoting the Education of the Poor, *Bombay Free School*, 1830–1, 1835–6.
Annual Reports of the Parental Academic Institution, *Doveton College Reports*, 1824–34.

Regent's Park College, Oxford

Reports relative to the Benevolent Institution at Calcutta, 1812–20.
Annual Reports of the Baptist Benevolent Institution, 1812, 1827.
Periodical Accounts of the Serampore Mission, 1829, 1832.
Reports of the Calcutta Baptist Missionary Society, 1819–29.

Rhodes House Library, Oxford

Annual Report of the Society for the Propagation of the Gospel in Foreign Parts, 1833–34.

School of Oriental and African Studies, London

Annual Reports of the Wesleyan Missionary Society, MMS Archives, 1814–57.

Private Ownership

East Indian Charitable Trust, Calcutta
  MS notes on the foundation of the European Female Orphan Asylum.
Family Records
  Records of the Stark family (Mrs C. Brown), the Ricketts family (Mrs S. Dyson), the Kirkpatrick family (Mr W. Kirkpatrick).
Roman Catholic Cathedral, Calcutta
  Baptismal, Marriage, and Burial Records, 1740–1804, 1808–55.
St Thomas's School, Calcutta
  Meeting of the Governors of the Free School, 1817.
Accounts of the Free School, Calcutta, to Midsummer 1818–19, 20–1, 21–2, 22–3, 33–5, (Church Mission Press, Calcutta).

B. Private Papers

British Library, London

Papers and Letters relative to the Affairs of Oude, 1795–7.
The Wellesley Papers.
Warren Hastings Papers.

India Office Library and Records

Alexander Macrabie's Papers.
Beechey, G., 'George Duncan Beechey, Portrait Painter, 1797–1852'.
Bentinck Correspondence.
Correspondence and Notes of the Hon. F.J. Shore.
Frederick Papers.
Jodrell Papers.
Massey, W.H., 'Eastern Sketches or Original Letters from India, 1826–7'.
Mudie, A., 'Arabella's Church'.
Palmer, E., 'The Palmers of Hyderabad'.
Prinsep, E., 'Memoirs of William Prinsep'.
James Rennell Papers.
Strachey, R., 'Letters from Lucknow, 1815–1816–1817'.

National Army Museum, London

Letters from Ensign A. Le Gallais.
Papers Relating to William Gardner.
Papers of Lieut.-Colonel Skinner.

Public Record Office, London

General Letters, East Indies, War Office Out Letters, 1789–92.

Regent's Park College, Oxford

India Missionary Papers and Correspondence; Correspondence of Jabez Carey and Rev. John Marshman.

Rhodes House Library, Oxford

Archives of the Society for the Propagation of the Gospel in Foreign Parts; Register of Marriages at Trichinopoly, 1805–42.
Madras Diocesan Minutes and Memoranda, 1836.

School of Oriental and African Studies, London

London Missionary Society Records, Council for World Mission Archives;
Annotated Register of Missionaries.
Board Minutes.
Candidate Papers, 1796–1899.
Home Odds Personal.
North India Bengal Correspondence, 1824–8.
South India Correspondence, 1817–57.
Travancore Correspondence, 1832–8.

C. Acts and Other Official Correspondence

Acts of Parliament.
Bannerjee, A.C. (ed.), *Fort William-India House Correspondence*, XX, 1792–6, (National Archives of India, Delhi, 1969).
Census of India, 1931, (Manager of Publications, Delhi, 1933).
Census of India, 1941, (Government of India Press, Simla, 1943).
The East India Military Calendar; containing the Services of General and Field Officers of the Indian Army, (Kingsbury, Parbury, and Allen, London, 1823).
Hansard, Mar.–June 1830.
Long, C. (ed.), *Selections from the Unpublished Records of the Government, for the Years 1748–1767 inclusive relating mainly to the Social Condition of Bengal*, (Superintendent of Government Printing, Calcutta, 1869).
Mukhtar, A. 'Non-Gazetted Railway Services', *Labour Investigation Committee*, (Government of India Press, 1946).
Proposals for the Institution of a Free School Society in Bengal, 1789, (Honourable Company's Press, Calcutta, 1796).
Report of the Calcutta Domiciled Community Enquiry Committee 1918–19, (Bengal Secretariat Press, Calcutta, 1920).
Select Committees on Affairs of the East India Company, 1832, 1837, 1852–3.
Standing Orders of the Tenth Regiment, (Army Printing Office, Palermo, 1815).

D. Contemporary Works

Diaries, Letters, Memoirs, Pamphlets

A Short Examination of the Hyderabad Papers as far as they relate to the House of William Palmer and Co. in a Letter addressed to the Proprietors of East India Stock by an Enemy of Oppression, (J.M.Richardson, London, 1825).

Barlow, H. and Yule, H. (eds.), *The Diary of William Hedges, during his Agency in Bengal, 1681–87*, (Hakluyt, London, 1887).

Browne, S.S., *Home Letters written from India, 1828–41*, (C.F. Roworth, London, 1878).

Bute, Marchioness of (ed.), *The Private Journal of the Marquess Hastings K.G.*, (Saunders and Otley, London, 1858).

Ricketts, J.W., *A Series of Letters and other Matter regarding a Certain Scheme for forming a Commercial and Patriotic Association avowedly for the Public Good of the East Indian Community*, (J.W.Ricketts, Calcutta, 1828).

Travellers' Accounts

Bernier, F., (A. Constable, ed.), *Travels in the Moghul Empire, 1656–1668*, (Constable, Westminster, 1891).

Cordiner, J., *A Voyage to India*, (Longman, Aberdeen, 1820).

Grose, J., *A Voyage to the East Indies with Observations on various parts there*, (Hooper and Morley, 2nd ed., London, 1766).

Fane, H.E., *Five Years in India*, (Henry Colburn, London, 1841).

Grandpré, L. *Voyage dans l'Inde et au Bengal*, (Dentu, Paris, 1801).

Heber, R., *Narrative of a Journey through the Upper Provinces of India*, (John Murray, London, 1827; 1829 ed.)

Kindersley, J., *Letters from the Island of Teneriffe, Brazil, the Cape of Good Hope and the East Indies*, (Nourse, London, 1777).

Parkes, F., *Wanderings of a Pilgrim in Search of the Picturesque*, (Pelham Richardson, London, 1850).

Pemble, J. (ed.), *Miss Fane in India*, (Alan Sutton, Gloucester, 1985).

Thompson, E., *Sailor's Letters written to his select friends in England, during his Voyages and Travels in Europe, Asia, Africa and America, from the year 1754 to 1759*, (Hoey and Potts, London, 1767).

Valentia, G., *Voyages and Travels to India, Ceylon, The Red Sea, Abyssinia, and Egypt 1802, 1803, 1804, 1805, and 1806*, (William Miller, London, 1809).

General Works

A Brief History of the Parental Academic Institution, (Athenaeum Press, Madras, 1854).

Anglo-India; Social, Moral and Political; Being a Collection of Papers from the Asiatic Journal, (W.H. Allen, London, 1838).

Badenach, W., *Inquiry into the State of the Bengal Army*, (John Murray, London, 1826).

Bell, A., *Report of the Military Male Orphan Asylum at Madras*, (John Murray, London, 1812).
Bellew, M.W., *Memoirs of a Griffin: or a Cadet's first year in India*, (W.H. Allen, London, 1843).
Cobbe, R., *Bombay Church, or a True Account of the Building and Finishing of the English Church at Bombay from 1745 to 1759*, (J. and W. Oliver, London, 1766).
D'Oyley, *Tom Raw, the Griffin: a Burlesque Poem in Twelve Cantos*, (R.Ackermann, London, 1828).
Fenwick, C.A., *Essay on the Colonization (sic) of Hindoostan by East Indians*, (Baptist Mission Press, Calcutta, 1828).
Forester, M.A. (ed.), *Dyce Sombre against Toup, Solaroli, Prinsep and the East India Company*, (Hansard, London, 1855).
Goldbourne, S. (J. Macfarlane, ed.), *Hartly House Calcutta*, (Calcutta, 1789; new ed., Thacker Spink, Calcutta, 1908).
Grand, G.F. (W.K. Firminger, ed.), *The Narrative of the Life of a Gentleman Long Resident in India*, (Cape of Good Hope, 1814; Calcutta Historical Society, 1910).
Grant, C., *Observations on the State of Society among Asiatic Subjects of Great Britain, particularly with respect to morals and on the means of improving it; written chiefly in the year 1792*, (House of Commons, London, 1813).
Grier, S.C., *Letters of Warren Hastings to his Wife*, (William Blackwood, Edinburgh, 1905).
Holwell, J.Z., *A Genuine Narrative of the Deplorable Deaths of the English Gentlemen and Others etc.*, (A. Millar, London, 2nd ed. 1758).
Huggins, W., *Sketches in India: Treating on Subjects connected with the Government, Civil and Military Establishments, Characters of the European and Customs of the Native Inhabitants*, (John Letts Jnr, London, 1842).
Kyd, J. (attrib.), *Thoughts, How to better the Condition of Indo-Britons*, (Calcutta, 1828).
Lushington, C., *The History, Design and Present State of the Religious, Benevolent and Charitable Institutions founded by the British in Calcutta and its Vicinity*, (Hindostanee Press, Calcutta, 1824).
Malcolm, J., (K.N. Pannikar, ed.), *The Political History of India from 1784 to 1823*, (John Murray, London, 1826; Associated Publishing House, New Delhi, 1970).
Martin, M. (ed.), *The Despatches, Minutes and Correspondence of the Marquess Wellesley K.G.*, (John Murray, London, 1836).
Montague, C.J. (attrib.), *Henry Louis Vivian Derozio*, (Reprint from the Oriental Magazine, I, No.10, Oct. 1843).
Monro, I., *A Narrative of Military Operations on the Coromandel Coast*

Bibliography

against the Combined Forces of the French, Dutch and Hyder Ally Cawn, (T. Bensley, London, 1789).

Murray, J., *On the Topography of Meerut*, (Military Orphan Press, Calcutta, 1839).

Pearson, H., *Memoirs of the Life and Writings of the Rev. Claudius Buchanan D.D.*, (Oxford University Press, Oxford, 1817).

Philips, C.H. (ed.), *The Correspondence of Lord William Bentinck, 1828–35*, (Oxford University Press, Oxford, 1977).

Report of Proceedings connected with the East Indians' Petition to Parliament, (Baptist Mission Press, Calcutta, 1831).

Roberts, E., *Scenes and Characteristics of Hindostan with Sketches of Anglo-Indian Society*, (W.H. Allen, London, 1835).

Ross, C. (ed.), *Correspondence of Charles, Lord Cornwallis*, (John Murray, London, 1859).

Sherwood, M.M., *The History of George Desmond*, (F. Houlston & Son, Wellington, 1821).

——, *The History of Little Henry and His Bearer*, (F. Houlston and Son, Wellington, 12th ed., 1818).

Shore, F.J., *Notes on Indian Affairs*, (John H. Palmer, London, 1837).

Smith, L.F., *A Sketch of the Rise, Progress, and Termination of the Regular Corps Formed and Commanded by Europeans in the Service of the Native Princes of India*, (John Stockdale, London, 1805).

Statham, J., *Indian Recollections*, (S. Bagster, London, 1832).

Stocqueler, J.H., *Handbook of India, a Guide to the Stranger and the Traveller, and a Companion to the Resident*, (W.H. Allen, London, 1844).

Tennant, W., *Indian Recreations, Consisting chiefly of Strictures on the Domestic and Rural Economy of the Mohammedans & Hindoos*, (Longman, London, 1803).

Wallace, R.G., *Fifteen Years in India, or, Sketches of a Soldier's life: being an attempt to describe Persons and Things in various parts of Hindostan*, (Longman, London, 1822).

Williamson, T., *The East India Vade-Mecum, or Complete Guide to Gentlemen intended for the Civil, Military, or Naval Service of the East India Company*, (Black, Parry and Kingsbury, London, 1810).

Newspapers and Periodicals

Alexander's East India Magazine, 1830–3.

Asiatic Journal and Monthly Register, 1823, 1825, 1837.

References to Madras in the Asiatic Journal, 1829–40, (Madras Mail, Madras, 1889).

The Bengal and Agra Directory and General Register, (Samuel Smith and Co., Calcutta, 1845).
Bengal Hurkaru, 1825, 1828–30.
The Calcutta Annual Register and Directory, (Scott and Co., Calcutta, 1831).
The Calcutta Annual Directory and Register, (Scott and Co., Calcutta, 1835).
Das Gupta, A.C. (ed.), *Selections from the Calcutta Gazette – The Days of John Company*, (West Bengal Government Press, Calcutta, 1959).
Sandeman, H.D. (ed.), *Selections from the Calcutta Gazettes of the years 1816 to 1823 inclusive, showing the Political and Social Condition of the English in India fifty years ago*, (Calcutta Central Press Company Ltd, Calcutta, 1869).
Oriental Herald, 1825.

II. SECONDARY SOURCES

Published Works

Abel, E., *The Anglo-Indian Community: Survival in India*, (Chanakya Press, Delhi, 1988).
Anderson, B., *Imagined Communities: Reflections on the Origins and Spread of Nationalism*, (Verso, London, 1983; Revised ed., 1991).
Anthony, F.R., *Britain's Betrayal in India: the Story of the Anglo-Indian Community*, (Allied Publishers, New Delhi, 1962).
Arthur, W., *A Mission to the Mysore; with Scenes and Facts illustrative of India, its People and its Religion*, (Partridge and Oakey, London, 1847).
Ballhatchet, K., *Race, Sex and Class under the Raj: Imperial Attitudes and Policies and their Critics, 1793–1905*, (Weidenfeld and Nicholson, London, 1980).
Banton, M., *Race Relations*, (Tavistock, London, 1967).
Bayly, C.A., *Imperial Meridian: The British Empire and the World, 1780–1830*, (Longman, London, 1989).
——, *Indian Society and the Making of the British Empire*, (Cambridge University Press, Cambridge, 1988; Paperback ed., 1990).
Boxer, C.R., *Race Relations in the Portuguese Colonial Empire, 1415–1825*, (Clarendon Press, Oxford, 1963).
——, *The Dutch Seaborne Empire, 1600–1800*, (Hutchinson, London, 1965; Penguin ed., 1990).
Burton, I., *The Life of Captain Richard F. Burton*, (Chapman and Hall, London, 1893).
Burton, R.G., *A History of the Hyderabad Contingent*, (Government Printing Office, Calcutta, 1905).
Busteed, H.E., *Echoes of Old Calcutta: being chiefly Reminiscences of the days of Warren Hastings, Francis and Impey*, (Thacker, Spink and Co., Calcutta, 2nd ed. 1888).

Bibliography

Callahan, R., *The East India Company and Army Reform, 1783–1798*, (Harvard University Press, Massachusetts, 1972).

Campos, J.J.A., *History of the Portuguese in Bengal*, (Butterworth, Calcutta, 1919).

Carman, W.Y., *Indian Army Uniforms under the British*, (Leonard Hill, London, 1969).

Chatterton, E.A., *A History of the Church of England in India since the Early Days of the East India Company*, (SPCK, London, 1924).

Chaudhuri, N.C., *The continent of Circe, being an Essay on the Peoples of India*, (Chatto and Windus, London, 1965).

Clarke, T.G., *The Fortunes of the Anglo-Indian Race*, (Higginbotham and Co., Madras, 1876).

Compton, H.E., *European Military Adventurers of Hindustan, 1784–1803*, (T.Fisher Unwin, London, 1892).

Crawford, D.G., *A History of the Indian Medical Service, 1600–1913*, (Thacker and Co., London, 1914).

Crawford, S.C., *Ram Mohan Roy: Social, Political and Religious Reform in 19th Century India*, (Paragon, New York, 1987).

Derozio, H.L.V. (F. Bradley-Birt and R. Das Gupta, eds.), *Poems of Henry Louis Vivian Derozio: A Forgotten Anglo-Indian Poet*, (Oxford University Press, Calcutta, 1923; 1980 ed.).

Dover, C., *Half-Caste*, (Secker and Warburg, London, 1937).

D'Souza, A.A., *Anglo-Indian Education: A Study of its Origins and Growth in Bengal up to 1960*, (Oxford University Press, Delhi, 1976).

Ernst, W., *Mad Tales from the Raj: The European Insane in British India, 1800–1858*, (Routledge, London, 1991).

Fraser, J.B., *Military Memoir of Lieut.-Col. James Skinner C.B., for many years a distinguished officer commanding a Corps of Irregular cavalry in the Service of the H.E.I.C.*, (Smith, Elder and Co., 1851; Amabala reprint, 1955).

Ghosh, S.C., *The Social Condition of the British Community in Bengal, 1757–1800*, (E.J.Brill, Leiden, 1970).

Gist, N.P., and Wright, R.D., *Marginality and Identity: Anglo-Indians as a Racially-mixed Minority in India*, (E.J. Brill, Leiden, 1970).

Grey, C. (H.L.O. Garrett, ed.), *European Adventurers of Northern India, 1745–1849*, (Government Printing Press, Lahore, 1929).

Guide to the Eurasian and Anglo-Indian Villages, (The Eurasian and Anglo-Indian Association, Madras, 1882).

Hobsbawm, E.J., *Industry and Empire: From 1750 to the Present Day*, (Weidenfeld and Nicolson, London, 1968; Penguin ed., 1990).

Hodgson, G.H., *Thomas Parry: Free Merchant, Madras, 1768–1824*, (Higginbothams, Madras, 1938).

Holman, D., *Sikander Sahib: The Life of Colonel James Skinner, 1778–1841*, (Heinemann, London, 1961).

Ilbert, C., *The Government of India, Being a Digest of the Statute Law Relating Thereto*, (Clarendon Press, Oxford, 1898).

Joarder, B., *Prostitution in Nineteenth and Early Twentieth Century Calcutta*, (Inter-India Publications, New Delhi, 1985).

Kail, O.C., *The Dutch in India*, (Macmillan, India, 1981).

Kelly, S. (ed.), *The Life of Mrs Sherwood*, (Darton & Co., London, 1854).

Kincaid, D., *British Social Life in India, 1608–1937*, (Routledge & Kegan Paul, London, 1973).

King, B.B., *The Blue Mutiny: The Indigo Disturbances in Bengal, 1859–62*, (University of Pennsylvania Press, Philadelphia, 1966).

Kopf, D., *British Orientalism and the Bengal Renaissance: The Dynamics of Indian Modernization, 1773–1835*, (University of California Press, Berkeley, 1963).

Llewellyn-Jones, R., *A Fatal Friendship: The Nawabs, the British and the City of Lucknow*, (Oxford University Press, Delhi, 1985).

——, *Claude Martin in Early Colonial India*, (Oxford University Press, Delhi, 1992).

Love, H.D., *Vestiges of Old Madras, traced from the East India Company's Records*, (John Murray, London, 1913).

Lunt, J. (ed.), *From Sepoy to Subedar: being the Life and Adventures of Subedar Sita Ram, a Native Officer of the Bengal Army written and related by himself*, (Lahore 1873; New ed., Macmillan, 1988).

Madge, E.W. (S.R. Choudhuri, ed.), *Henry Derozio, the Eurasian Poet and Reformer*, (Metropolitan Book Agency, Calcutta, 1967).

Misra, B.B., *The Indian Middle Classes: Their Growth in Modern Times*, (Oxford University Press, London, 1961).

——, *The Central Administration of the East India Company, 1773–1834*, (Manchester University Press, Manchester, 1959).

Mittra, P.C., *Biographical Sketch of David Hare*, (Calcutta, 1877, New ed., 1949).

Panckridge, H.R., *A Short History of the Bengal Club, 1827–1927*, (The Statesman Press, Calcutta, 1927).

Pandey, B.N., *The Introduction of English Law into India: The Career of Elijah Impey in Bengal, 1774–1783*, (Asia Publishing House, Bombay, 1929).

Parry, J.H. and Sherlock, P.M., *A Short History of the West Indies*, (Macmillan, London, 1965; 1971 ed.).

Pearse, H., *The Hearseys, Five Generations of an Anglo-Indian family*, (William Blackwood, Edinburgh, 1905).

Bibliography

Pearson, M.N., *The Portuguese in India*, (Cambridge University Press, Cambridge, 1987).

Pemble, J., *The Invasion of Nepal: John Company at War*, (Clarendon Press, Oxford, 1971).

——, *The Raj, the Indian Mutiny and the Kingdom of Oudh, 1801–1859*, (Harvester Press, Sussex, 1977).

Penner P. and Dale R., (eds), *The Rebel Bureaucrat – Frederick John Shore, 1799–1837, as Critic of William Bentinck's India*, (Chanakya Publications, Delhi, 1983).

Penny, F.E., *The Church in Madras: being the history of the Ecclesiastical and Missionary action of the East India Company in the Presidency of Madras in the Seventeenth and Eighteenth Centuries*, (Smith and Elder, London, 1904).

Philips, C.H., *The East India Company, 1784–1834*, (Manchester University Press, Manchester, 1940).

Porter, R., *English Society in the Eighteenth Century*, (Allen Lane, London, 1982; Penguin ed., 1990).

Potts, E.D., *British Baptist Missionaries In India, 1793–1837*, (Cambridge University Press, Cambridge, 1967).

Renford, R.K., *The Non-Official British in India to 1920*, (Oxford University Press, Delhi, 1987).

Rosselli, J., *Lord William Bentinck: The Making of a Liberal Imperialist, 1774–1839*, (Chatto and Windus, Sussex, 1974).

Sandys, E.T., *One Hundred and Fourty Five Years at the Old Mission Church*, (Valmiki Press, Calcutta, 1916).

Saroop, N., *A Squire of Hindoostan*, (Palit and Palit, New Delhi, 1983).

Sharp, H. (ed.), *Selections from Educational Records*, (Bureau of Education, Calcutta, 1920).

Stark, H.A., *Hostages to India, or the Life Story of the Anglo-Indian Race*, (Star Printing Works, Calcutta, 1936).

——, *John Ricketts and His Times*, (Wilson and Son, Calcutta, 1934).

—— and Madge E.W., *East Indian Worthies, being Memoirs of distinguished Indo-Europeans*, (Cambridge Steam Printing Works, Calcutta, 1892).

Stone, L., *The Family, Sex and Marriage in England, 1500–1800*, (Weidenfeld and Nicolson, London, 1977; Abridged ed., Peregrine, 1988).

——, *Road to Divorce: England, 1530–1987*, (Oxford University Press, Oxford, 1990).

Thompson, E.J., *The Life of Charles, Lord Metcalfe*, (Faber and Faber, London, 1937).

Thompson, E.P., *The Making of the English Working Class*, (Victor Gollancz, London, 1963; Penguin ed., 1991).

Toynbee, G., *A Sketch of the Administration of the Hooghly District from 1795 to 1845*, (Bengal Secretariat Press, Calcutta, 1888).

Tripathi, A., *Trade and Finance in the Bengal Presidency, 1793–1833*, (Orient Longmans, Calcutta, 1936).

Van den Berghe, P.L., *The Ethnic Phenomenon*, (Elsevier, New York, 1981).

Varma, L.B., *Anglo Indians: a Historical Study of Anglo Indian Community in 19th Century India*, (Reena Roy, New Delhi, 1979).

Wenger, E.S., *The Story of the Lall-Bazar Baptist Church*, (Edinburgh Press, Calcutta, 1908).

Wheeler, J.T., *Early Records of British India: a History of the English Settlement in India*, (Newman and Co., Calcutta, 1878).

Yalland, Z., *Traders and Nabobs: The British in Cawnpore, 1765–1857*, (Michael Russell, Salisbury, 1987).

——, *A Guide to the Kacheri Cemetery and the Early History of Kanpur*, (BACSA, Putney, 1983).

Yazdani, Z., *Hyderabad during the Residency of Henry Russell, 1811–1820*, (Oxford University Press, Oxford, 1976).

Articles

Anon., 'The East Indian Community', *Calcutta Review*, XI, Jan.–June 1849, pp.73–90.

Anon., 'Hyderabad, the Nizam's Contingent', *Calcutta Review*, XI, Jan.–June 1849, pp.141–219.

Anon., 'The Educational Establishments of Calcutta, Past and Present', *Calcutta Review*, XIII, Jan.–June 1850, pp.442–467.

Arnold, D., 'European Orphans and Vagrants in India in the Nineteenth Century', *Journal of Imperial and Commonwealth History*, VII:2, 1979, pp.104–27.

——, 'White Colonization and Labour in Nineteenth Century India', *Journal of Imperial and Commonwealth History*, XI:2, 1983, pp.133–58.

Callahan, R., 'Cornwallis and the Indian Army, 1786–97', *Military Affairs*, XXXIV, 1970, pp.93–7.

Dunn, T.O., 'An Anglo-Indian Romance', *Calcutta Review*, 295, Jan. 1919, pp.56–71.

Edwards, T., 'Henry Louis Vivian Derozio', *Calcutta Review*, CXLIII, 1881, pp.283–310.

——, 'Eurasians and Poor Europeans in India', *Calcutta Review*, CXLIII, 1881, pp.38–56.

Firminger, W.K., 'Some Fresh Light on the Old Bengal Lodges', *Transactions of the Quatuor Coronati Lodge*, No.2076, XVIII, 1905, pp.157–60, United Grand Lodge of England Library.

Fraser, T., 'Memoir on the Education of Indians', 7 Feb. 1827, *Bengal Past and Present*, Jan.-June 1919, XVIII, pp.73–156.

Madge, E.W., 'Baptisms in Calcutta, 1767–77, 1778–82', *Bengal Past and Present*, 1923, XXV:2, pp.131–55; XXVI:1–2, pp.142–68.

Seed, G., 'Lord William Bentinck and the Reform of the Education', *Journal of the Royal Asiatic Society*, Apr.1952, pp.66–77.

Stewart, A.F., 'Some Notes on the Position of Early Eurasians', *Asiatic Quarterly Review*, July 1913, pp.93–101.

Symonds, R., (N. Allen, ed.), 'Eurasians under British Rule', *Oxford University Papers on India*, (Oxford University Press, Delhi, 1987), I:2, pp.28–42.

Theses

Bingle, R.J., *The Marquess of Hastings, 1813–23*, (Oxford University D. Phil. thesis, 1964).

Hillicker, J.F., *British Educational Policy in Bengal, 1833–54*, (London University Ph. D. thesis, 1968).

Genealogical and Reference Works

Buckland, C.E., *Dictionary of Indian Biography*, (Swann Sonnenschein, London, 1906).

Dodwell E. and Miles, J.S., *Alphabetical List of the Officers of the Indian Army*, (Longman, Orme, Brown and Co., London, 1838).

——, *Alphabetical List of the HEIC Madras Civil Servants*, (Longman, Orme, Brown and Co., London, 1839).

Hodson, V.C.P., *List of Officers of the Bengal Army, 1758–1834*, (Constable and Co., London, 1927).

Nair, P.T., *A History of Calcutta's Streets*, (Firma KLM Private Ltd., Calcutta, 1987).

Prinsep, C.C., *Record of the Services of the Honourable Company's Civil Servants in the Madras Presidency, 1741–1858*, (London, 1885).

Stokes, W., *The Anglo-Indian Codes*, (Clarendon Press, Oxford, 1887).

Thacker and Co., W., *The Bengal Obituary*, (London, 1851: BACSA reprint, 1987).

Yule, H. and Burnell, A.C., *Hobson-Jobson*, (John Murray, London, 1886. New ed., Routledge and Kegan Paul, London, 1985).

Index

Abbott, Sarah, 25
Achmuty, family, 142, 158
Acts:
    Charter Act 1813, 86, Charter Act 1833, 147–8, *Jury Act 1826*, 143, *Regulating Act 1773*, 56, 138, *Test and Corporation Acts 1828*, 144, *Usury Act 1797*, 103, 106
Albuquerque, Alfonso de, 1, 77
Amherst, Governor General Lord, 130
Anglo-Indians:
    authors, vii–viii, 55, 64, *employment*, vii, 149, 157, *'golden age'*, 55, *numbers of*, vi, *poverty of*, vii, 153
Apothecaries, 42, 47
Ashley, Lord, 144

Baptisms, 4–5, 8, 18
Barretto, family, 52, 158
Bayley, Hon. W. 130
Beechey, George, 108
Bell, Dr. Alexander, 28, 32
Bentinck, Governor-General Lord, 39, 75, 78, 101, 117, 120, 130, 134, 140–2, 147, 150, 152
Bird, William, 151
Bishop's College, Calcutta, 86
Board of Control, 140, 144–5
Brightman, family, 88, 91, 158
British society:
    admission to Government House, 80–1, *class in society*, 36–7, 76, *concepts of moral virtue*, 58–9,

154–5, *Eurasian women in*, 76–7, *legal status*, 138, 149, *non-official immigrants*, 38–9, 52, 148, *numbers*, 149, *philosophy of rule*, 57
Browne, Samuel, 17, 100
Buchanan, Rev. Charles, 58–9, 67
Buckingham, William, 51, 159
Byrn, Wale, 87–8, 91, 124, 130, 150, 155, 159

Calcutta Apprenticing Society, 115
Campbell, William, 96
Carey, Maria, 77, 160
Carlisle, Earl of, 144
Carnatic Corps of Artificers, 41
Carstairs, Peter, 39, 71, 160
Charitable Funds, 66–8, 70–1
Charnock, Job, 3
Churches:
    Lal Bazaar Chapel, Calcutta, 86, *Old Mission Church, Calcutta*, 86–7, *St. John's, Calcutta*, 4–5, 18, 22, *St. Mary's, Madras*, 68, *St. Thomas's, Bombay*, 21, *'Tucker's Chapel', Madras* 86
Colonisation, 61–2, 115, 117–120, 139
Colour, 76–8
Commercial and Patriotic Association, 119
Companions, 6–10, 14–15, 17–18
Company, HEIC, 14, 23–4, 33–4, 37–40, 44, 55–8, 60, 62, 64–7, 70–2, 75, 97, 113, 117, 132–7, 140–9, 156

Index

Cornelius, Charles and family, 45, 54
Cortlandt, Henry Van, 97
Cornwallis, Governor-General Lord, 5, 12, 57, 61, 64, 97, 133
Costa, Willoughby Da, 43, 85, 91, 128, 143, 160
Cotton, Bishop George, 153
Covenanted civil servants, 43, 53, 56, 63, 66–7, 150

Derozio, H.V.L. and family, 85, 124–7, 160
Dick, family, 49, 88, 91, 161
Divorce, 6
Doctors, 49
Doveton, Captain John, 96, 129–30, 162
Dutch, 1–2

East Indian Association, Calcutta, 123
East Indian Colonization Committee, Bombay, 119–20
East Indian Colonization Fund, 119
Ellenborough, Lord, 145
Engineers, 42, 48
English language press, 119, 140–1
Eurasian Philanthropic Association, 119–20
Eurasians:
accent, 80, *alleged genetic inferiority*, 82–4, *bandsmen*, 40–1, 52, *banned from Company regular army*, 62, 64, *Calcutta Club*, 74–5, *competition from British immigrants*, 38–9, 52, *competition from Indians*, 151–2, *disinclination to farming and trade*, 118–9, 121, 131, *discouragement of marriage to British*, 80, *discrimination against*, 55–7, *discrimination, relaxation of measures*, 68–9, 143, *dress*, 79, *education in India*, 11, 112, 121–3, 127–31, *employment*, 39–41, 42–3, 48–53, 112, *exclusion from charitable benefits*, 66–8, 70, *exclusion from covenanted service*, 39, 55–6, 64–6, 137, *fears for job security*, 134, *intermarriage*, 87–8, *jury service*, 138, 144, *land ownership*, 38, 118, *legal status*, 137–9, 145–6, 148–9, *Lord Clive's Fund*, 68, 144, *marriage prospects for women*, 10–11, 17, 18–19, 77, *memorial of 1853*, 151, *names for*, 89–90, *Natives of India, classified as*, 55–6, 61, 71, 98–9, 106, 135, 138–9, 145, 156, *numbers of*, ix, 12, 21, 57, 60, 70, *pauperism*, 42, *petition of 1818*, 62, 140, *petition of 1830*, 133–49, 156, *place in society*, 28–9, 38, 53–4, *princely states, service in*, 93–111, *prospects of military employment reduced*, 113, *Protestantism*, 85–7, *railways, employment on*, 152, 157, *rejection of maternal ancestry*, 75–6, *resentment at social exclusion*, 84–5, 135, *residential area, Calcutta*, 88, *respect for, alleged lack of*, 151, *soldiers' wives and widows*, 40, 59–60, 69–70, *stereotype*, 81–5, 147, 155, *support for communal activities*, 114–5, *teachers*, 32, 50, 123–4
Evangelicals, 15–17

Fenwick, Charles, 113–5, 118–9, 121, 162
Fergusson, Cutlar, 145
Fink, Rev. R.C., 93, 162
Forjett, Charles, 151, 204
Fort St. George, Madras, 3, 4, 55, 60, 69
Fort William, Calcutta, 4, 59
Foster, Lieutenant-Colonel Henry, 96, 111, 163
Frith, Robert, 128

Gardner, Lieutenant-Colonel William, 8, 108
Gidney, Sir Henry, 91
Goa, 2
Gordon, alias Carron, 96
Grey, Sir Edward, 130

Hastings, Governor-General Warren, 61

Index

Hastings, Governor-General Lord, 80–1, 89, 100, 103–5, 118
Hearsey, Hyder, 96, 107, 111, 163
Heatly, Jacob, 143
Heber, Bishop Reginald, 20, 78, 85, 115, 128
Hindu College, Calcutta, 122, 124, 129, 137
Holmes, John, 96
Hopkins, George, 96
Huggins, William, 42, 84, 107
Hutteman, G.S., 87
Hyderabad, 7, 96, 101–7, 110, 113

Illegitimacy, 4–5, 18, 26, 33, 57, 59–60, 67, 148, 155
Imlach, Colonel Henry and family, 51, 91, 143, 163
Indians:
alleged indolence, 81, *colour*, 78, *exclusion from covenanted service*, 150, *from government service*, 38, *increase in numbers in uncovenanted service after 1833*, 151, *jury service*, 133, *preference for in government appointments*, 134, *princely states*, 93–111, *objections to Eurasians in authority*, 63, 151, *reliable business partners*, 107–8, *western education of*, 54, 113, 122–3, 131
Indigo, 42, 51, 93, 149

Johnston, Sir Alexander, 117, 147
Jones, Lieutenant-General Sir Richard, 66, 71, 164

Kellner, Sir George, 151, 164
Kerr, Dr., 32
Kirkpatrick, William Benjamin, 43, 91, 164
Kyd, James, 39, 52, 81, 88, 91, 114–5, 121–2, 128, 155, 164

Law Commission, 147–8
Lawrence, Sir Henry, 153
Lawyers, 49
Legacies, 11

Lindsay, Mr., 99
Linstedt, family, 50, 91, 127, 165
Lorimer, James, 124, 130, 165

Macaulay, Thomas, 152
Mackintosh, Sir James, 145
Madge, family, 54, 87, 88, 152, 165
Madrassa, Calcutta, 123–4
Malcolm, Governor Sir John, 19, 27, 28–9, 117, 141
Marathas, 94, 96–7, 100, 104, 106, 113
Marine Apprenticing Society, 116
Marriage, 5–7, 13–14, 17–19
Marshman, Rev. John, 27, 92
Martin Claude, 8, 99, 110
Martindell, Henry, 91, 166
Martinière, La, 8, 130
Masters, William, 130, 166
Maxwell, Adam, 38
Metcalfe, Sir Charles, and sons, 18, 65, 67, 101, 102, 104, 130, 141, 150, 166
Meyer, George, 150
Middleton, Bishop Thomas, 86
Military:
accommodation, 12–13, *cohabitation*, 19, *drunkenness*, 13, *irregular units*, 37, *legacies*, 11, *marriages*, 9–11, 13–14, 40, 68, 155, *marriage allowances*, 68, *Military Asylum, Chelsea*, 25, *minor cadets*, 56, *numbers*, 9, *pay*, 10, *private soldiers*, 12, *promotion prospects for officers*, 9–10, 61, *Royal Army*, 13, 24, 64–5, *social background*, 3, 12, 156, *venereal disease*, 155
Missionaries:
admission to India, 26, *Eurasian missionaries*, 50–1, 82–3, 86, *schools*, 26–7, 123
Missionary Organisations:
LMS, 50, 82–3, *Serampore Baptists*, 26–7, 50–1, 52, 86, 92, 123, *SPCK*, 26–7, 29, *USPG*, 51, 86, *Wesleyans*, 50
Montague, Charles, 166
Mughals, 76, 94

Index

Munro, Governor Sir Thomas, 34–5, 69–70
Mortality, 19, 22, 30–1

Nairn, John, 66
Nairne, Major Robert, 66, 167
Native Book Society, Bombay, 123
Nepal, 95
North America, 57

Oriental Society, Calcutta, 123
Orphan Societies:
  Benevolent Institution, Calcutta, 26–7, 31, 129, 137, *Civil Orphan Asylum, Madras*, 120, *European Female Orphan Asylum, Calcutta*, 25, *Free School, Bombay*, 24, 27, 32, *Free School, Calcutta*, 22, 25, 27, 29, 40, 42, *Lower Military Orphanage, Calcutta*, 24–5, 34, 41, *Male Military Orphan Asylum, Madras*, 28, 32, 46, *Military Orphan Society, Bengal*, 24, 121, *Society for the Education of the Poor, Bombay*, 21, 26, *SPCK, Tanjore*, 29, *Upper Military Orphanage, Calcutta*, 17, 24, 31, 124
Orphanages:
  Admissions, 24, 26, *austerity*, 29–30, *diet*, 30, *education*, 31–2, *funding*, 27–8, 33–4, *health*, 30–1, *management*, 27, *numbers*, 21, *printing*, 23, 32, *public dances*, 17, *regime*, 23, 29–30, *social usefulness*, 28, *trade training*, 32
Oudh, 78, 95–9, 108–110

Palmer, John, 51, 102, 105
Palmer, William, 39, 52, 101–6, 110, 167
Parental Academic Institution, 112, 115, 123–4, 126–31, 137
Parliament, 135–6, 138–9, 142–5, 148
Parry, Thomas, 107–8
Pater, Lieutenant-General Sir John, 11
Patronage, 44, 46, 59, 63, 96, 99, 113

Peel, Robert, 144
Pondicherry, 77
Poona College, 123
Poor Whites, 5, 12–13, 20–2, 27, 33, 35, 42, 60, 62, 86
Portuguese, 1–2, 34, 59, 86
Pote, Charles, 49, 91, 136, 167
Private Schools, 23
Prostitution, 6, 14, 16, 18
Punjab, 96, 108, 110

Reed, Charles, 128, 143
Regulations, Bengal, 137
Rennell, James, 6
Ricketts, John, 87, 89–92, 114, 118–19, 124, 126, 128, 134–7, 140, 143–5, 146, 152–3, 155, 168
Roberts, Emma, 63, 140
Roberts, Mr., 95, 110
Rochford, Marcus, 123, 168
Rotton, family, 109
Roy, Ram Mohan, 133
Rumbold, Sir William, 103, 105–6
Russell, Henry, 103–5

St. Helena, 65
San Domingo, 64
School and School Book Societies, Calcutta, 123
Sheriff, James, 87
Sherwood, Mary, 15–16
Shore, Frederick, 9, 37, 52, 107
Singh, Ranjit, 96, 108, 110
Skinner, Lieutenant-Colonel James, 39, 74, 80, 84, 96, 99–101, 108, 110–11, 122, 142, 155, 168
Sombre, David Ochterlony Dyce, 109, 168
Spanish America, 72
Stark, family, 152, 169
Stevenson, Major-General Sir Robert, 66, 80, 169
Supreme Courts, 138–9, 141, 143, 148
Surveyors, 42, 46–7
Sutherland, James, 135
Sutherland, Patrick, 43

Teachers, 32, 50

Index

Thomas, Jacob, 96
Thompson, Rev. J.T., 93, 169
Turing, family, 55, 169

Uncovenanted civil service, 42–6, 134–5, 150

Valentia, Lord, 60, 64
Vickers, Major, 110

Walters, George, 98–9, 108, 170
Wellesley, Governor-General Lord, 18, 57, 59, 81, 97–8, 133
Wellington, Duke of, 144
Weston, Charles, 22, 39, 52, 56, 138, 170
Wills, 7–9, 11
Wortley, Stuart, 144
Wynn, Charles, 139, 144